Communications
in Computer and Information Science

2230

Editorial Board Members

Joaquim Filipe ⓘ, *Polytechnic Institute of Setúbal, Setúbal, Portugal*
Ashish Ghosh ⓘ, *Indian Statistical Institute, Kolkata, India*
Lizhu Zhou, *Tsinghua University, Beijing, China*

Rationale

The CCIS series is devoted to the publication of proceedings of computer science conferences. Its aim is to efficiently disseminate original research results in informatics in printed and electronic form. While the focus is on publication of peer-reviewed full papers presenting mature work, inclusion of reviewed short papers reporting on work in progress is welcome, too. Besides globally relevant meetings with internationally representative program committees guaranteeing a strict peer-reviewing and paper selection process, conferences run by societies or of high regional or national relevance are also considered for publication.

Topics

The topical scope of CCIS spans the entire spectrum of informatics ranging from foundational topics in the theory of computing to information and communications science and technology and a broad variety of interdisciplinary application fields.

Information for Volume Editors and Authors

Publication in CCIS is free of charge. No royalties are paid, however, we offer registered conference participants temporary free access to the online version of the conference proceedings on SpringerLink (http://link.springer.com) by means of an http referrer from the conference website and/or a number of complimentary printed copies, as specified in the official acceptance email of the event.

CCIS proceedings can be published in time for distribution at conferences or as post-proceedings, and delivered in the form of printed books and/or electronically as USBs and/or e-content licenses for accessing proceedings at SpringerLink. Furthermore, CCIS proceedings are included in the CCIS electronic book series hosted in the SpringerLink digital library at http://link.springer.com/bookseries/7899. Conferences publishing in CCIS are allowed to use Online Conference Service (OCS) for managing the whole proceedings lifecycle (from submission and reviewing to preparing for publication) free of charge.

Publication process

The language of publication is exclusively English. Authors publishing in CCIS have to sign the Springer CCIS copyright transfer form, however, they are free to use their material published in CCIS for substantially changed, more elaborate subsequent publications elsewhere. For the preparation of the camera-ready papers/files, authors have to strictly adhere to the Springer CCIS Authors' Instructions and are strongly encouraged to use the CCIS LaTeX style files or templates.

Abstracting/Indexing

CCIS is abstracted/indexed in DBLP, Google Scholar, EI-Compendex, Mathematical Reviews, SCImago, Scopus. CCIS volumes are also submitted for the inclusion in ISI Proceedings.

How to start

To start the evaluation of your proposal for inclusion in the CCIS series, please send an e-mail to ccis@springer.com.

Angelo Ferrando · Rafael C. Cardoso
Editors

Agents and Robots for reliable Engineered Autonomy

4th Workshop, AREA 2024
Santiago de Compostela, Spain, October 19, 2024
Proceedings

Editors
Angelo Ferrando ⓘ
University of Modena and Reggio Emilia
Modena, Italy

Rafael C. Cardoso ⓘ
University of Aberdeen
Aberdeen, UK

ISSN 1865-0929　　　　　　　　ISSN 1865-0937 (electronic)
Communications in Computer and Information Science
ISBN 978-3-031-73179-2　　　ISBN 978-3-031-73180-8 (eBook)
https://doi.org/10.1007/978-3-031-73180-8

© The Editor(s) (if applicable) and The Author(s), under exclusive license to Springer Nature Switzerland AG 2025

This work is subject to copyright. All rights are solely and exclusively licensed by the Publisher, whether the whole or part of the material is concerned, specifically the rights of translation, reprinting, reuse of illustrations, recitation, broadcasting, reproduction on microfilms or in any other physical way, and transmission or information storage and retrieval, electronic adaptation, computer software, or by similar or dissimilar methodology now known or hereafter developed.
The use of general descriptive names, registered names, trademarks, service marks, etc. in this publication does not imply, even in the absence of a specific statement, that such names are exempt from the relevant protective laws and regulations and therefore free for general use.
The publisher, the authors and the editors are safe to assume that the advice and information in this book are believed to be true and accurate at the date of publication. Neither the publisher nor the authors or the editors give a warranty, expressed or implied, with respect to the material contained herein or for any errors or omissions that may have been made. The publisher remains neutral with regard to jurisdictional claims in published maps and institutional affiliations.

This Springer imprint is published by the registered company Springer Nature Switzerland AG
The registered company address is: Gewerbestrasse 11, 6330 Cham, Switzerland

If disposing of this product, please recycle the paper.

Preface

Autonomous agents have been extensively studied for decades in design and implementation. Nevertheless, their real-world use has been mostly limited to software applications rather than physical interaction contexts. Meanwhile, robotics has expanded beyond industrial settings into dynamic fields like robotic assistants and search and rescue, involving complex interactions with humans and other robots. This shift poses challenges to traditional software engineering methods.

Increased autonomy is key for robots to navigate these environments, with autonomous agents and multi-agent systems offering promising engineering approaches. However, as autonomy and interaction increase, ensuring reliable behaviour becomes more complex, highlighting the need for new verification and validation methods throughout the engineering lifecycle.

History

The workshop on Agents and Robots for reliable Engineered Autonomy (AREA) was formed in 2020 and seeks to bridge the gap between the autonomous agents, robotics, and software engineering communities.

Since its inception, AREA has been co-located with the European Conference on Artificial Intelligence (ECAI). AREA 2020 occurred online due to the COVID pandemic, with proceedings published as Electronic Proceedings in Theoretical Computer Science Volume 319 and a special issue in the Journal of Sensor and Actuator Networks, JSAN Volume 10, No. 3, 2021. AREA 2022 took place in Vienna, with proceedings published as Electronic Proceedings in Theoretical Computer Science Volume 362 and a special issue in the Robotics journal, Volume 12, No. 2, 2023. AREA 2023 was located in Kraków, with proceedings published as Electronic Proceedings in Theoretical Computer Science Volume 391 and a special issue in the Annals of Mathematics and Artificial Intelligence journal (ongoing).

Topics

- Agent-based modular architectures applicable to robots
- Agent-oriented software engineering to model high-level control in robotic development
- Agent programming languages and tools for developing robotic or intelligent autonomous systems
- Coordination, interaction, and negotiation protocols for agents and robots
- Distributed problem-solving and automated planning in autonomous systems
- Engineering reliable interactions between humans and autonomous robots or agents
- Fault tolerance, health management, and long-term autonomy

- Neuro-symbolic artificial intelligence
- Real-world applications of autonomous agents and multi-agent systems in robotics
- Runtime verification of autonomous agents and robotic systems
- Task and resource allocation in multi-robot systems
- Verification and validation of autonomous systems

AREA 2024

AREA 2024 was held in person as a 1-day workshop[1]. We received a total of 14 submissions, each of which was reviewed (single-blind) by three reviewers. In total, 10 papers were accepted for presentation at the workshop, with 9 regular papers and 1 short paper.

AREA 2024 provided a forum for researchers and practitioners in agent-oriented software engineering, robotic applications, formal verification, and artificial intelligence to present and discuss their work. The workshop's overall purpose was to facilitate the cross-fertilisation of ideas and experiences in these fields to:

- Enhance our understanding of the theory and practice of engineering intelligent agents and multi-agent systems in robotic applications;
- Showcase the application of agent methodologies, architectures, languages, and tools in the engineering of robotic systems;
- Identify new directions for the formal verification of multi-agent and robotics-based systems.

August 2024

Angelo Ferrando
Rafael C. Cardoso

---

[1] The complete workshop programme is available online at: https://areaworkshop.github.io/AREA2024/ (Accessed 2 August 2024).

Invited Talks

Two speakers were invited to the AREA 2024 workshop: Aniello Murano, for his work on the strategic reasoning and verification of Multi-Agent Systems, and Eva Onaindia, for her expertise in Automated Planning and Multi-Agent Path Planning. Their participation allowed us to comprehensively cover two critical areas of the workshop: formal verification of Multi-Agent Systems and Automated Planning.

Aniello Murano

Strategic reasoning is essential in numerous fields, including game theory, artificial intelligence, economics, and cybersecurity, as it involves devising and analysing strategies to achieve goals in both competitive and cooperative settings. This talk will explore the formal aspects of strategic reasoning, focusing on the mathematical and logical underpinnings that enable precise and effective strategy formulation. Key model frameworks, such as Alternating-time Temporal Logic (ATL) and Strategy Logic, one of the most powerful logics for strategic reasoning, will be discussed to illustrate their roles in understanding and predicting strategic interactions.

Eva Onaindia

A Hybrid system (HS) exhibits both continuous and discrete behaviours, and it is an essential tool for modeling complex real-world processes, such as those in robotics, automotive systems, and aerospace engineering. Continuous dynamics are typically governed by equations describing the evolution of the system state over time, and discrete dynamics are characterised by abrupt transitions between modes of operation, often representing control decisions or the logic of an automated system. A hybrid trajectory is a sequence of transitions that describes a particular execution of an HS over time.

A sequence of observations collected from an HS, such as sensor readings of the system variables, reflect the behaviour of the system. By generating a hybrid trajectory that matches a given sequence of observations, we can trace the operations of the system, identify the underlying factors leading to the observed behaviour, and verify that our understanding of the system matches its operations. In this talk, we will discover the power of AI planning technology to diagnose, understand, and verify the behaviour of an HS and compare its performance with model-checking tools for safety validation in hybrid systems.

Organisation

General and Program Committee Chairs

Angelo Ferrando	University of Modena and Reggio Emilia, Italy
Rafael C. Cardoso	University of Aberdeen, UK

Program Committee

Tobias Ahlbrecht	Clausthal University of Technology, Germany
Gleifer Alves	Universidade Tecnológica Federal do Paraná, Brazil
Mehrnoosh Askarpour	McMaster University, Canada
Francesco Belardinelli	Imperial College London, UK
Rafael H. Bordini	PUCRS, Brazil
Daniela Briola	University of Milano-Bicocca, Italy
Christian Colombo	University of Malta, Malta
Louise Dennis	University of Manchester, UK
Babak Esfandiari	Carleton University, Canada
Marie Farrell	University of Manchester, UK
Ian Gray	University of York, UK
Jomi Fred Hübner	Federal University of Santa Catarina, Brazil
Erez Karpas	Technion, Israel
Bettina Könighofer	Graz University of Technology, Austria
Bruno Lacerda	University of Oxford, UK
Charles Lesire	ONERA, France
Livia Lestingi	Polytechnic University of Milan, Italy
Matt Luckcuck	University of Nottingham, UK
Vadim Malvone	Télécom Paris, France
Viviana Mascardi	University of Genoa, Italy
Claudio Menghi	University of Bergamo, Italy
Stefania Monica	University of Modena and Reggio Emilia, Italy
Chunyan Mu	University of Aberdeen, UK
Eva Onaindia	Valencia Polytechnic University, Spain
Fabio Papacchini	Lancaster University Leipzig, Germany
Pedro Ribeiro	University of York, UK
Ana Paula Rocha	University of Porto, Portugal
Matteo Rossi	Polytechnic University of Milan, Italy

Stefano Tedeschi   University of Aosta Valley, Italy
Christos Tsigkanos University of Athens, Greece

Contents

Risk-Aware On-the-Fly Solving of Physical Vehicle Routing Problems 1
   Jáchym Herynek and Stefan Edelkamp

Agents as a Design Paradigm for Robotic Systems Leveraging ROS
and Gazebo 21
   Valeria Seidita and Antonio Chella

Verification-Oriented Specification of Multi-agent Interaction Patterns 38
   Alberto Tagliaferro, Livia Lestingi, and Matteo Rossi

Evaluation of Human Interaction with Fleets of Automated Vehicles
in Dynamic Underground Mining Environments 54
   Olga Mironenko, Hadi Banaee, and Amy Loutfi

Signal Sparsity Considerations for Using VAE with Non-visual Data: Case
Study of Proximity Sensors on a Mobile Robot 73
   Oksana Hagen and Swen Gaudl

Planning with Non-deterministic Actions in Jason 83
   Josh Blondin and Babak Esfandiari

Bid Intercession to Unlock Human Control in Decentralized
Consensus-Based Multi-robot Task Allocation Algorithms 99
   Victor Guillet, Christophe Grand, Charles Lesire, and Gauthier Picard

Reason Logically, Move Continuously 115
   Andrea Gatti

Attentive A* for Visual Cue Based Path Planning in Complex Environments ... 128
   Abhay Kumar, Kunal Verma, Armaan Garg, and Shashi Shekhar Jha

Centralized Stochastic Multi-agent Pathfinding Under Partial Observability 145
   Guy Shani, Roni Stern, Itay Raveh, and Inon Katz

Author Index 165

Risk-Aware On-the-Fly Solving of Physical Vehicle Routing Problems

Jáchym Herynek[1] and Stefan Edelkamp[1,2]

[1] Computer Science Department, Artificial Intelligence Center Faculty of Electrical Engineering Czech Technical University, Prague, Czech Republic
{heryjac,edelkste}@fel.cvut.cz
[2] Department of Theoretical Computer Science and Mathematical Logic Faculty of Mathematics and Physics Charles University, Prague, Czech Republic
edelkamp@ktiml.mff.cuni.cz

Abstract. In missions for a set of autonomous vehicles given a complex environment with obstacles and many waypoints to visit, risk-aware routing plays an important role. In this paper, we consider multi-robot, multi-goal motion planning where unsafe areas should be avoided. We assume a geometric environment for a set of high-dimensional robots, providing a motion model with nonlinear dynamics that, for a given state and a small time step, applies a control action and provides a next state or reports a collision. As there are anonymous goals meaning there is no predefined assignment of goals to the robots, the approach assigns goals to them on-the-fly during the solution process. We study the computational limits and possibilities of our approach, derive a scaling framework system that plans and executes the safe travel for the given fleet of robots, and we conduct experiments for benchmark scenarios.

1 Introduction

Safe mission planning is at the core of modern robotics [46]. There are many critical risk scenarios. Consider, for example, a robot rover mission on a different planet as in Deep Space 1 [7] or in the Mars rover mission [2], where transmission time windows are dependent on visibility to the ground station on earth, and energy is consumed by the rover. In our setting, we consider an unstructured, complex environment for a team of high-dimensional robotic systems with nonlinear dynamics and nonholonomic constraints to visit a set of goal regions in a suitable cost-minimizing order. The task is to efficiently compute maximally safe, collision-free, and dynamically feasible trajectories that enable the robots to complete the mission.

Robots have size, heading, and velocity, and their motions can often only be described according to a dynamic simulator or set of nonlinear differential equations. While the multi-goal route planning problem for one agent is already computationally hard [4], the physical motion planning problem for a fleet of mobile robots is computationally even more demanding [8] and considered to be one the most challenging problems in computational robotics nowadays.

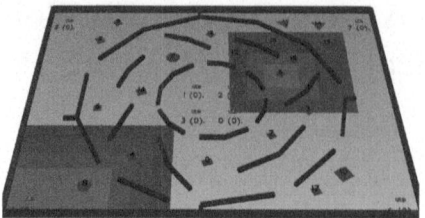

Fig. 1. Sample scenario for safe physical vehicle routing. The map show several obstacles (blue), goals to be visited (red), and risk areas (yellow to orange). There are eight vehicles found at their starting location (four in the middle and four in the corners of the arena)(Color figure online) .

Risk-aware travel planning is crucial in many applications as not all routes warrant the same safety level. Potential vehicle damage may be one critical source of mission risk. Other risk factors are timing constraints, obstacles being hit, dynamically infeasible trajectories, and further aspects. This paper studies the safe physical vehicle routing problem (see Fig 1). It models safety in terms of minimizing the time spent in risk areas and integrates dynamic feasibility in form of motion constraints.We propose a multi-robot multi-goal motion planning framework generic in terms of the applied vehicle models (given by their shape and motions as differential equations or via a simulator); and the geometric environments with obstacles, safety terrains, and goal regions. These inputs can be modified non-intrusively in text files without changing the implementation. During the search, we traverse randomized roadmaps and assume that the multi-criteria cost function can be linearized to a single-objective [16]. We exploit a motion tree for the continuous execution of valid trajectories [35], and employ discrete solvers for guiding the routing.

The contributions of the paper are manifold. We study general mission planning problems for k geometrically shaped robots with nonlinear motion dynamics, with g goal regions and geometric areas of various mission risk levels, while handling both robot-robot and robot-obstacle collisions. Different to many multi-agent path finding scenarios (see [44]), we have anonymous goals. A subsequent feature of our approach is the on-the-fly assignments of goals to the robots. While we derive that the considered physical safe vehicle routing problem is semi-decidable, experimentally we always secured convincing solutions to a our set of mission tasks. For the discrete abstraction we prove polynomial solubility, which may surprise, as many tour-finding problems are at least NP-hard even without weights and direction. The ants-on-a-stick puzzle helps understanding the proof concept, its generalization from singular goals to goal agendas, possible improvements to the solution qualities, and the completeness of solution finding. In the selection of inputs we vary the number of robots, the cost function, the discrete solver parameters, and separate parallel from sequential planning. Risk is modeled as an integral over a curve in the continuous case, and the sum of edge costs in the discrete case, added or maximized for the robots. A central planner runs a loop of alternating discrete and continuous problem solving, calling a state-of-the-art solver of the vehicle routing problem [10]. For moderately sized maps the complete solution process of planning and simulating the robots runs in real-time.

The paper is structured as follows. Firstly, we review safe motion planning for a robot fleet. Then, we present a geometric model of the mobile robots acting in the potentially unsafe environment with an ensemble of polytopes and differential equations. Next, we study complexities for the continuous and the discrete vehicle routing problems, and the effect of adding risk. After explaining some implementation considerations in more detail, we demonstrate the capabilities of our solver in a number of different artificial and benchmark scenarios.

2 Related Work

Physical Vehicle Routing. We consider robot motion extension of the vehicle routing problem (VRP) known from Operations Research [14], where the objective is to find optimized tours for a fleet of vehicles to service a given set of customer requests. Usually, the assignment of the goals to the vehicles has to be found by the solver. Dynamic VRPs were studied by [9], and vehicle routing for robots with temporal constraints by [24]. They use a high-level task planner to statically assign waypoints to the vehicles and a low-level motion planner that generates a feasible path that respects the vehicle' motion models; while [17] tackles pickup and delivery VRPs over a discrete abstraction using sampling-based motion planning to guide the search in an obstacle-rich environment, which produces paths that maximize the number of customers that could be visited. The authors of [51] developed an approach that tackles the vehicle routing problem with uncertain customer demands and travel distances by applying fuzzy theory; [30] presented an approach that combines A* and a genetic algorithm to solve a variant of the TSP with energy and capacity constraints, where A* is used to compute the shortest path for each combination of waypoint pairs.

Multi-agent pathfinding (MAPF) executed on a graph with a fixed assignment of k robots to k goals has a body of research [44] simply too large to be covered in detail. There has been work on multi-agent multi-goal path finding, one introducing CBSS, an approach for multiagent combinatorial path finding [39], and one considering MAPF for precedence-constrained goal sequences [52]. The authors of [3] highlight that the simplifying discretized time limits the applicability of multi-agent path-finding algorithms in real-world applications and raise questions of how to discretize time in an effective manner, proposing an algorithms for finding optimal solutions that do not rely on any time discretization: while [34] introduced the multi-objective physical TSP as a real-time game where the player controls a ship that must visit a series of waypoints in a maze while minimizing three opposing goals: time spent, fuel consumed and damage taken, and the proposed controller was based on single-objective Monte-Carlo tree search, while the evaluation stressed multi-objective concepts.

There is upcoming related work on multi-robot multi-goal mission planning in terrains of varying energy consumption [21], but which comes with no theory and a different focus, given that energy to be planned for needs to be repleted.

Risk-Aware Planning. Safe planning is often considered in the aircraft domain, as any in-flight failure may lead to a crash with immense consequences [15]. The risk induced by an aircraft accident can be defined in various ways, such as economic evaluation and casualties on the ground [13,22]. Possible risk to people, ground vehicles, and aircraft for small UAVs ground risk map is proposed in [22], and the induced risk as a result of three consecutive events is discussed in [13], i.e., loss of control with an uncontrolled crash on the ground; impact with someone; and fatal injury to the hit person. However, a precise impact location cannot be predicted, and a stochastic model has to be used in the case of an uncontrolled fall of the aircraft [12], the use of which may be computationally demanding. Thus, routing is employed in surveillance planning with safe emergency landing trajectories [47]. Safe planning was also proposed in the existing approach of risk map assessment [37] and to find the trajectory with minimal risk in [38]. The plan in dynamic environments by the concept of the lifelong A* [25] and RRTX [33] achieve computationally feasible generalization towards dynamic environments. On the contrary, the risk related to car-like vehicles is often associated with on-road accidents and collisions. A risk model based on roads' physical conditions, such as friction and allowed travel, speed is proposed in [11], providing a weighted graph with the risk associated with roads. A more detailed road risk model is proposed in [29], where both travel time and risk are considered during the planning phase. However, the problem of finding the optimal path is regarded as a network flow problem and [42] applied planning space discretization and efficient risk propagation through a riskmap for airplanes. The approach can find the least risky landing site and corresponding forced landing trajectory for any configuration in the planning space.

Similar to cost-efficient planning, the least risky trajectory can be obtained by various approaches based on the environmental representation. Moreover, [37] define trajectory risk as a accumulation of risks taken over areas and propose using a graph-based variant of the A* algorithm, called Risk-A*, to find the least risky trajectory in a given roadmap graph. Further assumptions about the risk, such as its limits, are utilized. Risk-A* relies on a multi-layer precomputed risk map for a static environment. Constructing a whole risk map can be computationally demanding. Therefore, [38] further explored the idea of a multi-layer ground risk map and proposed an online evaluation of the risk instead of creating a full ground risk map. Hence, an RRT*-based algorithm called Risk-based RRT* is proposed for finding the least risky trajectory. The algorithm randomly samples the configuration space, and an impact probability is predicted for the taken sample. Then, the risk is calculated similarly to the construction of the ground risk map, assuming various map layers such as the population density and sheltering factors. The new sample is added to the roadmap such that the risk is minimized, and the process continues until a trajectory to the goal location is found. The main surplus of risk-based RRT* to RRT* is in incorporating the risk assessment routines. Plaku [36] addresses risk-aware planning for a single robot with the same vehicle models to ours, but where the objective to secure a secondary rescue route at each point executing the overall route was completely different.

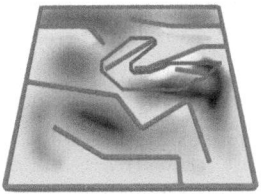
(a) Sample heatmap with solution paths

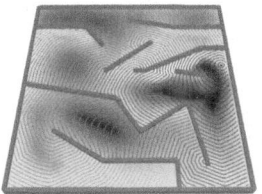
(b) Same heatmap wth iso-distance contours

Fig. 2. An example of a risk heatmap: (**a**): with example solutions, (**b**): with iso-distance contours. The heatmap shows high-risk areas (in bright yellow) and low-risk areas (in black). Notice that the risk-aware trajectory (in green) between two configurations is longer than the shortest path (in blue), but its risk is significantly reduced. Iso-distance contours, points with the same risk-aware distance from the start (shown as a black dot) are also shown (Color figure online).

3 Towards a Problem Formulation

Figure 2 shows an example of a risk heatmap together with two trajectories, a longer one that avoids risks and a shorter one that does not. The heatmap influences the shortest paths, as illustrated in the figure, where we have some areas of risk that induce higher costs. We may project risks onto the edge weight function of the randomized roadmap and minimize the cost function $g(s) + h(s)$ where $g(s)$ is the motion cost from the start node s_0 to the node s, and $h(s)$ is the heuristic cost that estimates the motion cost between s and the goal node t. The main difference is to encapsulates the risk into the cost function. The motion cost $g(s)$ and heuristic cost $h(s)$ for node s can be expressed as $g(s) = \int_{s_0}^{s} r(x)\ dx$ and $h(s) = \int_{s}^{t} r(x)\ dx$, where $r(x)$ is the risk function.

In our approach, mission risk can be traded-off with solution time and also be encoded in terms of enforcing limits on energy consumption, travel time, and vehicle load, which we will not dwell on, as well as in obstacle avoidance and motion feasibility. We are able to efficiently provide a full-fledged missions for high-dimensional robotic systems with nonlinear dynamics and nonholonomic constraints that visit a maximized number of goal regions in a suitable risk-minimizing order within an unstructured, complex environment. It efficiently computes collision-free, dynamically-feasible, low-cost, risk-minimizing trajectories that enable the robot to satisfy the task. In safe motion planning, we select the regions to avoid risks during travel [6].

As we compute cost-minimizing dynamically feasible tours, not trajectories for individual (initial/goal) location pairs, even in the abstraction, we precompute shortest paths between all pairs of waypoints, add distances to the current location, and provide an according distance matrix of shortest-path distances to a discrete solver. During travel, the starting robot location is exchanged with the current location leading to a modification of one row and one column in the distance matrix. In general terms, the different objectives risk and travel cost lead to multi-criteria optimization [18]. We approximate such bi-criteria path-finding problem by using a user-defined linear combination of the two, and generate a randomized risk roadmap for our motion planning algorithm. We assume that the multi-criteria cost function of travel cost and travel risk is linearized and remains additive in order to support shortest-path search as in Dijkstra's shortest path algorithm or A*. It is well-known that the optimal value of this function will be located on the so-called Pareto frontier.

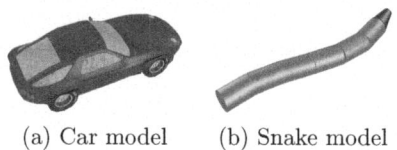

(a) Car model   (b) Snake model

Fig. 3. Vehicle models used in the experiments.

The robots are defined as a tuple $\langle \mathcal{M}, \mathcal{Q}, \mathcal{S}, \mathcal{U}, f \rangle$, where $s \in \mathcal{S}$ augments the configuration by including other variables, such as velocity and steering angle. We further have the geometric robot shape $\mathcal{M}$, the configuration space $\mathcal{Q}$, the state-space $\mathcal{S}$, the control space $\mathcal{U}$, and the motion equations f. A configuration $q \in \mathcal{Q}$ defines the position and orientation. A control $u \in \mathcal{U}$ defines external inputs, such as acceleration and steering angle that is used to control the robot. The motion equations are often expressed as a set of differential equations of the form $\dot{s} \leftarrow f(s, u)$. As an example, the motion equations of the car model shown in Fig. 3(a) are defined as

$$\begin{bmatrix} \dot{x} \\ \dot{y} \\ \dot{\theta} \\ \dot{v} \\ \dot{\psi} \end{bmatrix} = \begin{bmatrix} v\cos(\theta)\cos(\psi) \\ v\sin(\theta)\cos(\psi) \\ v\sin(\psi) \\ a \\ \omega \end{bmatrix}, \quad (1)$$

where the state $s = (x, y, \theta, \psi, v)$ defines the position (x, y), orientation θ, steering angle ψ, and velocity v, while the control $u = (a, \omega)$ defines the acceleration a and steering rate ω. As another example shown in Fig. 3(b), a snake model can be obtained by attaching N trailers to the car and augmenting f as

$$\dot{\theta}_i = (v/H)(\sin(\theta_{i-1}) - \sin(\theta_0))\prod_{j=1}^{i-1}\cos(\theta_{j-1} - \theta_j), \quad (2)$$

where θ_i is the orientation of the i-th trailer, with $\theta_0 = \theta$, and where H is the hitch distance [27]. When applying a control $u \in \mathcal{U}$ to a state $s \in \mathcal{S}$ for a time step dt, the new state $s_{\text{new}} \in \mathcal{S}$ is computed by a function:

$$s_{\text{new}} \leftarrow \text{SIMULATE}(s, u, f, dt), \qquad (3)$$

which numerically integrates f for one time step dt. Applying a sequence of controls $\langle u_1, \ldots, u_{\ell-1} \rangle$ gives rise to a dynamically-feasible motion trajectory $\pi : \{1, \ldots, \ell\} \to \mathcal{S}$, where $\pi(1) \leftarrow s$ and for all $i \in \{2, \ldots, \ell\}$ we have

$$\pi(i) \leftarrow \text{SIMULATE}(\pi(i-1), u_{i-1}, f, dt). \qquad (4)$$

Robot navigation in geometric environments has been studied for decades in the area of computational geometry and robotics [28]. We consider geometric objects as a selection of polytopes [32]. For our framework we use an input model that is an arrangement of geometric objects, i.e., all obstacles and even safety areas are encoded as polytopes in $\mathbb{R}^d$, e.g., polygons in 2D and polyhedra in 3D (w.l.o.g., this paper sticks to 2D, while we support 3D robot models and environments). A rough problem definition looks as follows. For the sake of the simplicity of notation, we also assume a homogeneous fleet, while we can also deal with heterogeneous ones.

Definition 1 (Safe Physical Vehicle Routing). *We are given a geometric autonomous vehicle model $\langle \mathcal{M}, \mathcal{Q}, \mathcal{S}, \mathcal{U}, f \rangle$ and its simulation semantics for a fleet of k robots with nonlinear dynamics, operating in the the geometric world $\mathcal{W}$ of connected regions, obstacles $\mathcal{O}$, and goals $\mathcal{G}$, and travel cost function c together with an arrangement of geometric shapes for risk that incur damage to the vehicle. The task in safe physical vehicle routing is to dynamically plan valid trajectories π^i, via determining the control actions of every robot i, $i \in \{1, \ldots, k\}$, that in combination visit all the goals, while avoiding robot-obstacle and robot-robot collisions and minimizing accumulated damage and travel cost.*

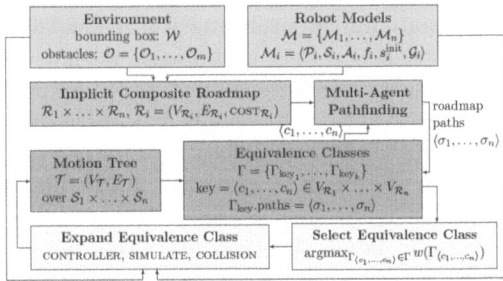

Fig. 4. General framework multi-robot architecture, following [35].

To guide the search in the continuous case, building on [35], we use a graph abstraction of the above problem that will be solved at each node of the constructed motion tree of feasible trajectories and that is utilized as a heuristic function. The general multi-robot architecture is reviewed in Fig. 4. We extended it with safety regions and anonymous multi-goals (inducing one common goal set for all the robots), as well as with a risk-aware VRP solver for multi-agent safe tour finding.

4 Complexity Considerations

In this section, we consider the complexity of the problem.

Continuous Case. It is well known that the computational complexity of motion planning with dynamics is huge. Even rearranging rectangles, with no rotations, inside of a rectangular box is NP-hard, and motion planning with robots for the Dubin's car setting is barely decidable, while with general nonlinear dynamics, it is undecidable [8]. Undecidability is a harsh limitation, but it does not mean that all instances of the problem are unsolvable and that we cannot try solving them. In fact, this complexity results refers to the notion of semi-decidability, as Branicky [8] showed that smooth ordinary differential equations in $\mathbb{R}^3$ can simulate arbitrary Turing machines and, hence, possess the power of universal computation. If we are lucky with the instance and the exploration, we can generate a solution by enumeration. But as we cannot enforce a bound on the solution length, in general we are not able decide if the algorithm runs forever not being able to solve it, or if it takes too long to find one. Hence, the effectiveness of the approach boils down to the design of good search heuristics.

Discrete Case. To analyze the discrete case, we start with some initial observations. The traveling-salesman problem (TSP) is NP-complete and, thus, as generalizations, all multi-vehicle VRPs with exclusive node visits are at least NP-hard [4]. Note that algorithms are exponential in the number of waypoints to visit, not in the size of the graph, as there is a polynomial-time shortest paths reduction for the graph that can be applied in time cubic to the graph size.

In an undirected graph with n nodes and a set of k moving robots, we consider a multi-agent multi-goal path finding problem with k robot tours for n waypoints. For a fixed assignment from k robots to k goals, we have the (non-optimal) MAPF problem that has been solved for an undirected graph [26,40]. The work goes back to [49], who proved this for $k = n-1$. A tractable algorithm for MAPF on undirected graphs was given by [48]. Recently, it was shown that the directed MAPF is NP-complete [31]. While it was known that the problem was NP-hard, Nebel proved that it is also in NP, showing that the short solution hypothesis for strongly connected digraphs holds. Another interesting recent MAPF variant is the option to disconnect trailers or containers from the vehicle agents [5]. Turning to multiple goals, we obtain the following definition.

For the optimal anonymous MAPF problem with k agents and goals, there are polynomial algorithms. The main idea is to replicate the underlying problem graph with the solution depth and searching for an optimal network flow [50]. The approach, however, does not easily carry over to multiple goals as even for one agent we have a TSP. Next, we turn to multiple goals.

Definition 2 (Safe Anonymous Vehicle Routing). Let $G = (V, E, r, c)$ be a weighted graph with edge functions $r : E \to \mathbb{R}^{\geq 0}$ for risk, and cost $c : E \to \mathbb{R}_{\geq 0}$ for travel distance. For a given $\alpha \in [0,1] \cap \mathbb{R}$ we define a linear combination travel weight $w : E \to \mathbb{R}_{\geq 0}$ so that for all $(u,v) \in E$ we have $w(u,v) = \alpha \cdot r(u,v) + (1-\alpha) \cdot c(u,v)$. We assume that the graph is undirected, so that for all $(u,v) \in E$ we have $(v,u) \in E$ and $w(u,v) = w(v,u)$. In the safe vehicle routing routing problem, for a set of agents R with $k = |R|$, and a set of waypoints $W \subseteq V$ with $m = |W|$ a route has to be found that visits all the waypoints and minimizes accumulated travel weight.

If we do not impose optimality on the travel and allow nodes to be visited more than once during the travel, the edge weights do not matter, and we obtain the following result, which adapts the goal agendas of the individual robots on-the-fly. As the proof in fact uses edge costs, the constructed solution will have an optimized solution quality. The beauty of our approach is that it dynamically assigns the goals to the robots, so that swapping agendas on robot-robot interaction is supported during the replanning.

Theorem 1 (Polynomial-Time Solubility of Anonymous Vehicle Routing in Undirected Graphs). In an undirected weighted graph $G = (V, E, w)$ with $n = |V|$, $e = |E| \subseteq V \times V$, given a set of $W \subseteq V$ waypoints with $m = |W|$, and k agents moving along edges via graph nodes, the safe vehicle routing problem is solvable in polynomial time.

Proof. The proof is based on the following intriguing puzzle[1]. A number of ants are dropped on a $1m$ stick. Each ant is traveling either to the left or the right with constant speed $1m$/minute. When two ants meet, they bounce off each other and reverse direction. When an ant reaches an end of the stick, it falls off. At some point all the ants will have fallen off. The time at which this happens will depend on the initial configuration of the ants. While ants bouncing off each other seems difficult to keep track of, we observe that two ants bouncing off each other is equivalent to two ants that pass through each other, or exchanging their intended goal direction. Viewed in this way, all ants fall off after traversing the length of the stick, and it will be empty after one minute.

Back to the original graph problem in the theorem. If the graph is disconnected, we first compute the connected components in linear time and solve the problem in each connected component individually. So, w.l.o.g., we may assume that the undirected graph is connected. Any given assignment of (still unvisited) waypoints to the agents induces a partitioning $W_1 \ldots, W_k$ of the set of waypoints W with $\cup_{i=1} W_i = W$ and $W_i \cap W_j = \emptyset$ for all $1 \leq i \neq j \leq k$.

We use a shortest path reduction of the graph and a greedy vehicle routing solver on the pairwise distances to find initial routes in form of waypoint agendas for each of the agents. The shortest path from any two adjacent waypoints in any tour can be computed by Dijkstra's algorithm in time $O(e + n \log n)$, e.g.,

---

[1] discussed, e.g., by Su, Francis E., et al. in blog "Ants on a Stick." Math Fun Facts. See https://www.math.hmc.edu/funfacts.

with Fibonacci heaps. For m waypoints to visit in a given order by k agents, we have $O((k+m) \cdot (e + n \log n)) = O(n^3)$ and, thus, polynomial time.

We start with a greedy initial ordered assignments of goals to the agents, which may be found by graph partitioning or weighted clustering approximation methods, or by time-limited VRP solving. Suppose that during the travel imposed by the shortest paths between subsequent goals, agent r_i has waypoint g_j on top of its goal agenda, and another agent $r_{i'}$ has waypoint $g_{j'}$ with $i \neq i'$ and $j \neq j'$ on top of its agenda. In case of collision of the two we apply the argument from the ant-on-stick example. The two agents exchange their agendas, so that $r_{i'}$ next turns to wayoint g_j with r_i next turns to waypoint $g_{j'}$. This is done for each of the agents at each collision, so that all waypoints are reached in polynomial time. □

Note first, that using breadth-first search instead of Dijkstra's shortest path search would of also yield solubility in undirected roadmap graphs, but it leads to much worse solutions, as the underlying problem graph is weighted. Note second, we may even argue that no de-facto collision occurs in solving the problem in undirected graphs, as we could stop on the robots on the nodes right before the collision to exchange the direction and the waypoint agendas. This, however, assumes at least some space in between the robots.

Therefore, the conditions that make discrete tour planning hard are a) the direction of the graph, b) the optimization criterion, and, c) the inherent complexity of the robots' movements such as speed and acceleration. Note that we allow the shortest paths to overlap on both nodes and edges, which in the NP-hard Hamiltonian Path problem is not allowed. Also note that when relaxing revisiting nodes and searching for edge-disjoint Eulerian paths, the tour construction, in contrast to the TSP, is already linear-time.

Risk-awareness, however, is essential. The agent traversing the graph might have limited risk that it can take, so that the shortest path found via the metric might become infeasible. While the single-objective shortest-path problem is general is solvable in polynomial time, as these methods utilize the optimal substructure of the problem, the addition of risk may violate this property.

Theorem 2 (Complexity Anonymous Safe Shortest Paths). *Let graph $G = (V, E, r, c, s, t)$ with nodes V, edges E, weight $r : E \to \mathbb{R}$ for risk, and cost $c : E \to \mathbb{R}$ for travel distance have one start s and one target node t. For our case, as is commonly true for path metrics, both of these costs are additive over edges, i.e. $c(\pi) = \sum_{e \in \pi} c(e)$ and $r(\pi) = \sum_{e \in \pi} r(e)$. Minimizing $c(\pi)$ such that $r(\pi) < B$, where π is a path from s to t and B is a bound on the accumulated risks, is NP-hard.*

Proof. This scenario refers to a *weight constrained shortest path problem* [20], which is the problem of minimizing one metric over paths in a graph, subject to a bound on another metric, which has to be shown to be NP-complete by [19] by a reduction from the PARTITION problem, i.e., the task of deciding whether a S of positive integers can be partitioned into two non-empty subsets S_1 and $S_2 = S \setminus S_1$ such that $\sum_{s_1 \in S_1} s_1 = \sum_{s_2 \in S_2} s_2$. □

The weight constrained shortest path problem can, however, be solved by dynamic programming approaches in exponential time [43]. Also, heuristic search approaches have been studied [1].

Wide Corridors. Back to the continuous risk-aware multi-robot multi-goal tour-finding problem. We discussed that though the problem is undecidable in general, particular instances might be solvable. But if we suppose the continuous problem to robots to always bypass each other even in narrow corridors, essentially casting each undirected way in the discrete setting into two directed ways for the continuous setting. In that case, we can establish trajectories based on a found discrete order. This can be done by increasing the size of the robot in the randomized roadmap that constituted the graph. The geometric reasoning behind this method for reducing the size of the robot and inflating the object is related to taking Minkowski sum of obstacles and robots. In simulation practice, we observed that our construction of the discrete graph actually satisfied this property, so that solvable instances in the discrete case usually lead to solvable instances in the continuous case. If not, we dynamically increase the edge weight and prune the branch in the motion tree.

Geometric Environments. In a geometric world, besides robot-obstacle collision in each node of the motion tree, we need to check $r(r-1)/2 = O(r^2)$ robot-to-robot collisions, each of which can be computationally demanding for complex robots. However, experimentally the time for this collision checking was negligible, as collision checks are accellerated with with bounding boxes or sphere trees. In most cases, the solver recognizes infeasibility due to agent collisions quickly enough to fully replan on the high-level.

5 Implementation Considerations

To find a trajectory that satisfies the motion planning problem, we use a sampling-based motion planning approach; namely, a simplified probabilistic roadmap [23] PRM to construct a search graph over the configuration space, which is the set of all abstract configurations and positions that the vehicle can obtain. The PRM computes random samples around the environment as nodes and connects neighboring nodes if the edges between the nodes do not collide with an obstacle. We ensure the graph is dense by generating numerous samples to construct many routes to reach the goals regions. We continue this process by adding new nodes and connecting them until all the goal regions are connected to the same component.

After constructing the roadmap and integrating risk-awareness in the cost function, Dijkstra's shortest-path algorithm is invoked from each of the regions of interest to compute the minimum cost paths to every roadmap vertex. The cost between the vertices is used in the form of a distance matrix, which is used in the subsequent stage. The benefit of this approach is that it considers the obstacles in the environment, and with the discrete abstraction, we can ignore the obstacle and still have the shortest distance between the goals that consider the obstacles.

For an efficient discrete vehicle routing routine as invoked several time in our algorithm, we used nested-rollout policy adaption (NRPA) as the applied search procedure [41]. NRPA is a Monte-Carlo search algorithm for single-player games. It learns a rollout policy by adapting weights on each action and initializes all weights to zero. During the rollout phase, an action is sampled with a probability proportional to the exponential of the associated weight encoded in the policy. The approach has been shown to be effective approach to the vehicle route planning by [10] and applied to motion planning e.g., by [17]. NRPA mainly has two parameters: the recursion depth and the iteration width.

NRPA was proposed as a way to use gradient ascent rather than navigating the tree directly. The algorithm consists of three elements: the policy, the rollout, and the policy adaptation. The algorithm simplified to a single robot (see Fig. 5) starts with nestedness *level*, which is defined by a user and performs a sequential call to $level - 1$, $level - 2$, and if they reach the lowest recursion level, the rollout occurs. Iterations correspond to the recursion width and helps replacing the best solution found. To extend the search to more than one robot, we can simulate the tour of multiple robots, as a combined tour of one robot by resetting the time and location at each end of a subtour.

Algorithm Search
Input: recursion *level*, policy *pol*
Output: best *score* and *route*
if ($level = 0$)
　　($score, route$) ← $Rollout(pol)$
　　return ($score, route$)
$best \leftarrow \infty$
for (N iterations) **do**
　　($result, newroute$) ←
　　　　Search($level - 1, pol$)
　　if ($result < best$)
　　　　$best \leftarrow result$;
　　　　$pol \leftarrow$ Adapt($pol, newroute$)
return ($best, route$)

Algorithm Adapt
Input: policy *pol*, improving *route*
Output: updated policy *pol'*
$node \leftarrow root(), pol' \leftarrow pol$
for ($j \leftarrow 0..|route| - 1$) **do**
　　$pol'[node, route_j] \leftarrow pol'[node, route_j] + 1$
　　$z \leftarrow \sum_i e^{pol[node,i]}$
　　for (children i of $node$) **do**
　　　　$pol'[node, i] \leftarrow pol'[node, i] - e^{pol[node,i]}/z$
　　$node \leftarrow route_j$
return pol'

Fig. 5. Nested rollout with policy adaptation.

An important principle of NRPA is to bias rollouts through learning by weighting possible actions. The weights for the actions are updated in each step of the algorithm to prioritize the movements of the best routing sequence found. In addition, each simulation state is coded differently to prevent the policy of the simulation state from affecting the selection of subsequent simulation state steps. The choices of the simulation steps are random, but the probability is not the same in each step. Policy adaptation adds value to the action of the best sequence and decreases the weight of other possible actions by an amount proportional to their weight.

Algorithm Rollout
Input policy *pol*
Global big factor M, #agents r, #waypoints n,
  time windows $[l_i, r_i]$ for agent r_i, metric $dist[0..n-1][0..n]$
Output score *val*; vehicle tours *route*
$(visits_1, \ldots, visits_{n-1}) \leftarrow (1, \ldots, 1); visits_0 \leftarrow k-1; route_0 \leftarrow 0;$
$node \leftarrow prev \leftarrow makespan \leftarrow violations \leftarrow cost \leftarrow 0; length \leftarrow 1$
while $(length \leq n+k)$
  $sum \leftarrow succs \leftarrow 0$
  for $(i \leftarrow 0..n-1)$
    if $(visits_i > 0)$
      $moves_{succ} \leftarrow i; succ \leftarrow succ + 1$
      for $(j \leftarrow 0..n-1), (i \neq j)$ **do**
        if $(visits_j > 0)$
          if $(l_i > r_j \lor makespan + dist_{node,i} > r_j)$ $succ \leftarrow succ - 1$ **break**
  if $(succs = 0)$
    for $(i \leftarrow 0..n-1)$ **do**
      if $(visits_i > 0)$ $moves_{succ} \leftarrow i; succ \leftarrow succ + 1$
  for $(i \leftarrow 0..succ - 1)$
    $value_i \leftarrow e^{pol[node][moves_i]}; sum \leftarrow sum + value_i$
  $mrand \leftarrow rand(0, sum); i \leftarrow 0; sum \leftarrow value_0$
  while $(sum < mrand)$
    $i \leftarrow i+1; sum \leftarrow sum + value_i$
  $node' \leftarrow moves_i; prev' \leftarrow node$
  $makespan' \leftarrow makespan' + dist_{prev',node'} > l_{node'}$?
      $makespan' + dist_{prev',node'} : l_{node'}$
  $visits_{node'} \leftarrow visits_{node'} - 1$
  if $(makespan' > r_{node'})$ $violations \leftarrow violations + 1$
  $prev \leftarrow prev'; node \leftarrow node'$
  $route_{length} \leftarrow node; length \leftarrow length + 1$
  $cost \leftarrow cost + dist_{prev,node}$
  $makespan \leftarrow makespan'$
  if $(node = node_0)$ $prev \leftarrow makespan \leftarrow 0$
return $(M \cdot violations + cost, route)$

Fig. 6. Rollout function for vehicle routing problem.

6 Experiments

We implemented the framework in GNU g++ on Ubuntu 22.04 using one core of a AMD Ryzen 7 7840U processor with 2×16 GB DDR5-5600. As inputs (see Figs. 1 and 7) we used manually created geometric benchmarks and automatically converted grid benchmarks [45] into this format, which itself is a viable

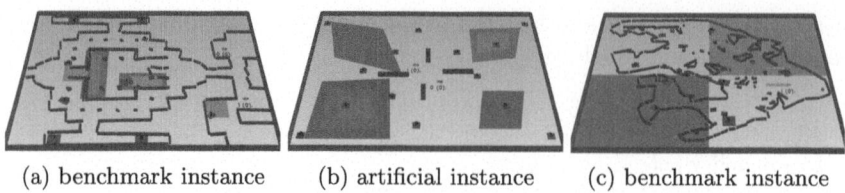

(a) benchmark instance (b) artificial instance (c) benchmark instance

Fig. 7. Three example inputs with 2 robots at their starting location, several obstacles (blue),and goals (red) to be visited. The maps also shows risk areas (in yellow to orange alias high-risk to low-risk). Scene (b) was manually designed, while (a) and (c) are converted grid benchmark instances from video game maps; (a) and (b) feature the car model, (c) the snake model (Color figure online) .

research avenue [32]. Input conversion and evaluation scripts were written in modern interpreter languages. We use median bar plots (with 90% quantiles) to visualize the distribution of the data in repeated runs with 50 different random seeds. In our graphs specifically, the bar in the middle is the median, not the mean. The upper bar is the maximum, and the lower bar is the minimum value observed in the various runs.

The problems are designed in a way to highlight the difference in the density of obstacles, in the performance of hand-crafted vs real maps, in the number of goals, in the number of robots, and the type of robots. The evaluation is based on illustrating the distributions over the 50 runs and displays the maximum and the sum of individual robot costs, as well as the overall CPU time in seconds.

For the sake of simplicity, for evaluating the risk-awareness we set value α in weight function $\alpha \cdot r + (1 - \alpha) \cdot c$ to either 0 or 1, so that either the solution length or the minimizing damage is interpreted most important to the solver.

Multi-Robot Multi-Goal Planning with Risk. We first consider a set of examples with varying domains, added areas of risk, and fixed parameter setting. *Arena 1* is a converted video game benchmark. *Arena 2* is *Arena 1* with a slight variation to the risk terrain. *Low obstacle* is a simplified scene with a few obstacles only. Snake scenarios include the second robot models, and *circle domains* are the same as the example of the intro with a scaling number of robots.

The results are shown in Fig. 8. While the robot initial positions have an influence on the search, one can clearly see that while increasing the number of robots does not necessarily improve the overall cost of the paths (this is where the positions of the robots make a huge difference), the most expensive path executed by a single robot reduction is much more significant. Snake robots do not lead to more complexity in the search.

Different Discrete Solver Settings. Secondly, in Fig. 9 we compare the time-quality trade-off with various discrete solver settings. In NRPA, we have the depth and the iteration width of the search, were we used the combinations (6,9) in Circle A, (6,8) in B, (6,7) in C, (5,7) in D, (5,6) in E, and (4,6) in F.

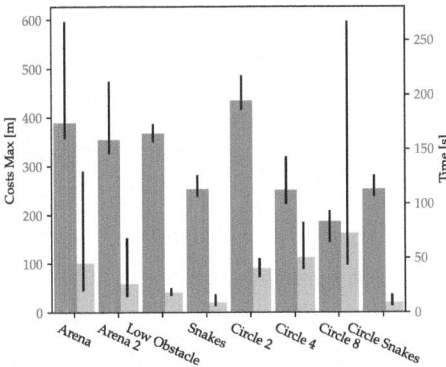

Fig. 8. Total CPU time for the entire simulation (red scale) together with maximum of risk costs (blue scale) in eight different examples (Color figure online).

As CPU time includes all computation and the simulation times regarding robot application, we judge these results as acceptable and efficient for real-time navigation. We can observe that lower parameter settings have significantly lower computational times at the cost of overall solution quality. The solver setting (B) was selected for all of the other experiments, as it provides the best compromise between solving time and solution quality. We also see that we have a few outliers, but most data values are clustered well around the median. Therefore we conclude the solutions to be robust with respect to different seeds.

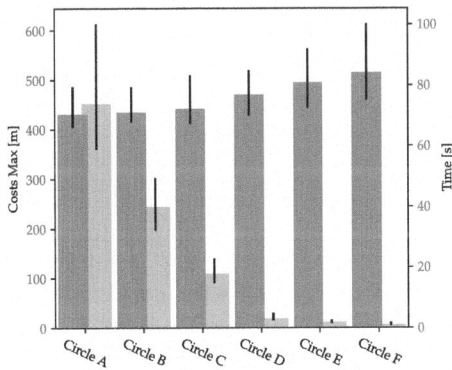

Fig. 9. Total CPU time for the entire simulation (red scale) together with maximum of risk costs (blue scale) in one example with seven different discrete solver parameterization (Color figure online).

Influence of Risks. Thirdly, we consider experiments comparing a risk-aware setting, i.e. $\alpha = 1$. with the one without, i.e. $\alpha = 0$. The outcome displayed in

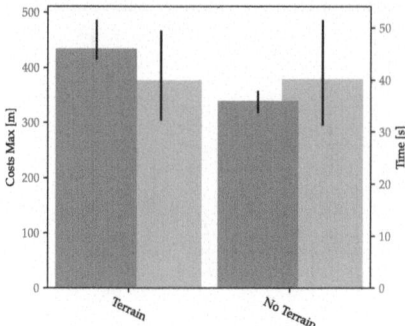

Fig. 10. Total CPU time for the entire simulation (red scale) together with maximum of risk costs (blue scale) for unsafe (Terrain) and safe routing (No Terrain) (Color figure online).

Fig. 10. As expected, the solution cost is generally smaller if risk is not considered in the search. In the case without considering risk, the cost is simply the distance, and (in this specific scenario) the risk is never lower than the distance. The running time is similar for the most part, as beyond the precomputation stage, the algorithm is almost the same regardless of the selected objective.

7 Conclusion

We introduced the risk-aware multi-robot multi-goal motion planning problem, which requires the integration of the motion planning problem and the vehicle routing problem to solve a challenging multi-robot multi-goal task-motion planning minimizing travel time and risk. The emphasis was on the framework to feature the dynamic change of the ordering of the goals during the ongoing navigation. Deadlocks were avoided implicitly in the motion tree via replanning the goal ordering on the fly by calling the discrete solver in the motion tree.

We also studied the computational limits and possibilities for solving the physical vehicle routing problem that, even for the discrete case, combines subproblems known to be NP-hard. A non-optimal solution was found in polynomial-time for undirected graphs with neglected cost and allowed overlaps of individual shortest paths. The counter-intuitive aspect of polynomiality matches the observation of Eulerian paths, whose construction in contrast to the TSP is linear-time.

We were able to solve and simulate challenging benchmark problems for safe robot navigation in real time, which has not been considered for expressive robot models before, despite their apparent relevance. We demonstrated how a probabilistic risk roadmap was used for abstraction and to calculate the distance cost between interest regions amongst obstacles, which allowed us to scale our work to more complex environments and solve the planning problem with obstacles.

Acknowledgements. Thanks to Jazz Warsame for the introduction to the motion planning framework implementation, and to Jakub Sláma for some references and Fig. 2. We also thank Jiří Švancara for insights to solutions to MAPF based network flow. The presented work has been supported by the Czech Science Foundation (GAČR) under the research project number 22-30043S.

References

1. Ahmadi, S., Tack, G., Harabor, D., Kilby, P.: Weight constrained path finding with bidirectional A. In: Proceedings of the Fifteenth International Symposium on Combinatorial Search, SOCS 2022, pp. 2–10. AAAI Press (2022)
2. Ai-Chang, M., et al.: MAPGEN: mixed-initiative planning and scheduling for the mars exploration rover mission. IEEE Intell. Syst. **19**(1), 8–12 (2004)
3. Andreychuk, A., Yakovlev, K.S., Surynek, P., Atzmon, D., Stern, R.: Multi-agent pathfinding with continuous time. Artif. Intell. **305**, 103662 (2022)
4. Applegate, D.L., Bixby, R.E., Chvatál, V., Cook, W.J.: The Traveling Salesman Problem: A Computational Study. Princeton University Press (2006). http://www.jstor.org/stable/j.ctt7s8xg
5. Bachor, P., Bergdoll, R., Nebel, B.: The multi-agent transportation problem. In: Williams, B., Chen, Y., Neville, J. (eds.) AAAI, pp. 11525–11532. AAAI Press (2023)
6. Barbosa, F.S.: Towards safer and risk-aware motion planning and control for robotic systems, Ph.D. thesis, KTH Royal Institute of Technology, Sweden (2022). https://urn.kb.se/resolve?urn=urn:nbn:se:kth:diva-307094
7. Bernard, D.E., et al.: Remote agent experiment DS1 technology validation report, Technical report, Ames Research Center and JPL (2000)
8. Branicky, M.S.: Universal computation and other capabilities of hybrid and continuous dynamical systems. Theor. Comput. Sci. **138**(1), 67–100 (1995)
9. Bullo, F., Frazzoli, E., Pavone, M., Savla, K., Smith, S.L.: Dynamic vehicle routing for robotic systems. Proc. IEEE **99**(9), 1482–1504 (2011). https://doi.org/10.1109/JPROC.2011.2158181
10. Cazenave, T., Lucas, J., Triboulet, T., Kim, H.: Policy adaptation for vehicle routing. AI Commun. **34**(1), 21–35 (2021)
11. Chandra, S.: Safety-based path finding in urban areas for older drivers and bicyclists. Transp. Res. Part C Emerg. Tech. **48**, 143–157 (2014)
12. la Cour-Harbo, A.: Ground impact probability distribution for small unmanned aircraft in ballistic descent. In: International Conference on Unmanned Aircraft Systems, ICUAS, No. 9213990, pp. 1442–1451 (2020)
13. Dalamagkidis, K., Valavanis, K.P., Piegl, L.A.: On Integrating Unmanned Aircraft Systems into the National Airspace System: Issues, Challenges, Operational Restrictions, Certification, and Recommendations. Intelligent Systems, Control, and Automation: Science and Engineering. Springer, Dordrecht (2009). https://doi.org/10.1007/978-94-007-2479-2
14. Dantzig, G.B., Ramser, J.H.: The truck dispatching problem. Manage. Sci. **6**(1), 80–91 (1959)

15. Di, K., Zhou, Y., Jiang, J., Yan, F., Yang, S., Jiang, Y.: Risk-aware collection strategies for multirobot foraging in hazardous environments. ACM Trans. Auton. Adapt. Syst. **16**(3–4), 1–38 (2022)
16. Edelkamp, S., Jabbar, S., Lluch-Lafuente, A.: Cost-algebraic heuristic search. In: Veloso, M.M., Kambhampati, S. (eds.) AAAI, pp. 1362–1367. AAAI Press/The MIT Press (2005)
17. Edelkamp, S., Plaku, E., Warsame, Y.: Monte-Carlo search for prize-collecting robot motion planning with time windows, capacities, pickups, and deliveries. In: Benzmüller, C., Stuckenschmidt, H. (eds.) KI 2019: Advances in Artificial Intelligence, pp. 154–167. Springer, Cham (2019). https://doi.org/10.1007/978-3-030-30179-8_13
18. Ehrgott, M.: Multicriteria Optimization. 2 edn. Springer, Heidelberg (2005). https://doi.org/10.1007/3-540-27659-9
19. Garey, M.R., Johnson, D.S.: Computers and Intractability: A Guide to the Theory of NP-Completeness. W. H. Freeman (1979)
20. Handler, G.Y., Zang, I.: A dual algorithm for the constrained shortest path problem. Networks **10**(4), 293–309 (1980)
21. Herynek, J., Edelkamp, S.: Multi-robot multi-goal mission planning in terrains of varying energy consumption. In: 2024 IEEE/RSJ International Conference on Intelligent Robots and Systems (IROS). IEEE (2024)
22. Hu, X., Pang, B., Dai, F., Low, K.H.: Risk assessment model for UAV cost-effective path planning in urban environments. IEEE Access **8**, 150162–150173 (2020)
23. Kavraki, L.E., Švestka, P., Latombe, J.C., Overmars, M.H.: Probabilistic roadmaps for path planning in high-dimensional configuration spaces. IEEE Trans. Rob. **12**(4), 566–580 (1996)
24. Kiesel, S., Burns, E., Wilt, C., Ruml, W.: Integrating vehicle routing and motion planning. In: Twenty-Second International Conference on Automated Planning and Scheduling (2012)
25. Koenig, S., Likhachev, M.: Incremental A*. In: Dietterich, T.G., Becker, S., Ghahramani, Z. (eds.) NIPS, pp. 1539–1546. MIT Press (2001)
26. Kornhauser, D., Miller, G.L., Spirakis, P.G.: Coordinating pebble motion on graphs, the diameter of permutation groups, and applications. In: 25th Annual Symposium on Foundations of Computer Science, pp. 241–250. IEEE Computer Society (1984)
27. LaValle, S.M.: Planning Algorithms. Cambridge University Press, Cambridge, U.K. (2006)
28. Lavalle, S.M.: Planning Algorithms. Cambridge University Press (2006)
29. Li, Z., Kolmanovsky, I., Atkins, E., Lu, J., Filev, D.P., Michelini, J.: Road risk modeling and cloud-aided safety-based route planning. IEEE Trans. Cybern. **46**(11), 2473–2483 (2015)
30. Liangou, T., Dentsoras, A.: Optimization of motion and energy consumption of an industrial automated ground vehicle. In: 2021 12th International Conference on Information, Intelligence, Systems and Applications (IISA), pp. 1–7. IEEE (2021)
31. Nebel, B.: The Small Solution Hypothesis for MAPF on Strongly Connected Directed Graphs is True. In: Koenig, S., Stern, R., Vallati, M. (eds.) ICAPS, pp. 304–313. AAAI Press (2023)
32. Nguyen, N.T., Gangavarapu, P.T., Kompe, N.F., Schildbach, G., Ernst, F.: Navigation with polytopes: a toolbox for optimal path planning with polytope maps and B-spline curves. Sensors **23**(7) (2023). https://www.mdpi.com/1424-8220/23/7/3532

33. Otte, M., Frazzoli, E.: RRT X: asymptotically optimal single-query sampling-based motion planning with quick replanning. Int. J. Rob. Res. **35**(7), 797–822 (2016)
34. Perez, D., Powley, E., Whitehouse, D., Samothrakis, S., Lucas, S., Cowling, P.I.: The 2013 multi-objective physical travelling salesman problem competition. In: 2014 IEEE Congress on Evolutionary Computation (CEC), pp. 2314–2321 (2014)
35. Plaku, E.: Motion planning with differential constraints as guided search over continuous and discrete spaces. In: Symposium of Combinatorial Search (SOCS), pp. 171–172. AAAI Press (2012)
36. Plaku, E., Çela, A., Plaku, E.: Robot path planning with safety zones. In: Gini, G., Nijmeijer, H., Filev, D.P. (eds.) Proceedings of the 20th International Conference on Informatics in Control, Automation and Robotics, ICINCO 2023, vol. 1, pp. 405–412. SCITEPRESS (2023). https://doi.org/10.5220/0012162100003543
37. Primatesta, S., Guglieri, G., Rizzo, A.: A risk-aware path planning strategy for UAVs in urban environments. J. Intell. Rob. Syst. **95**(2), 629–643 (2019)
38. Primatesta, S., Rizzo, A., la Cour-Harbo, A.: Ground risk map for unmanned aircraft in urban environments. J. Intell. Rob. Syst. **97**(3), 489–509 (2020)
39. Ren, Z., Rathinam, S., Choset, H.: CBSS: a new approach for multiagent combinatorial path finding. In: IEEE Transactions on Robotics (2023)
40. Röger, G., Helmert, M.: Non-optimal multi-agent pathfinding is solved (since 1984). In: Multiagent Pathfinding, Papers from the 2012 AAAI Workshop, AAAI Technical Report, vol. WS-12-10. AAAI Press (2012). http://www.aaai.org/ocs/index.php/WS/AAAIW12/paper/view/5206
41. Rosin, C.D.: Nested rollout policy adaptation for Monte Carlo tree search. In: IJCAI, pp. 649–654. IJCAI/AAAI (2011)
42. Sláma, J., Herynek, J., Faigl, J.: Risk-aware emergency landing planning for gliding aircraft model in urban environments. In: IROS, pp. 4820–4826 (2023)
43. Smith, O.J., Boland, N., Waterer, H.: Solving shortest path problems with a weight constraint and replenishment arcs. Comput. Oper. Res. **39**(5), 964–984 (2012)
44. Stern, R., et al.: Multi-agent pathfinding: definitions, variants, and benchmarks. In: Proceedings of the Twelfth International Symposium on Combinatorial Search, SOCS, pp. 151–158. AAAI Press (2019). https://doi.org/10.1609/SOCS.V10I1.18510
45. Sturtevant, N.: Benchmarks for grid-based pathfinding. Trans. Comput. Intell. AI Games **4**(2), 144 – 148 (2012). http://web.cs.du.edu/~sturtevant/papers/benchmarks.pdf
46. Tihanyi, D., Lu, Y., Karaca, O., Kamgarpour, M.: Multi-robot task allocation for safe planning against stochastic hazard dynamics. In: 2023 European Control Conference (ECC), pp. 1–6 (2023)
47. Vána, P., Sláma, J., Faigl, J.: Surveillance planning with safe emergency landing guarantee for fixed-wing aircraft. Rob. Auton. Syst. **133**, 103644 (2020)
48. Wang, K.C., Botea, A.: MAPP: a scalable multi-agent path planning algorithm with tractability and completeness guarantees. arXiv preprint arXiv:abs/1401.3905 (2014)
49. Wilson, R.M.: Graph puzzles, homotopy, and the alternating group. J. Comb. Theory Ser. **B16**, 86–96 (1974)
50. Yu, J., LaValle, S.M.: Multi-agent path planning and network flow. In: Frazzoli, E., Lozano-Perez, T., Roy, N., Rus, D. (eds.) Algorithmic Foundations of Robotics X, pp. 157–173. Springer, Berlin Heidelberg, Berlin, Heidelberg (2013). https://doi.org/10.1007/978-3-642-36279-8_10

51. Zacharia, P.T., Xidias, E.K.: AGV routing and motion planning in a flexible manufacturing system using a fuzzy-based genetic algorithm. Int. J. Adv. Manuf. Technol. **109**(7), 1801–1813 (2020). https://doi.org/10.1007/s00170-020-05755-3
52. Zhang, H., Chen, J., Li, J., Williams, B.C., Koenig, S.: Multi-agent path finding for precedence-constrained goal sequences. In: International Conference on Autonomous Agents and Multiagent Systems, pp. 1464–1472 (2022)

Agents as a Design Paradigm for Robotic Systems Leveraging ROS and Gazebo

Valeria Seidita[1,2](✉) and Antonio Chella[1,2]

[1] Department of Engineering, University of Palermo, Palermo, Italy
{antonio.chella,valeria.seidita}@unipa.it
[2] ICAR-CNR National Research Council, Palermo, Italy

Abstract. The integration of ROS (Robot Operating System) and Gazebo as a simulator is becoming increasingly vital in the field of robotic system design and development. Like any complex software, robotic software development requires disciplined processes to ensure efficiency and robustness. Despite the potent capabilities of ROS and Gazebo, current methodologies for developing robotic systems often omit a dedicated design phase, leading to the absence of a structured design process. This oversight can undermine the potential for developing sophisticated and reliable systems. In this paper, we argue for the adoption of the agent-based design paradigm as a systematic approach to robotic development. By employing this paradigm, we aim to leverage the modular and flexible architecture inherent in agent-based models, enhancing the capabilities of ROS and Gazebo.

Keywords: Healthcare robotics · Robotic simulation · Robotic Operating System (ROS)

1 Introduction

Robotics is an evolving field that deals with the design, construction, control and use of robots. Robots are complex systems that incorporate multiple disciplines such as mechanical engineering, electrical engineering, computer science and artificial intelligence. Their complexity makes the design and development of robotic systems a challenging task.

In the evolving field of robotics, the development of robust and effective systems increasingly demands engineering approaches that are both disciplined and adaptable. This is particularly evident in the domain of assistive healthcare robotics [17,27], where the systems are required not only to perform complex interactions with humans and their environment but also to do so with high reliability and flexibility. As the global population ages, the healthcare sector faces unprecedented challenges, making the role of robotics more critical than ever in providing care and support. The same is happening in several other fields. This has spurred significant interest in innovative approaches to robotic design that can meet these complex needs. Robotic systems in healthcare must navigate dynamic and unpredictable environments, interact safely and effectively with patients, and perform a wide range of tasks from monitoring vital signs to assisting with mobility or daily life activities. The inherent complexity of these tasks, coupled with the high standards required for safety and user-friendliness, calls for a design methodology that goes beyond traditional engineering approaches [6,7,29]. The focus of this work is on healthcare sector since it arise from our work in research projects in the field of healthcare robotics.

Agent-based design paradigms [11,31] offer a promising solution to these challenges. By conceptualizing robotic systems as collections of interacting agents, each with their own roles and responsibilities, this approach enables a modular and flexible architecture inherently suited to the demands of complex, dynamic environments. Moreover, the agent-based paradigm aligns well with the principles of software engineering, providing a disciplined framework that facilitates robust, reusable, and scalable software development and offers a modular and flexible approach to the design and development of robotic systems. In this paradigm, the robotic system is viewed as a collection of software agents that work together to achieve a common goal. Each agent is responsible for a specific task and has its own intelligence and autonomy.

Today, ROS [15,22] and Gazebo [16,19] are extensively used to develop a variety of robotic systems, ranging from autonomous vehicles and industrial robots to complex service and personal assistant robots. These tools provide an essential foundation for building and testing robotic applications in simulated environments that mimic real-world conditions. However, despite their widespread adoption, there remains a lack of a structured engineering approach to the design and development of these systems.

There is a notable gap in the literature and in practice when it comes to an engineering discipline that systematically addresses the complexities of designing agent-based robotic systems with ROS and Gazebo. This gap underscores the need for further research to develop methodologies that not only embrace the technical capabilities of ROS and Gazebo but also exploit the conceptual and operational benefits of agent-based architectures. The integration of these paradigms promises to yield robotic systems that are not only robust and efficient but also capable of exhibiting high degrees of intelligence and adaptability in complex environments.

In the following sections, we delve into the specifics of agent-based design paradigm, elucidating their advantages and implementation strategies using ROS and Gazebo. The main contribution of this work is the mapping between the central elements for agent-based design and the technical and implementation elements of ROS and Gazebo. The resulting model is a very preliminary attempt to form the basis for a methodological approach that closes the gaps mentioned above.

The rest of the paper is organized as follows: in Sect. 2 we discuss some related works, in Sect. 3 we outline the basic principles of a design process and the abstraction of the agent domain, in Sect. 4 we take a detailed look at the features of ROS and Gazebo and how they are used to program a robotic system, in Sect. 5 we identify a mapping between agents and ROS and Gazebo and the results using a case study that we used for our analysis, and finally in Sect. 6 we draw some conclusions.

2 Related Work

In the area of robotic system development that takes advantage of ROS and simulators in general, and Gazebo in particular, research is still open with respect to specific design methods. In this section, we provide an overview of what we believe to be the most recent and compelling work on the integration of BDI agents and ROS for robot programming.

A work in the field of mobile robotics is presented in [12]. The authors in the field of navigation of autonomous mobile robots use BDI agents and their natural connection with AgentSpeak to automatically generate navigation plans in the form of intermediate destinations (waypoints) that allow the robot to monitor, pause and resume the plans in case of unexpected events. The navigation process is integrated into the agent itself, unlike traditional solutions that tend to delegate this task to external modules, as is often the case in the context of ROS. This internal approach takes full advantage of the logical capabilities of BDI agents and allows them to directly handle plan interruptions, such as collision avoidance or map updating, without relying on additional components for logical processing. The proposed work represents a kind of architecture onto which a planning process can be grafted. In fact, the proposed architecture integrates the navigation planning process into the reasoning cycle of the agent, allowing a close interaction between decision logic and action execution. However, the approach remains bottom-up in the sense that the rationale for using ROS is dictated by its specificity and the topic mechanism which, in conjunction with the particular application domain, enables an efficient outcome. It does not propose a top-down approach that provides a supporting methodology that can then be replicated.

Often the use of BDIs is reduced to pure programming considerations. In [28], for example, a very interesting method for integrating BDI agents into ROS is presented, which improves the level of abstraction when programming autonomous robots. The proposed architecture makes it possible to program the robot's intelligence through cognitive agents to control perceptions and actions, while ROS facilitates the robot's interaction with sensors and actuators. In addition, the paper includes experiments with simulated drones that illustrate the performance benefits of the proposed approach. However, the use of Gazebo is not considered, although the context and nature of the simulation suggest that tools such as Gazebo could be used to further extend and test the proposed results and architecture. In the work proposed by Cardoso et al. [9] they go a little deeper into the integration between agents and ROS and present an interface to integrate agents based on the Belief-Desire-Intention model into robotic systems developed with ROS. This work shows how such agents can be implemented using the Gwendolen programming language and verified by the AJPF

Model Checker. The focus of the work is on the formal verification of the properties of agents, especially those related to decision making. The work also shows how ROS can be used to develop modular robotic applications, taking advantage of the node-based structure to manage communication and task distribution. Another, even more application-oriented work is presented in [20], where the development and implementation of an autonomous robotic system for mail delivery on a university campus using the Belief-Desire-Intention architecture together with the Robot Operating System is described. The authors propose an approach that combines the BDI reasoning system in its Jason implementation with ROS, which manages the connections to the robot's sensors and actuators. The ultimate goal is to create a robotic agent that autonomously navigates through the tunnels on campus, picks up mail from specific stations, delivers it to recipients, and notifies them via a mobile application. An important aspect of the proposed system is the integration of the BDI reasoning system on a Raspberry Pi computer that has been connected to the iRobot Create2 robot. The system includes a line sensor and a camera that provide data to the BDI reasoning system via ROS. Thus, the proposed integration operates at a very low-level, functioning as a quasi-hardware solution that emphasizes the power of BDI and ROS from an implementation perspective. In most of the papers we have studied, agents are primarily considered as a programming paradigm rather than a design paradigm, which is, however, one of the strengths of this technology.

While some studies [8,13,21] have explored the use of ROS with agent-based models-highlighting the potential for enhanced modularity and system robustness-comprehensive integration strategies and design practices are still in their nascent stages. Essentially, and to the best of our knowledge, the literature presented so far only considers the lowest levels of a design approach, which we will refer to as M0 and M1 in the next sections. It lacks a disciplined approach to the verticalization of concepts related to agents, ROS and Gazebo, from specification to code.

3 Design Concepts and the Agent Paradigm

Since the late 1960s, the need for a disciplined approach to software production has been recognized. Complex software systems require specific design activities to analyze the problem domain, identify potential goals and requirements, and then convert them into software. It is good practice to tie a design methodology to the programming language to be used.

The logic normally followed in an engineering approach is shown in Fig. 1 with reference to object-oriented design and programming. A real-world object at level M0 becomes an instance of a user model level object. A model is a representation of the world that is intended to be studied or analyzed and follows a specific syntax that refers to a modeling language. In the example figure, the modeling language at level M1 is UML [3], whose elements, or rather the main design abstractions of the metamodel, are the class, attribute, and instance, and are in turn instances of the more general concept of class defined in MOF at level M3 [1,2]. With this logic, software development, using a design process, is nothing but a sequence of activities that allow the transformation of models in order to instantiate the abstractions of level M2 into elements of level M1 (objects in the case of object-oriented programming) and finally into objects in real-world elements at level M0. Following this vertical reading of the figure, one can easily understand how the elements required for a software project depend on the programming language used for code development.

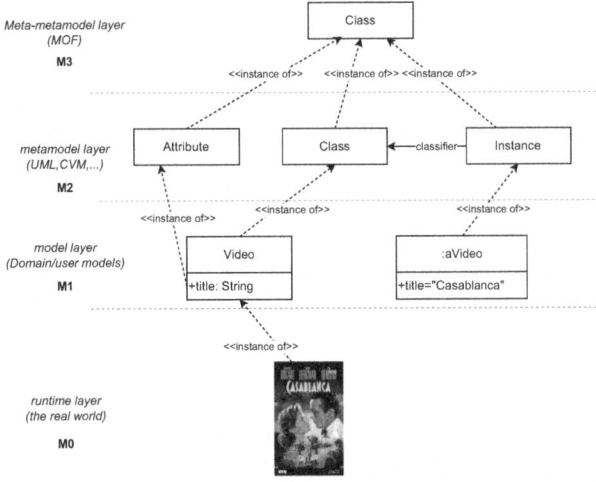

Fig. 1. Metamodeling layers (redrawn from MOF [2])

With this in mind, we can also state that the elements considered at various levels are closely linked to the problem domain under examination. In the case of objects, these are particularly useful in domains where the world elements, the objects themselves, need to be computerized.

In the application domain of a robotic system, the software in question must take into account the fact that a robot interacts with the surrounding environment through sensors and actuators, and the sensory data influence the robot's ability to make decisions to interact with the environment. A robot typically has a specific goal to achieve in the environment; thus, robotic systems must be capable of planning actions by interpreting sensory data to understand the surrounding environment. This may involve object recognition, position and orientation estimation, environment segmentation, and many other tasks. *And what if the environment is not fully known or interaction with other intelligent elements, such as humans, is required to achieve a goal? The problem domain becomes increasingly complex.* The agent-based design paradigm [14,30,33] can manage this complexity efficiently and scalably. By using autonomous agents operating in a dynamic environment, it is possible to address challenges related to perception, planning, and interaction, enabling the creation of robots capable of adapting and performing a wide range of tasks efficiently and reliably.

The agent-based design paradigm is based on the idea of modeling complex systems as sets of autonomous agents acting in a dynamic environment to achieve specific goals. Agents are computational entities capable of perceiving their surrounding environment, processing information, making decisions, and acting autonomously to achieve predefined objectives. An agent is an autonomous entity situated in an environment and is capable of perceiving this environment through sensors, processing information internally, and acting on the environment through actuators to pursue specific goals or tasks [11,31]. An agent is autonomous, proactive, and social. According to Wooldridge and Jennings [14,31], who first defined an agent, some key elements that lead to the use of agents as a design paradigm include:

- Autonomy: An agent is autonomous in that it can operate independently, making decisions and acting without the direct control of a human operator.
- Perception and Action: Agents have the ability to perceive the environment through sensors and act upon it through actuators. This perception-action cycle allows agents to dynamically interact with their environment.
- Goals or Tasks: Agents are designed to achieve specific goals or perform assigned tasks. These goals may be defined by the agent itself or imposed by a human operator.
- Environment: Agents operate within an environment that may be physical, virtual, or a combination of both. The environment provides the context in which agents operate and influences their actions and decisions.
- Society: The real world is a multi-agent environment; a single agent cannot undertake actions to achieve a goal without considering others, communicating with them, and requesting their services, thus cooperating.

We claim that *adopting the agent-based design paradigm for the development of robotic systems through ROS and Gazebo represents a strategic and innovative choice that addresses the challenges inherent in complex dynamic and interactive environments.* In contexts such as assistive robotics, where the variability of the environment and the need for autonomous interaction with humans and objects are significant, the ability of agents to operate independently becomes crucial. Using the agent-based design paradigm thus offers a series of decisive operational advantages such as scalability, robustness, and the identification of the main software elements that realize the intended functionalities.

Following the logic of Fig. 1, we can schematize the use of the agent paradigm with a minimal set of elements that we present in Fig. 2. From this figure, one can see that at level M2 there are abstractions like Agent, Role, Task, Action, etc. Here are some general definitions of these elements useful for understanding the proposed mapping with the technical level offered by ROS and Gazebo:

- Agent - An autonomous computational entity capable of perceiving its environment through sensors and acting on that environment through actuators to achieve specific objectives.

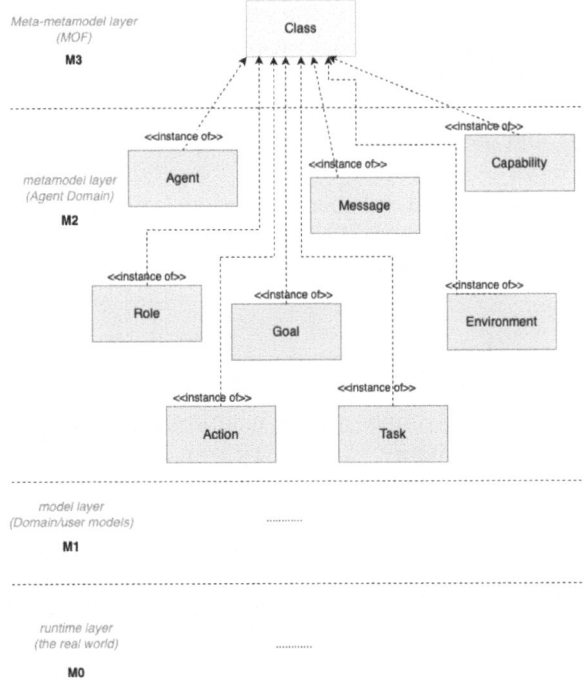

Fig. 2. The metamodeling layers in the agent oriented paradigm.

- Task - A task is a specific activity or set of activities that an agent is designated to complete. Tasks can vary in complexity and may require the agent to perform a series of actions in a particular sequence or respond to environmental changes in real-time.
- Role - A role defines a set of behaviors and responsibilities associated with an agent in a particular context or in collaboration with other agents. An agent's role might include specific privileges, tasks, or rules of behavior within a multi-agent system. For example, in a disaster relief team of robots, one robot might have the role of "scout" to explore the area, while another might have the role of "carrier" to bring necessary tools. The role is thus related to a Goal.
- Goal - A goal, or objective, is the desired final state that an agent aims to realize through its actions. The concept of a goal is fundamental in agent-based design since it guides the agent's decision-making and behavior. A goal can be simple, such as achieving a certain temperature in a room, or complex, such as coordinating a group of robots to complete a construction.
- Action - An action is an operation or intervention that an agent performs on the environment to advance towards its goal. Actions can be physical, such as the movement of a robot, or digital, such as updating a database. An agent's actions are determined by its planning strategy and its perception of the environment.

- Environment - the set of objects in the world in which the agent acts, and the actions that can be performed with them, may also include elements of each agent's inner world to model complex capabilities with respect to the self.
- Message - A message defines a functional dependency between agents to achieve a goal, and the content of the message provides the elements to receive or provide a service.
- Capability - Capability is the element that models what the agent can do and therefore what actions it can perform. In complex contexts, it can be used to stably determine which action an agent can perform or which it can delegate and to whom.

In this section, we deliberately do not consider the relationships between the elements in Fig. 2, as these are dependent on the specific design methodology used. To enter the context simply and as mentioned earlier, a design methodology is a sequence of activities that allows transitioning from one model to another through transformation, and in doing this, we follow the chosen M2 level where the relationships between the elements dictate the execution path of the design activities. The relationships between the elements are defined based on the application domain and thus also on the implementation domain. For example, in previous work [18,25,26] , we used the agent programming language Jason [4,5] and CArTaGo [23] to implement agents in robotic systems capable of exhibiting self-disclosure activities. The relationships identified in that case were dependent on a BDI agent context as seen from the paper.

Here, we can initially, based on our experience with agent-based design methodologies, consider relationships that take into account the simple concept of a robot as the agent defined by Russel and Norvig [24] (an agent is endowed by sensors and actuators and it is able to interact with the environment) and the technological aspect involving the use of ROS and Gazebo. In the following section, we will illustrate the main features of ROS and Gazebo and attempt to discuss what is needed to design a complex robotic application using these tools.

4 Developing Robotic Systems with ROS and Gazebo

ROS (Robot Operating System) is a flexible framework for writing robot software. It is a suite of tools and libraries designed to assist developers in creating complex and robust robotic applications across different hardware platforms.

ROS provides the services of an operating system on a heterogeneous network of computers, including low-level hardware device control, implementation of commonly required functionalities, message passing between processes, and software package maintenance. It is particularly useful in the development of complex robots that require software modules to communicate efficiently with each other. The primary goal of ROS is to provide capabilities to create powerful robotic applications that can be reused on other robots. ROS has a collection of software tools, libraries, and a set of packages that make robotic software development straightforward and intuitive.

All these tools have been analyzed in this work to identify the design abstractions which, as mentioned in the previous section, are the elements that enable the transformation of models from specifications to code, regardless of the system being built. Moreover, the use of ROS is based on what is called the *ROS computation graph*, which provides all the tools to process data from a robotic application and is fundamental to the programming process of a robotic system. The nodes, messages, topics, and services are elements of the graph that we have analyzed in detail.

A ROS *Node* is a process that utilizes *ROS functionalities* to perform computations on data. *A ROS robot consists of many nodes* that communicate with each other. Each node performs a specific task and has the capability to communicate with other nodes via messages. For example, a node might process a laser scanner to ensure there are no collisions. A ROS node is written with the help of ROS client libraries (such as roscpp or rospy, thus at a low level it uses object-oriented programming languages).

Messages are data structures used for *communication* between nodes via topics or services. Messages can contain various types of data such as integers, floating points, booleans, arrays, etc. A topic can send one message at a time.

Topics are communication channels through which nodes exchange messages. A node sends messages by publishing them on a topic and any interested node can subscribe to that topic to receive the messages.

Services in ROS are another form of communication between nodes, allowing a node to invoke a function in another node and await a response. Unlike topics, which are asynchronous, services are synchronous, meaning that the calling node will wait for a response from the node providing the service. The type of communication is one-to-many, therefore the topic can be subscribed to by multiple nodes.

Furthermore, in the graph, there are parameters that allow nodes to configure their values at runtime. The parameter server maintains a collection of names and values that nodes can dynamically modify and update, and the bags, which are files in ROS used to save and reproduce topic data. This is useful for testing the behavior of robots without having to operate in real time. At the implementation level, which is not particularly relevant to the analyses we are conducting in this work, there is also the ROS Master that serves as a link between the nodes.

Another important ROS tool is *Plugin*. Plugins in ROS allow developers to use and integrate existing software without having to modify the original code. This is particularly useful for extending the capabilities of simulators like Gazebo, where components such as sensors or control algorithms can be added as plugins. A developer must be aware of the existing plugins, or be able to create new ones, to create complex functionalities through integration.

A developer aiming to develop a robotic application with ROS should: *(i)* define the system architecture by dividing the robot's functionalities into separate nodes, *(ii)* identify the communications these exchange, *(iii)* implement the processes in the nodes to handle tasks, *(iv)* establish the types of messages exchanged by the topics, and *(v)* define the topics on which nodes will publish or from which they will subscribe. If necessary, messages can be customized. After identifying the functionalities that require synchronous communication, services should be implemented. Finally, before testing and debugging, integration with Gazebo proceeds. Plugins are used to integrate specific functionalities into the Gazebo simulator and to test the robot's behavior in a virtual environment.

Gazebo is an advanced robotic simulator that offers the ability to simulate robots in complex and dynamic environments with realistic physics. It is widely used in robotics research and development because it provides a controlled and flexible environment for testing algorithms, hardware designs, and robot-environment interaction scenarios without the risks or costs associated with real-world experiments. Gazebo integrates seamlessly with ROS, allowing developers to use their ROS nodes, messages, and services directly within the Gazebo simulated environment. Thanks to specific plugins, commands and data can flow seamlessly between ROS systems and the Gazebo simulation. One of Gazebo's strengths is its ability to simulate accurate physical interactions between robot components and between the robot and the environment. Gazebo provides a vast library of simulated sensors and ready-to-use robot models. These elements can be easily integrated and configured in projects, allowing developers to simulate complex scenarios with various types of sensors and actuators without having to build them from scratch. Users can create and modify detailed simulated environments to test their robots in a variety of contexts. This is essential to ensure that robots can operate under diverse conditions, from simple indoor spaces to complex outdoor scenarios with various obstacles and weather conditions.

Gazebo plugins are specifically designed to extend the capabilities of the Gazebo simulator. They are primarily used to add specific behaviors directly to models within the simulation, such as controlling a robot's movements, simulating sensors, or interacting with the simulated physical environment.

It is necessary to emphasize that ROS nodes are software components that perform specific computational, control, or data processing functions within the ROS framework. They can handle a wide range of tasks, from processing sensory data to controlling actuators, managing route planning, and managing communication between different nodes. While Gazebo plugins operate within the Gazebo simulation environment with direct access to the APIs and consequently can realize detailed and low-level operational behaviors, ROS nodes are more flexible and modular, capable of communicating via a messaging system on topics or services, and are therefore suited for implementing and orchestrating high-level logics and can be directly transferred to real robots without depending on Gazebo. Gazebo plugins can be used to simulate behaviors that are then managed by ROS nodes in the context of the simulation.

Figure 3 summarizes, through key elements of ROS and Gazebo and how they relate to each other, the analysis illustrated in this section.

5 Agents for ROS and Gazebo Designing

From our perspective, a robot can have multiple nodes that perform tasks at different levels of granularity. The question then is: *how do I identify ROS Nodes for a complex robotic application?* Our proposal is simply to instantiate a node from an agent, and below we explain the reasoning process we followed and the advantages that ensue.

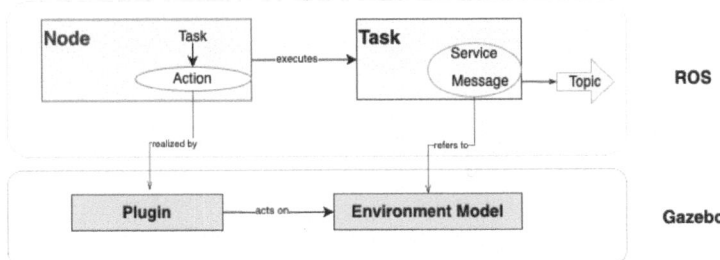

Fig. 3. ROS and Gazebo elements related to the process for programming robots.

Agents are autonomous entities that communicate with each other through messages. In ROS, this translates into the use of nodes that operate as independent agents. This decentralized architecture allows for greater modularity, where each agent (node) can be developed, tested, and maintained independently from others. Modularity facilitates system upgrades and maintenance without requiring a complete overhaul, making the system more manageable and scalable.

ROS promotes a communication system based on topics, services, and actions, which is natural for an agent-based paradigm. Agents in ROS (nodes) publish and subscribe to topics to exchange messages in a structured format, invoke services to perform synchronous operations, and use actions for asynchronous interactions that require feedback on prolonged operations. This communication model supports effective interaction among agents, essential for coordinating complex tasks and dynamically responding to environmental changes.

In the agent paradigm, each agent has the ability to operate autonomously to make decisions based on its own perceptions of the environment, just like nodes in ROS. This level of autonomy is crucial in robotic applications where rapid and informed decisions are necessary to react to continually changing environmental conditions, such as navigating crowded spaces or interacting with humans and other robots.

In Fig. 4, the complete modeling layers for designing with ROS and Gazebo using an agent paradigm are shown.

The M2 layer provides guidance on the design methodology that can be followed, which is beyond the scope of this paper where we have identified an initial mapping between ROS elements and agents. As our research progresses, we will further refine the M2 layer also in light of additional experiments on

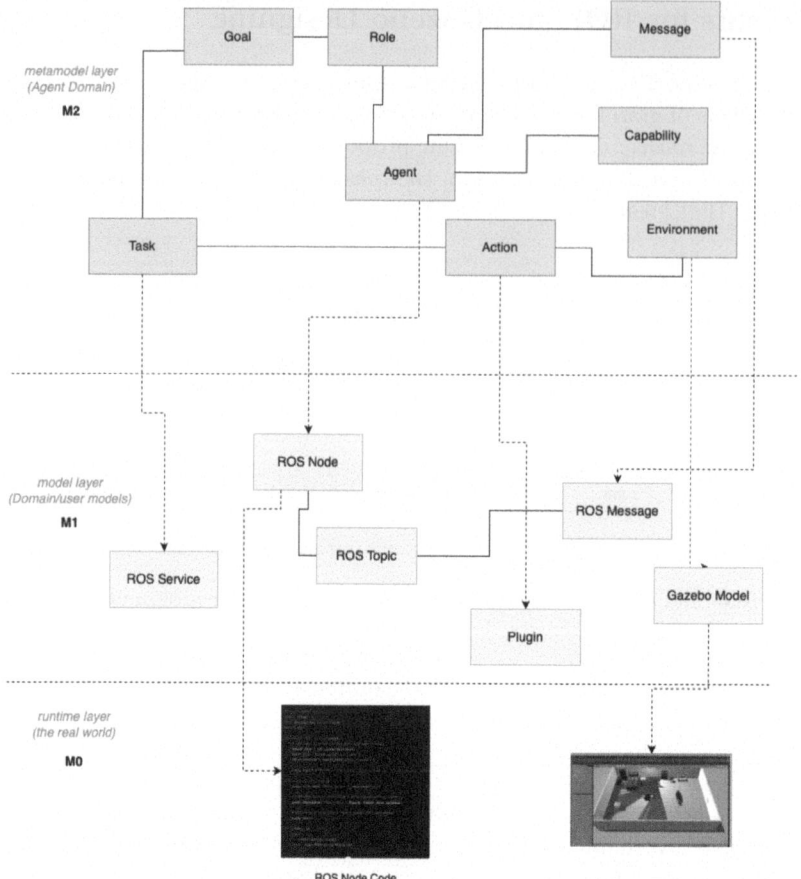

Fig. 4. Our proposal for mapping agent paradigm to ROS and Gazebo (arrows between layers model *instance-of* relationship).

the development of robotic systems, to ultimately identify and detail a well-structured and comprehensive design approach.

5.1 Case Study and Validation

The work presented here is part of research from two projects we are currently undertaking, and in this paper, we illustrate the initial theoretical results. The goal of the first project is to develop a robotic support system for patients with metabolic deficits to provide suggestions to them and their physiotherapists in following physical exercises and monitoring the results. The second project, also in the healthcare domain, aims to analyze and study the effects of explainability and trustworthiness in supporting patients on a post-hospitalization journey and their caregivers. The main focuses of our robotic research include *how to model*

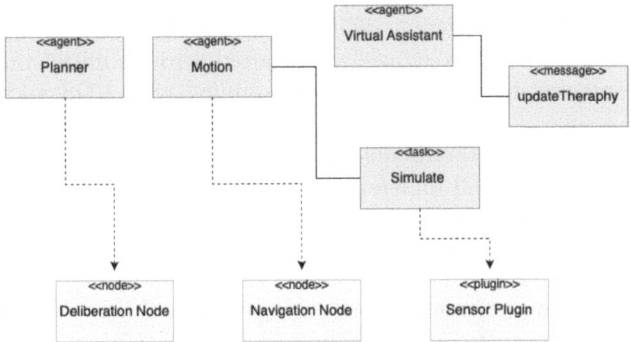

Fig. 5. A very simple excerpt of the design model for the case study illustrated in Subsect. 4.1.

the knowledge of robots about a highly dynamic environment and how to update this at design time, as well as how to model and implement the decision-making process that also includes explaining what has been decided and why.

In the initial part of both projects, it was necessary to conduct a theoretical analysis to identify the application domains in details, decide which technologies to use, and then, as illustrated in previous sections, how to apply the agent paradigm to the implementation of the robotic system.

A common initial scenario used to validate the approach, from level M2 to M0, involves monitoring a patient who has returned home after hospitalization, has been diagnosed, and given a therapy to follow, and who must be constantly monitored to provide suggestions on following the therapy and to alert doctors and nurses in case of sudden issues. The scenario description we used is as follows: *An elderly person with type 2 diabetes is assisted at home by a home care robot programmed to monitor their health and the surrounding environment. This robot collects data on the elderly person's health, such as blood glucose levels, and regularly sends it to a health database. A doctor, through a dedicated application, accesses this data to assess the elderly person's health status and adjust therapies as necessary. If the data indicate that the health conditions are stable, treatment continues without interruption. Otherwise, the robot can receive and implement updates on the therapeutic regime or other assistance needs, always under the doctor's supervision. Suppose the robot detects a sudden drop in the elderly person's glucose levels while it is set to administer insulin at the usual time. However, the robot identifies that the elderly person's food intake has been lower than usual and decides to consult the doctor before proceeding. If the robot does not have a predefined action line for this specific scenario, it sends an alert to the doctor to get further instructions. The doctor can then decide to temporarily modify the insulin dosage or provide other specific directions, which the robot is authorized to execute.*

Following a hybrid approach to requirements analysis that took into account the activities of two well-known agent design methodologies, PASSI and GAIA

[10,32], we identified the agents, their goals, and the main tasks along with the messages they need to exchange, and drafted a rough initial version of the design before moving immediately to programming with ROS and simulation with Gazebo.

In Fig. 5, a snippet of the model where, so as not to complicate the model and to make it readable and understandable for the purposes of this paper, we report only some agents, tasks, etc., that then led to the identification of the following high-level ROS nodes and Gazebo plugins:

- Navigation - manages the map of the environment and the robot's localization within the structure. It uses algorithms like AMCL (Adaptive Monte Carlo Localization) for localization and the move_base system for route planning;
- Health Monitoring - receives input from sensors monitoring vital parameters such as blood glucose, heart rate, blood pressure, and other health indicators;
- Social Interaction - handles verbal and non-verbal communication with the elderly person. It may use speech synthesis to speak and voice recognition algorithms to listen and understand requests (this part of the process is still under development).
- Plan Deliberation - selects the most suitable plan to achieve a goal, listens to the collected information, and deliberates the set of actions and plans to be activated for each node and to be executed using topics for communication. This node communicates directly with the node for doctor support, which is responsible for updating the library of plans of the planner to add plans and enable plan review in runtime;
- Doctor Support - functions as a dashboard console where doctors retrieve data monitored by the robot and collected by the system. The agent allows doctors to communicate new therapies to the robot, which will be translated into plans and added to the planner agent's plan library. The therapy will be executed during the next reasoning cycle of the agent instance;
- Robot Control: Manages the robot's hardware, including motors, sensors, and actuators. This node takes care of the low-level control of the robot's movements, ensuring safe and precise operations.

- Sensor Plugin: To accurately simulate sensors like cameras, motion sensors, or proximity sensors. These plugins help test how the robot perceives its surrounding environment in the RSA.
- Motion Control Plugin: Simulate the robot's motor control systems, allowing the testing of navigation and handling strategies within the simulated structure.
- Physical Interaction Plugins: Simulate physical interaction with the environment, such as the ability to open doors or move objects, crucial elements for an assistive robot.
- Environmental Plugin: To create and modify dynamic environments within Gazebo, these plugins can simulate environmental changes, such as the opening and closing of doors or variations in lighting.

This study not only demonstrates the practical implementation of agent-based design in ROS and Gazebo but also highlights the crucial role of a structured design phase in developing reliable and effective robotic systems for complex healthcare scenarios.

6 Conclusions

In this paper, we have explored the integration of an agent-based design paradigm with the advanced simulation capabilities of Gazebo and the architectural flexibility of ROS. This synergy enables the creation of robotic systems that are not merely reactive to environmental changes but are also capable of moving in dynamic environments, being autonomous, adapting to new contexts, and cooperating effectively with other agents and humans. Such systems transition from being simple automated machines to becoming true intelligent companions, capable of assisting users in a wide range of daily activities.

Agent-based design inherently contributes to the robustness and fault tolerance of robotic systems. In the ROS framework, if one node (agent) fails, others can continue to operate, thereby enhancing system reliability. Moreover, nodes can be configured to detect failures and autonomously restart or employ backup mechanisms to ensure operational continuity. This approach not only reduces downtime but also facilitates maintenance and updates without disrupting the overall functionality of the system. By employing agents in the design process, robotic systems are architected to be highly flexible, adapting seamlessly to a broad spectrum of operational scenarios. Agents can be programmed with learning capabilities that allow them to adapt and improve from past experiences, continuously enhancing their performance over time. Within ROS, this adaptability is further augmented through the integration of advanced machine learning and computer vision packages, enabling robots to tackle complex, real-world tasks more effectively.

Additionally, with the support of Gazebo, the interaction among agents can be simulated in a controlled environment prior to real-world deployment. This allows developers to test and refine coordination and communication algorithms in complex scenarios safely and economically, minimizing the risks and costs associated with direct real-world testing. Such simulations are crucial in ensuring that the robotic systems are not only functional but also optimized for performance and safety before they operate alongside humans in sensitive environments such as healthcare.

In conclusion, the agent-based design paradigm, when integrated with ROS and Gazebo, provides a powerful framework for developing advanced robotic systems. This approach supports the evolution of robotics from simple task executors to complex, intelligent entities capable of significant autonomy and interaction. Future work will focus on refining the integration of these technologies to enhance the scalability and efficiency of robotic systems, pushing the boundaries of what is possible in robotics today and creating ad-hoc methodological approaches.

Acknowledgments.. The work has been supported by the PRIN 2022 project I-TROPHYTS ("IoT and humanoid RObotics for autonomic PHYsio-Therapeutic monitoring, coaching and supervising in smart Spaces: a feasibility study", P20224TAETP)

References

1. Model-driven development: a metamodeling foundation. IEEE softw. **20**(5), 36–41 (2003)
2. ptc/04 10-15.: OMG, Meta Object Facility (MOF) 2.0 Core Specification
3. Booch, G., Jacobson, I., Rumbaugh, J., et al.: The unified modeling language. Unix Review **14**(13), 5 (1996)
4. Bordini, R.H., Hübner, J.F.: BDI Agent Programming in AgentSpeak Using *Jason*. In: Toni, F., Torroni, P. (eds.) CLIMA 2005. LNCS (LNAI), vol. 3900, pp. 143–164. Springer, Heidelberg (2006). https://doi.org/10.1007/11750734_9
5. Bordini, R.H., Hübner, J.F., Wooldridge, M.: Programming multi-agent systems in AgentSpeak using Jason. John Wiley and Sons (2007)
6. Brugali, D.: Software engineering for experimental robotics, vol. 30. Springer (2007)
7. Bruyninckx, H., Klotzbücher, M., Hochgeschwender, N., Kraetzschmar, G., Gherardi, L., Brugali, D.: The brics component model: a model-based development paradigm for complex robotics software systems. In: Proceedings of the 28th Annual ACM Symposium on Applied Computing, pp. 1758–1764 (2013)
8. Cardoso, R.C., Ferrando, A.: A review of agent-based programming for multi-agent systems. Computers **10**(2), 16 (2021)
9. Cardoso, R.C., Ferrando, A., Dennis, L.A., Fisher, M.: An interface for programming verifiable autonomous agents in ROS. In: Bassiliades, N., Chalkiadakis, G., de Jonge, D. (eds.) EUMAS/AT -2020. LNCS (LNAI), vol. 12520, pp. 191–205. Springer, Cham (2020). https://doi.org/10.1007/978-3-030-66412-1_13
10. Cossentino, M.: From requirements to code with passi methodology. In: Agent-oriented methodologies, pp. 79–106. IGI Global (2005)
11. Ferber, J., Weiss, G.: Multi-agent systems: an introduction to distributed artificial intelligence, vol. 1. Addison-wesley Reading (1999)
12. Gavigan, P., Esfandiari, B.: Bdi for autonomous mobile robot navigation. In: International Workshop on Engineering Multi-Agent Systems, pp. 137–155. Springer (2021). https://doi.org/10.1007/978-3-030-97457-2_8
13. Iñigo-Blasco, P., Diaz-del Rio, F., Romero-Ternero, M.C., Cagigas-Muñiz, D., Vicente-Diaz, S.: Robotics software frameworks for multi-agent robotic systems development. Robot. Auton. Syst. **60**(6), 803–821 (2012)
14. Jennings, N.R.: Agent-oriented software engineering. In: Multi-Agent System Engineering: 9th European Workshop on Modelling Autonomous Agents in a Multi-Agent World, MAAMAW'99 Valencia, Spain, June 30–July 2, 1999 Proceedings 9. pp. 1–7. Springer (1999). https://doi.org/10.1007/3-540-48437-X_1
15. Joseph, L., Cacace, J.: Mastering ROS for Robotics Programming: Design, build, and simulate complex robots using the Robot Operating System. Packt Publishing Ltd (2018)
16. Koenig, N., Howard, A.: Design and use paradigms for Gazebo, an open-source multi-robot simulator. In: 2004 IEEE/RSJ International Conference on Intelligent Robots and Systems (IROS)(IEEE Cat. No. 04CH37566), vol. 3, pp. 2149–2154. IEEE (2004)

17. Kuo, I.H., Broadbent, E., MacDonald, B.: Designing a robotic assistant for healthcare applications. In: the 7th conference of Health Informatics New Zealand, Rotorua (2008)
18. Lanza, F., Seidita, V., Chella, A.: Agents and robots for collaborating and supporting physicians in healthcare scenarios. J. Biomed. Inform. **108**, 103483 (2020)
19. Marian, M., Stîngă, F., Georgescu, M.T., Roibu, H., Popescu, D., Manta, F.: A ROS-based control application for a robotic platform using the Gazebo 3d simulator. In: 2020 21th International Carpathian Control Conference (ICCC), pp. 1–5. IEEE (2020)
20. Onyedinma, C., Gavigan, P., Esfandiari, B.: Toward campus mail delivery using BDI. J. Sens. Actuator Netw. **9**(4), 56 (2020)
21. Park, J., Delgado, R., Choi, B.W.: Real-time characteristics of ros 2.0 in multiagent robot systems: an empirical study. IEEE Access **8**, 154637–154651 (2020)
22. Quigley, M., et al.: Ros: an open-source robot operating system. In: ICRA workshop on open source software. vol. 3, p. 5. Kobe, Japan (2009)
23. Ricci, A., Piunti, M., Viroli, M., Omicini, A.: Environment programming in cartago. Multi-agent programming: Languages, tools and applications, pp. 259–288 (2009)
24. Russell, S.J., Norvig, P.: Artificial intelligence: a modern approach. Pearson (2016)
25. Seidita, V., Lanza, F., Sabella, A.M.P., Chella, A.: Can agents talk about what they are doing? a proposal with jason and speech acts. In: CEUR Workshop Proceedings. vol. 3261, pp. 17–29. CEUR-WS (2022)
26. Seidita, V., Sabella, A.M.P., Lanza, F., Chella, A.: Agent talks about itself: an implementation using jason, cartago and speech acts. Intelligenza Artificiale **17**(1), 7–18 (2023)
27. Shubha, P., Meenakshi, M.: Design and implementation of healthcare assistive robot. In: 2019 5th International Conference on Advanced Computing and Communication Systems (ICACCS), pp. 61–65. IEEE (2019)
28. Silva, G.R., Becker, L.B., Hübner, J.F.: Embedded architecture composed of cognitive agents and ROS for programming intelligent robots. IFAC-PapersOnLine **53**(2), 10000–10005 (2020)
29. Sommerville, I.: Softw. Eng. 9'd. Education Limited, England (2010)
30. Winikoff, M., Padgham, L.: Agent oriented software engineering. Multiagent systems, pp. 695–757 (2013)
31. Wooldridge, M.: An introduction to multiagent systems. John wiley and sons (2009)
32. Wooldridge, M., Jennings, N.R., Kinny, D.: The gaia methodology for agent-oriented analysis and design. Auton. Agent. Multi-Agent Syst. **3**, 285–312 (2000)
33. Wooldridgey, M., Ciancarini, P.: Agent-oriented software engineering: The state of the art. In: International Workshop on Agent-oriented Software Engineering, pp. 1–28. Springer (2000). https://doi.org/10.1007/3-540-44564-1_1

Verification-Oriented Specification of Multi-agent Interaction Patterns

Alberto Tagliaferro(✉), Livia Lestingi, and Matteo Rossi

Politecnico Di Milano, Milan, Italy
{alberto.tagliaferro,livia.lestingi,matteo.rossi}@polimi.it

Abstract. Smart cyber agents are pivotal in software-intensive systems such as smart manufacturing, robotics, and the Internet of Things. These agents monitor physical surroundings through sensors and make impactful decisions that influence the environment. Software engineering challenges in this domain include the specification of interactive multi-agent tasks. The general-purpose Domain-Specific Language named LIrAs, Language for Interactive Agents, is a high-level language that allows for unambiguous custom pattern definition. Additionally, LIrAs facilitates interactions with human agents, a safety-critical situation requiring particular attention. This paper lays the foundation for LIrAs specifications translation to Stochastic Hybrid Automaton (SHA). The target SHA model structure follows a three-layer hierarchical structure and makes LIrAs specifications amenable to formal verification, specifically Statistical Model Checking, through the Uppaal tool, capable of including time-dependent physical phenomena, such as human fatigue and robot dynamics.

Keywords: Multi-Agent Patterns Specification · Domain-Specific Language · Stochastic Hybrid Automata

1 Introduction

Assistive robotics, Internet of Things (IoT), and intelligent manufacturing systems are examples of increasingly widespread and complex software-intensive systems. These systems feature smart cyber agents equipped with sensors to gather environmental data and make decisions influencing their surroundings. Including multiple interacting agents—i.e., Multi-Agent Systems (MASs)—adds complexity to these environments since agents must interact with both the environment and each other to be effective. The involvement of human agents (often unavoidable, if not desirable) is an additional challenge since well-tailored programming and decision-making on the robotic agents' side can spare stakeholders from financial losses or physical harm.

Specifying MAS interactive tasks poses a critical challenge in software engineering [10]. The inherent complexity of these systems often necessitates expert users for task specification, making the process both time-consuming and error-prone. To address this issue, a common solution is developing a Domain-Specific

Language (DSL) to be used as a high-level language. This approach significantly reduces the complexity of specifications, the time required to develop them, the likelihood of errors, and the amount of technical knowledge needed. Often, DSLs can be translated into formal models, enabling the verification of correctness properties through formal verification techniques.

This work builds upon a DSL-based toolchain for MAS specifications, illustrated in Fig. 1, centered around the LIrAs DSL [25]. LIrAs enables the specification of tasks for various types of agents (software-based or human) with a high degree of versatility across different applications. In LIrAs, the interaction patterns are flexible concerning the type and quantity of actions involved since they are not bound to a specific application. LIrAs agents are endowed with basic atomic abilities, referred to as *skills*, such as a translational motion for a robot or a quadcopter. Through LIrAs, it is possible to define *patterns*, as depicted in Fig. 1, combining different skills that multiple agents must perform in a coordinated fashion through user-friendly primitives. LIrAs patterns are parametric with respect to the context in which they will be executed—i.e., all aspects related to specifying the operational environment, such as layout or Points of Interest (PoIs), are defined externally from LIrAs. Several LIrAs specifications constitute a custom pattern *library*.

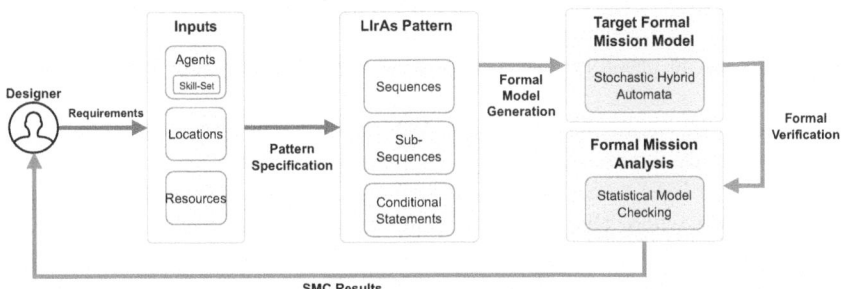

Fig. 1. LIrAs-based toolchain for MAS specification. Pre-existing elements are in grey, while the contributions of this paper are highlighted in blue. The inputs on the left are defined externally from LIrAs and depend on the application field. In the middle, there are the main elements of a LIrAs pattern and on the right, the target mission analysis framework, selected to be compatible with the actual framework for the analysis of Human-Robot Interaction (HRI) missions [16].

The semantics of LIrAs patterns, specifically the custom synchronization dynamics among different agents, are defined starting from Deterministic Finites-tate Automata (DFA), allowing for the verification of basic well-formedness properties, such as ensuring that the pattern can be completed. Interested readers can refer to [25] for the presentation of the fundamental primitives of LIrAs and their mapping to DFA semantics.

However, formal models of the agents' skills involve a broader range of features than can be expressed through DFA (e.g., physical variables, such as a robot's battery charge, and sources of uncertainty, such as human choices). Furthermore, LIrAs pattern libraries, when *contextualized* within a layout with specific agents instances, lend themselves to richer analyses than basic well-formedness properties, such as the computation of *quality metrics* concerning the effort required on the human agent's side or the timeliness of a contextualized custom pattern. Lestingi et al. [16] introduce a framework for formally modeling and analyzing HRIs. The framework relies on a textual DSL, distinct from LIrAs, specifically tailored for tasks involving both human and robotic agents. However, a limitation of this DSL is its reliance on a finite set of predefined patterns, which may not be sufficient to cover all real-world scenarios.

The hereby presented vision builds upon both sides by bridging the LIrAs toolchain with the framework for HRI analysis, hereinafter referred to as the *target* framework. LIrAs libraries of *ad-hoc* patterns can be imported into the DSL for HRI mission specification, with *mission* referring to a sequence of LIrAs patterns selected from the pattern library, thus enhancing the flexibility in mission specification.

The target framework models HRIs missions as networks of Stochastic Hybrid Automata (SHA), analyzed through Statistical Model Checking (SMC). SHA capture the physical components of the cyber-physical system under modeling, including factors such as battery charge and discharge or human fatigue, whose time dynamics are represented through differential equations [16]. Additionally, SHA enable the representation of stochastic behavior arising from human free will, capturing the possibility of a human agent acting differently from expectations.

Therefore, for the incorporation of LIrAs patterns into the target framework and mission analysis through SMC to be possible, a model-to-model conversion principle from LIrAs to SHA must be defined. This work introduces the stage of the toolchain where the pattern specification is transformed into a network of SHA, which is then analyzed using SMC. The translation from LIrAs to SHA follows a three-layer hierarchical structure. The top layer manages the synchronization of sub-sequences among agents; the middle one controls the actions' execution; the bottom layer contains the action skill set for the agents belonging to the mission.

The contributions of this paper pave the way towards the computation of quality metrics associated with the mission, such as the time required for completing each pattern and the physical effort required from humans. Once these metrics are computed, reconfiguration measures can be applied to satisfy specific design constraints. Given the hybrid nature of SHA, the components considered in the formal analysis in this newly developed stage of the toolchain encompass both cyber and physical components. Verified properties may encompass physical phenomena over time with continuous dynamics, such as the battery charge of a robot, and may also address compatibility with the environment and custom-defined patterns.

The paper is structured as follows: Sect. 2 provides an analysis of related work; Sect. 3 presents the technical background for SHA; Sect. 4 offers an illustrative example; Sect. 5 describes the translation from LIrAs to SHA; Sect. 6 concludes and presents possible future developments.

2 Related Work

The aim of LIrAs is to encompass a wide range of requirements specification in multi-agent systems, such as robotic applications or smart manufacturing. LIrAs' distinctive features are the possibility to customize patterns instead of relying on a predefined set and to include human agents in a pattern, making it particularly suitable for human-robot interaction patterns.

Various formal notations, such as Petri Nets [23], Automata [14], Linear Temporal Logic (LTL) [26], and Temporal Plan Networks [17] have been used to model the workflow of different agents' tasks. However, these approaches are less accessible to users without expertise in formal modeling. For this, especially in scenarios where a human-in-the-loop approach is essential, a common practice is to employ a high-level DSL for specifying requirements. This allows users to articulate specifications that might otherwise be ambiguous in natural language.

The DSLs developed for task specification can be general-purpose [5,21,28] or bounded to specific agent categories, such as autonomous vehicles [24], multi-copters [6,22], or medical rehabilitation robots [12]. In the field of robotics, Nordmann et al. in 2014 surveyed 137 such languages [20]. More recently, PsALM, a grammar-based DSL, was introduced, defining 22 patterns for robotic missions [18]. Additionally, PROMISE focuses on specifying concurrent robot missions through sequences of basic actions without relying on predefined patterns [13]. PuRSUE is a modeling language for human-robot interactions compiled into Timed Game Automata [4]. However, its language features lower-level primitives, as it targets users with a stronger technical background, making it complementary to LIrAs.

LIrAs provides high flexibility in specifications by combining agents' primitives into patterns without being constrained to a predefined set. This unique characteristic enables LIrAs to accommodate any type of agent, including humans, overcoming a common limitation in existing languages [27]: the limited support for patterns involving human agents. In conclusion, LIrAs offers a high level of abstraction, allowing patterns to be parametric to the environment and the various agent characteristics, such as the angular and translational velocities of robots.

3 Background

This section recaps the theoretical foundation of this paper's contribution, concerning SHA and SMC [2,9,11].

SHA features are illustrated through a running example inspired from [8, Sect. 4]. The system depicted in Fig. 2 [16] consists of two distinct components:

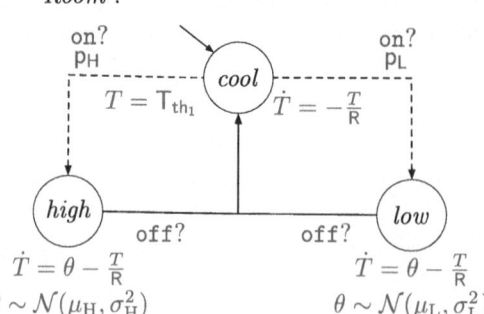
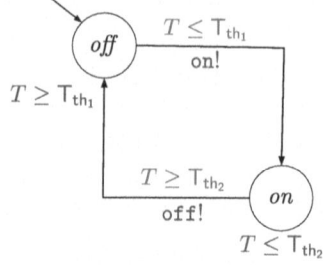

(a) Room SHA model, receiving events from the thermostat.

(b) Thermostat SHA model, initiating events that influence the room.

Fig. 2. Example of SHA network [16]. Dashed arrows represent probabilistic transitions, characterized by weights (in brown) denoted with p_H and p_L, while solid arrows are deterministic transitions. Color-coding is as follows: channels are red, probability distributions, flow conditions, exponential rates are purple, guard conditions are green, and updates are blue. (Color figure online)

a heating system (Fig. 2b) and a room (Fig. 2a). The physical phenomenon measured in this system is the temperature of the room, modeled as a real-valued variable, denoted by T, in the depicted automaton.

The thermostat's model has two locations, *on* and *off*. While in *off*, if the temperature falls below threshold T_{th_1} (as per invariant $T \geq T_{th_1}$ labeling the *off* location), the thermostat switches to the *on* location, activating the heating system. Similarly, the thermostat switches *off* the heating system when, while in *on*, the temperature exceeds the threshold T_{th_2}. Three locations model the room temperature's behavior, as illustrated in Fig. 2a. The temperature decreases naturally in the *cool* location with the heating system *off*. Locations *high* and *low* represent the room while the heating system is active, with the temperature increasing at different rates.

The temperature evolution follows differential equations, referred to as flow conditions. When the thermostat is *on*, the associated differential equation is $\dot{T} = \theta - \frac{T}{R}$, while it is $\dot{T} = -\frac{T}{R}$ when the heating system is *off*. Here, R is a constant, and θ is a randomly distributed parameter whose variability is based on a probability distribution. At the onset of the system, the thermostat is in *off*, and the temperature is initialized to T_{th_1}.

The parameter θ in Fig. 2a represents a realization of a normal distribution. When the room is heating at a high rate, it has a standard deviation of σ_H and a mean of μ_H (denoted as $\mathcal{N}(\mu_H, \sigma_H^2)$), where "H" stands for high. The probability distribution is $\mathcal{N}(\mu_L, \sigma_L^2)$ when the room is heating slowly, as there is an open window; here, the subscript "L" indicates low. The notation $\theta \sim \mathcal{N}(\mu, \sigma)$ is used to express that a random parameter θ is a realization of a random variable Θ governed by the distribution $\mathcal{N}(\mu, \sigma)$.

SHA switch locations through edges, and edges can be labeled by the events that trigger the corresponding switch. Event labels are either of the form e? or e! depending on whether the automaton receives or triggers the event, respectively. For example, once the thermostat triggers the on! event, the room reacts (label on?), realizing the synchronization between the two automata. The decision regarding the heating rate (whether high or low) when on! fires is probabilistic with weights p_H and p_L, respectively.

SHA are amenable to SMC [1] and can be modeled and analyzed through the UPPAAL tool [15]. SMC requires a stochastic model M (the SHA network in our case) and a property ψ formulated in Metric Interval Temporal Logic (MITL) over atomic propositions taken from the set AP [3]. These propositions include constraints in the set of symbols W (e.g., $w < 10$) or automata locations (such as $high$ in Fig. 2a). In our work, the property ψ is of the form $\diamond_{\leq \tau} ap$, where $\diamond$ is the "eventually" operator, $ap \in AP$ and τ is a time bound (i.e., the formula is true if ap holds within τ units of time from the onset). SMC estimates the probability of ψ holding for M—i.e., the value of expression $\mathbb{P}_M(\psi)$ [8].

In this paper, LIrAs specifications are translated into SHA network M. Through SMC, the framework calculates the probability of SHA o eventually reaching the location l within a time-bound τ, expressed as $\mathbb{P}_M(\diamond_{\leq \tau} o.l)$.

4 Illustrative Example

In this section, we propose an example of specification using LIrAs, based on the primitives of this language. We first present a MAS specification exemplar in natural language, followed by its associated LIrAs specification, highlighting LIrAs's compact and unambiguous syntax. In Sect. 5, to describe the contribution of this work, the exemplar is translated to DFA and SHA, and then analyzed through SMC.

The illustrative example focuses on HRI, involving two agents: a Human and a Robot. In LIrAs, each agent is associated with a set of *actions*, i.e., the atomic skills available to them to complete the mission. Agents operate in a known layout characterized by its geometry and a set of *points of interest*, intended as potential targets of their actions (e.g., significant locations to move to or equipment they can interact with). In this example, the set of actions available to these agents is: stop, moveTo, and follow. The stop action simply halts the involved agent, while the moveTo action requires a parameter, PoI, indicating the destination towards which the associated agent must move. The follow action can have one or two parameters: the mandatory one is the agent to be followed, and the optional second parameter specifies the target destination where the followed agent should bring the followers. A pattern consists of sequences, which dictate the order in which the following sub-sequences are executed by the agent. This element is crucial for enforcing synchronization stages across agents. A more formal explanation of these basic elements, including conditional statements and atomic predicates, is provided in [25].

Firstly, the two agents must reach the poi1, but the Robot will start its movement only once the Human has reached the destination. Notice that the

Listing 1.1. LIrAs specification of the motivating example.

```
Human:
  1: moveTo poi1
  2: moveTo poi2
Robot:
  1: moveTo poi1 if position(Human,poi1)
                 else stop
  2: follow Human (poi2)
```

DSL introduced in [16] does not envisage a pre-determined pattern for independent movement as in this case, hence justifying the specification a LIrAs custom pattern for this example. This is reached by using an if/else conditional statement and the `position` atomic predicate. Once both agents have reached the destination, the `Human` starts moving towards the `poi2`; meanwhile, the `Robot` follows. This simple specification is captured in LIrAs as shown in Listing 1.1, which is parametric to all the elements concerning the operational environment.

5 Translating LIrAs patterns to SHA

This section firstly introduces the SHA structure for a LIrAs pattern, then presents the DFA model capturing the illustrative example, followed by the translation of the LIrAs code to SHA. Finally, it reports the results from the validation of the SHA network.

5.1 Hierarchical LIrAs Pattern Structure

The SHA will be structured using the three-layer hierarchical design of Fig. 3, which thanks to its modularity is suitable for scenarios with different domains, and not only for HRI. This structure follows a top-to-bottom approach and consists of the Pattern Orchestrator, the Sequence Orchestrator, and the Action Set. These three categories comprise automata, with adjacent layers communicating through synchronized transitions, global variables, and guards.

At the top level of Fig. 3, the Pattern Orchestrator oversees the pattern by synchronizing all the sub-sequences of the involved agents. The orchestrator provides the conditioned starting signal for the passage from one sub-sequence to the next, communicating via shared synchronized transitions with the layer below, the Sequence Orchestrator. Each sub-sequence i is associated with a channel, s_i; more precisely, in the Pattern Orchestrator the transition label is of the form $s_i!$ (sending), while in the Sequence Orchestrator, it is $s_i?$ (receiving). Once the Pattern Orchestrator provides the starting commands, it no longer intervenes in executing that sub-sequence. For example, in Listing 1.1, the Pattern Orchestrator allows Line 2 and Line 5 to start simultaneously (firing channel s_1), and once both end, it provides the starting signal for Line 3 and Line 7 (channel s_2). However, LIrAs is limited to series-parallel networks. While this might be true from

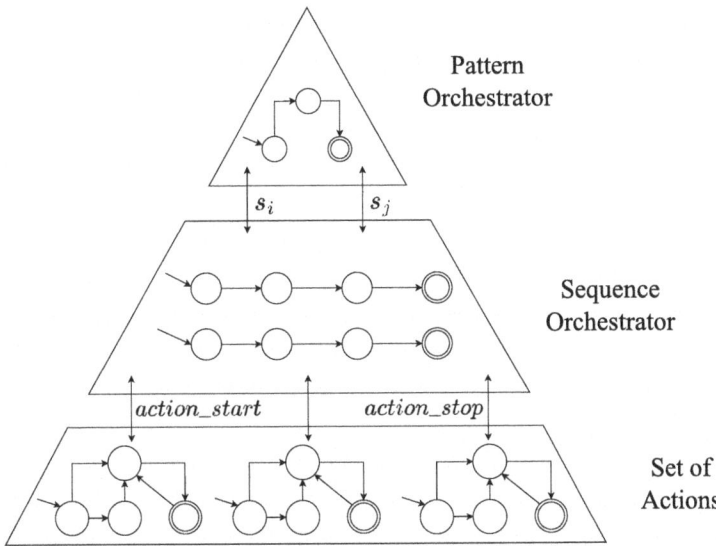

Fig. 3. Schematic representation of the three-layer hierarchical structure of the SHA in the LIrAs framework. The double arrows indicate the sharing of information between layers.

the Pattern Orchestrator's perspective, the managed sub-sequences can incorporate choices, dependencies, and loops through conditional statements and atomic predicates, thus adding more flexibility to the DSL.

Each mission corresponds to one Pattern Orchestrator. The number of orchestrator locations is one for each sub-sequence associated with the pattern, plus an initial and a final location. In Listing 1.1, having two sub-sequences, the number of locations for the Pattern Orchestrator is four.

The middle layer of Fig. 3 consists of as many automata as the number of agent sequences within the pattern; thus, there are only two for Listing 1.1. This layer forms the Sequence Orchestrator and communicates with the other two layers by sending and receiving synchronization signals, or by updating and checking global variables that indicate the execution status of actions and sub-sequences. In Listing 1.1, there are no sub-sequences with more than one action. However, if such sub-sequences exist, the Sequence Orchestrator must manage the start and stop conditions for the sequential execution of actions in the bottom layer. The only exception is in Line 5, where two actions are due to a conditional statement. In this case, the Sequence Orchestrator manages both the atomic predicate and the corresponding decision, as discussed in more detail in Sect. 5.3. LIrAs is currently limited to managing actions that do not include multitasking, meaning multiple actions cannot be executed simultaneously by the same agent. However, we plan to add this feature to the DSL with a suitable grammar.

Finally, the bottom layer of Fig. 3 collects all the expert-defined SHA representing the tasks executable by each agent. In Listing 1.1, only three automata are required: one for the human `moveTo` action, and two for the robot `moveTo` and `follow` actions. The `stop` action does not require a dedicated automaton as it simply halts the robot by terminating the execution of an action or movement. The primary focus for this layer is understanding why and how it must communicate with the Sequence Orchestrator. It receives start and stop commands for initiating and concluding the execution of an action, whether at the natural end of the task or due to a conditional statement that necessitates an early interruption. Sensor measurements are passed from the action layers to the Sequence Orchestrator to determine when an action can end or to compute the values of atomic predicates. These considerations imply that the actions do have not a predetermined duration for their execution, but they depend on the passed parameters like the PoI to be reached during a `moveTo` action, and the measurement of sensors. The random time required by each action is compensated with the reprogrammable *action_end* locations [25] at the end of each sub-sequence in the Sequence Orchestrator, where we can set a default behavior to be followed while waiting for the next synchronization stages.

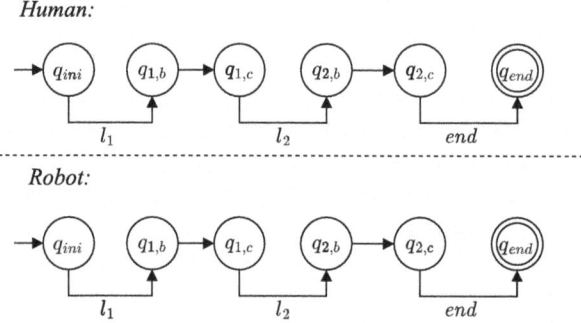

Fig. 4. DFA network of the example discussed in Sect. 4. Each action corresponds to two locations: $q_{1,b}$ when executing and $q_{1,c}$ when completed.

5.2 DFA Representation

The DFA in Fig. 4 formalizes the synchronization among agents in the illustrative example. This does not include conditional statements, which involve physical variables and are, thus, only handled by the SHA model.

In Fig. 4, both agents start from the initial location q_{ini}. From here, the transition labeled l_1 fires simultaneously, moving both agents to the busy location $q_{1,b}$ for the first action in the first sub-sequence (the `moveTo` actions in our example). After completing these actions, both agents transition to the complete locations $q_{1,c}$ for the first sub-sequences, as there is only one action in it. This sequence of events repeats for the second sub-sequences with the transition labeled l_2. A labeled transition can fire only if all agents sharing this label can do so simultaneously. This strategy ensures the synchronization requirements imposed by LIrAs in a multi-agent environment.

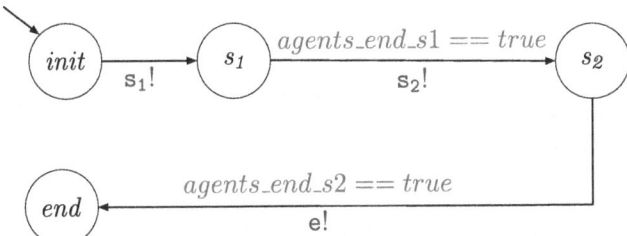

Fig. 5. Simplified automaton of the Pattern Orchestrator for the illustrative example in Sect. 4.

In the model of Fig. 4, the following Timed Computation Tree Logic (TCTL) properties can be verified. As captured by Formula (1), it is verified that there exists a path such that eventually all agents reach the final state.

$$\text{EF} \bigwedge_{a_{id} \in AG} a_{id}.q_{end} \qquad (1)$$

On the other hand, the property that, for all paths, eventually all agents reach the final state—captured by Formula (2)—is not verified for the network because an agent can remain indefinitely in any state, and not only in the q_{end} location.

$$\text{AF} \bigwedge_{a_{id} \in AG} a_{id}.q_{end} \qquad (2)$$

5.3 SHA Representation

We now present the SHA[1] associated with the illustrative example from Sect. 4, one for each layer depicted in Fig. 3.

The Pattern Orchestrator is depicted in the concise representation of Fig. 5, managing transitions between sub-sequences in the layer below using labels s_1! and s_2! for the first and second sub-sequences, respectively. Guards, shown in green, impose conditions on these transitions to ensure that all agents complete their sub-sequences before progressing. In the example involving a human and a robot, each agent must await authorization from the Pattern Orchestrator upon completing a sub-sequence. This authorization is granted based on

---

[1] The complete Uppaal model associated with the illustrative example is available at https://zenodo.org/records/12667806.

the Pattern Orchestrator's monitoring of all agents through global variables. These global variables are $a\_end\_s_i$, $\forall a \in Agents$ and $\forall s_i \in Subsequences$. Hence, in the example these variables are: $robot\_end\_s_1$, $robot\_end\_s_2$, $human\_end\_s1$ and $human\_end\_s2$, which in Fig. 5 are represented compactly through $agents\_end\_s_1$ and $agents\_end\_s_2$.

Figure 6 illustrates the automaton of the Sequence Orchestrator for the robotic agent. The number of locations in Fig. 6 is determined as follows: two for the initial and final locations, two locations per action, two for the busy and end locations, one for each committed location (i.e., equivalent to having an invariant $t \leq 0$ on the location and a guard $t \geq 0$ for each exit edge from that location) per sub-sequence, and one for each if/else conditional statement. This layer synchronizes with the Pattern Orchestrator through transitions labeled with s_1? and s_2? to know when to initiate sub-sequences. It updates the global variable representing the agent's sub-sequence status—i.e., $Robot\_end\_s1 = true$ and $Robot\_end\_s2 = true$ (the blue text in Fig. 6). These annotations indicate when an agent's sub-sequence concludes, and it is used by the Pattern Orchestrator to determine the starting commands for the next sub-sequence.

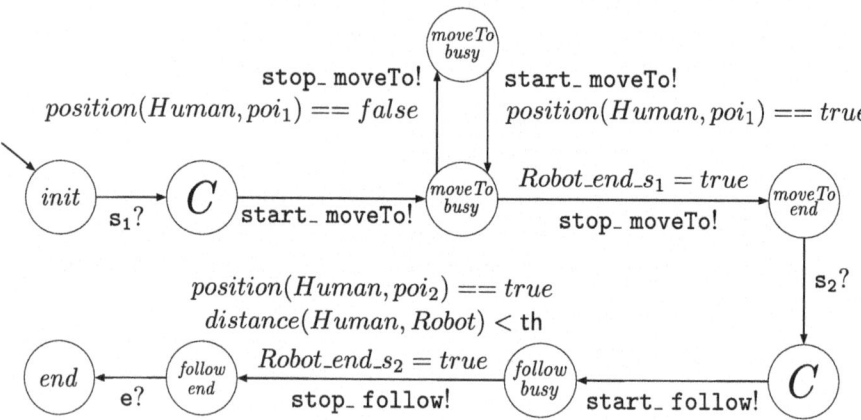

Fig. 6. Simplified automaton of the Sequence Orchestrator for the robot in the illustrative example in Sect. 4. Locations marked with C denote committed locations, which trigger instantaneously upon reaching them.

The robot's Sequence Orchestrator also communicates with the bottom layer of Fig. 3 using labels start_action! and stop_action!. These labels respectively initiate and terminate the execution of a task. The execution process can be influenced by guards from Fig. 6, which facilitate the completion of tasks and evaluate atomic predicates in conditional statements.

All the custom-defined skills for each agent in the pattern are consolidated in the bottom layer of Fig. 3, labeled as Action Set. Figure 7 presents the core features of the SHA modeling of the human agent's moveTo action. We recall that LIrAs specifications define the orchestration of expert-defined SHA in the Action Set layer into a SHA network, so even if the orchestration itself can be described through DFA (see Sect. 5.2), the overall model is SHA.

The moveTo SHA includes features capturing human decision-making and physical variables related to human physiology. Specifically, the SHA includes probabilistic edges capturing the fact that, once a command is received by the Sequence Orchestrator (e.g., through label start_moveTo?), the human may choose to ignore it with weight ignore $\in \mathbb{R}_{\geq 0}$ or abide by it with weight listen $\in \mathbb{R}_{\geq 0}$. Each location models a specific human behavioral state. Specifically, locations differ based on the time dynamics of a physiological variable—i.e., human physical fatigue modeled through a real-valued variable F. Fatigue decreases gradually in the *idle* location, indicating rest, and increases during movement phases (i.e., while in *busy*). Each location is, thus, labeled with a flow condition constraining the evolution of F while in such a location. In this specific case, flow conditions $\dot{F} = -\mathsf{F}_\mathsf{p}\mu e^{-\mu t}$ and $\dot{F} = \mathsf{F}_\mathsf{p}\lambda e^{-\lambda t}$ exploit Merletti et al.'s model of physical fatigue [19], where $\mu, \lambda \in \mathbb{R}_{\geq 0}$ represent the recovery and fatigue rates, respectively, and $\mathsf{F}_\mathsf{p} \in \mathbb{R}_{\geq 0}$ is the residual fatigue from the previous cycle. Interested readers may refer to [16] for the description of the human action's SHA.

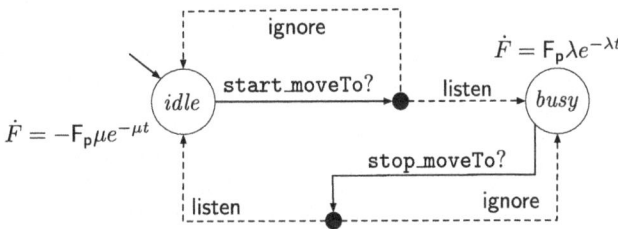

Fig. 7. Simplified SHA of the moveTo action for the human agent [16]. Dashed arrows represent probabilistic transitions, and purple equations denote differential equations used to compute the evolution of human fatigue.

This work's specific action set selection is due to the contextualization of LIrAs within the specific target framework. We recall that LIrAs is agnostic concerning the application domain and agents' skill sets and that the expressiveness of SHA extends to any generic agent with comparable features (e.g., choices subject to uncertainty and physical variables with non-linear time dynamics).

5.4 Validation

In the following, we present the results from the validation of the SHA network, obtained through the manual translation from LIrAs to automata using the Uppaal tool. This translation, based on the described methodology, aims to assess the feasibility of automating the entire process. Additionally, translating into SHA is necessary to analyze a pattern specified with LIrAs and verify SHA properties that provide relevant information about the specification. This analysis is performed for simplicity just for the illustrative example; other examples, which show similar results, are reported in [25]. Specifically, Fig. 8 illustrates a simulation run to demonstrate the behavior of the full system, followed by the results of the SMC query.

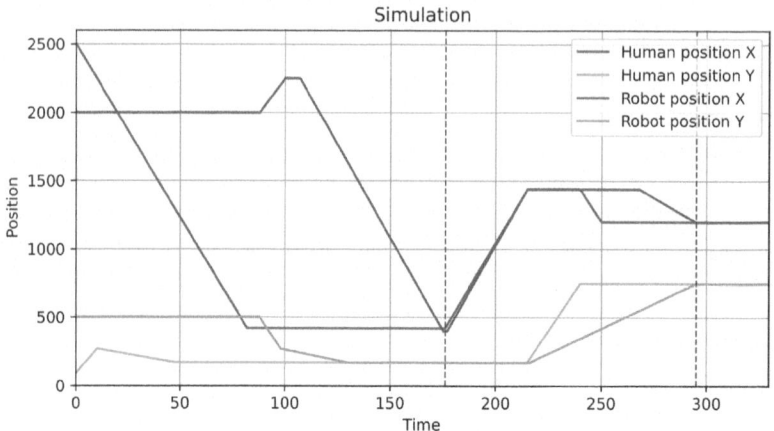

Fig. 8. Simulation of agents' behavior captured by Listing 1.1.

The simulation starts by executing the first sub-sequence, having the two agents in different locations. For the first 85 units of time, where a time unit corresponds to a second, the robotic agent is not moving, due to the if/else conditional statement, until the human does not reach the first PoI. After that, the human concludes the first sub-sequence and the robot starts moving. When the robot reaches the first PoI, too (around 175s), the first sub-sequence ends also for it. Now the Pattern Orchestrator is allowed to provide the start for the second sub-sequence, corresponding to the blue dashed line in the simulation of Fig. 8, where the robot starts the follow action until both agents reach the second PoI. After that, at around time 300 (marked with the pink dashed line), the pattern concludes having reached the final location in all the orchestrator automata.

Thanks to the Uppaal tool we use SMC to compute the probability of desired properties holding. Expression $\mathbb{P}_M(\psi)$ amounts to a confidence interval for the probability of ψ holding for M, which Uppaal computes through the Clopper-Pearson method [7]. Specifically, given hyperparameter ϵ, Uppaal concludes the verification experiment when the Clopper-Pearson confidence interval is smaller than ϵ. All results reported in the following are run with default value $\epsilon = 0.05$. Therefore, the highest confidence interval that can be obtained (approximating to near certainty of property ψ holding) is $[0.95, 1]$.

The first properties checked are $\mathbb{P}_M(\diamond_{\leq 300}\ o.\text{end})$, $\mathbb{P}_M(\diamond_{\leq 300}\ h.\text{end})$, and $\mathbb{P}_M(\diamond_{\leq 300}\ r.\text{end})$; they correspond to the probability for the Pattern Orchestrator (o), the Sequence Orchestrator for the Human (h), and the one for the Robot (r), respectively, to reach the final location within $300s$. The resulting confidence interval is $[0.95, 1]$, signifying the likelihood of these properties holding for M. We use the same time bound ($300s$) for all three properties because the shared synchronization label and status guards lead to the synchronous firing of the three terminal locations.

Since the probability $\mathbb{P}_M(\diamond_{\leq 175}\ o.\text{start}_{s2})$ has a confidence interval ranging from 0.95 to 1, we can assert that the first sub-sequence concludes within 175 s with near certainty. Given that the entire specification, which has two sub-sequences, completes within 300 s, it is apparent that s_1 and s_2 have similar durations. The first sub-sequence is slower between the two due to the idle action introduced by the `if/else` conditional statement in the robotic agent's sub-sequence, as seen in Lines 5 and 6 of Listing 1.1.

Lastly, since we do not want an automaton to reach the *end* location while the others do not, we can check the probability $\mathbb{P}_M((\diamond_{\leq 300}\ (o.\text{end} \wedge \neg h.\text{end}) \vee (o.\text{end} \wedge \neg r.\text{end}))$ is violated. It represents the probability of reaching the terminal location in the Pattern Orchestrator while not in the Sequence Orchestrators (for both the Human and the Robot). The resulting confidence interval in this case is $[0, 0.05]$, stemming from the guards and synchronization in the last transition, being almost zero we can assert that this property, as desired, is violated.

6 Conclusions and Future Developments

This paper builds upon the toolchain relying on LIrAs (whose syntax and semantics are presented in [25]) by demonstrating the translation of LIrAs specifications to SHA through an illustrative example and showcasing how SMC applies to the resulting formal model.

Through this translation process, we can derive a complex formal model based on SHA from a high-level specification with LIrAs, which would otherwise require an expert to generate. This model can then be verified with Uppaal by checking properties as reported in Sect. 5 and others. The validation presented in Sect. 5 demonstrates that our model efficiently represents the specification created with LIrAs, showing the probability of satisfying the desired properties.

Although the translation is currently performed manually, we plan to automate it in the future by leveraging the three-layer hierarchical structure presented in Sect. 5.1. This will simplify the validation of this approach on more examples. Additionally, we intend to extend this validation analysis to different fields to ensure the domain-agnostic capabilities of LIrAs in MAS applications. Finally, we aim to conduct a user study to assess the user-friendliness and clarity of LIrAs for non-expert users.

References

1. Agha, G., Palmskog, K.: A survey of statistical model checking. ACM Trans. Model. Comput. Simul. (TOMACS) **28**(1), 1–39 (2018)
2. Alur, R., Dill, D.L.: A theory of timed automata. Theoret. Comput. Sci. **126**(2), 183–235 (1994)
3. Alur, R., Feder, T., Henzinger, T.A.: The benefits of relaxing punctuality. J. ACM (JACM) **43**(1), 116–146 (1996)
4. Bersani, M.M., Soldo, M., Menghi, C., Pelliccione, P., Rossi, M.: PuRSUE-from specification of robotic environments to synthesis of controllers. Formal Aspects Comput. **32**, 187–227 (2020)
5. Bolton, M.L., Siminiceanu, R.I., Bass, E.J.: A systematic approach to model checking human-automation interaction using task analytic models. IEEE Trans. Syst. Man, Cybern.-Part A: Syst. Humans **41**(5), 961–976 (2011)
6. Bozhinoski, D., Di Ruscio, D., Malavolta, I., Pelliccione, P., Tivoli, M.: Flyaq: enabling non-expert users to specify and generate missions of autonomous multi-copters. In: 2015 30th IEEE/ACM International Conference on Automated Software Engineering (ASE), pp. 801–806. IEEE (2015)
7. Clopper, C.J., Pearson, E.S.: The use of confidence or fiducial limits illustrated in the case of the binomial. Biometrika **26**(4), 404–413 (1934)
8. David, A., Larsen, K.G., Legay, A., Mikučionis, M., Poulsen, D.B.: Uppaal smc tutorial. Int. J. Softw. Tools Technol. Transfer **17**, 397–415 (2015)
9. David, A., et al.: Statistical model checking for networks of priced timed automata. In: Fahrenberg, U., Tripakis, S. (eds.) FORMATS 2011. LNCS, vol. 6919, pp. 80–96. Springer, Heidelberg (2011). https://doi.org/10.1007/978-3-642-24310-3_7
10. Dragule, S., Gonzalo, S.G., Berger, T., Pelliccione, P.: Languages for specifying missions of robotic applications. In: Software Engineering for Robotics, pp. 377–411. Springer, Cham (2021). https://doi.org/10.1007/978-3-030-66494-7_12
11. Bouyer, P., Larsen, K.G., Markey, N., Sankur, O., Thrane, C.: Timed automata can always be made implementable. In: Katoen, J.-P., König, B. (eds.) CONCUR 2011. LNCS, vol. 6901, pp. 76–91. Springer, Heidelberg (2011). https://doi.org/10.1007/978-3-642-23217-6_6
12. Forbrig, P., Bundea, A.-N.: Modelling the collaboration of a patient and an assisting humanoid robot during training tasks. In: Kurosu, M. (ed.) HCII 2020. LNCS, vol. 12182, pp. 592–602. Springer, Cham (2020). https://doi.org/10.1007/978-3-030-49062-1_40
13. García, S., Pelliccione, P., Menghi, C., Berger, T., Bures, T.: High-level mission specification for multiple robots. In: ACM SIGPLAN International Conference on Software Language Engineering, pp. 127–140 (2019)
14. Lacerda, B., Lima, P.: Ltl plan specification for robotic tasks modelled as finite state automata. In: Proceedings of Workshop ADAPT–Agent Design: Advancing from Practice to Theory, Workshop at AAMAS, vol. 9 (2009)
15. Larsen, K.G., Pettersson, P., Yi, W.: UPPAAL in a nutshell. Int. J. on Softw. Tools for Tech. Transf. **1**(1-2), 134–152 (1997)
16. Lestingi, L., Zerla, D., Bersani, M.M., Rossi, M.: Specification, stochastic modeling and analysis of interactive service robotic applications. Robot. Auton. Syst. **163**, 104387 (2023)
17. Levine, S.J., Williams, B.C.: Watching and acting together: concurrent plan recognition and adaptation for human-robot teams. J. Artif. Intell. Res. **63**, 281–359 (2018)

18. Menghi, C., Tsigkanos, C., Pelliccione, P., Ghezzi, C., Berger, T.: Specification patterns for robotic missions. IEEE Transactions on Software Engineering (2019)
19. Merletti, R., Conte, L.L., Orizio, C.: Indices of muscle fatigue. J. Electromyogr. Kinesiol. **1**(1), 20–33 (1991)
20. Nordmann, A., Hochgeschwender, N., Wrede, S.: A survey on domain-specific languages in robotics. In: Brugali, D., Broenink, J.F., Kroeger, T., MacDonald, B.A. (eds.) Simulation, Modeling, and Programming for Autonomous Robots, pp. 195–206. Springer International Publishing, Cham (2014). https://doi.org/10.1007/978-3-319-11900-7_17
21. Paterno, F., Mancini, C., Meniconi, S.: ConcurTaskTrees: a diagrammatic notation for specifying task models. In: Howard, S., Hammond, J., Lindgaard, G. (eds.) Human-Computer Interaction INTERACT '97, pp. 362–369. Springer US, Boston, MA (1997). https://doi.org/10.1007/978-0-387-35175-9_58
22. Ruscio, D.D., Malavolta, I., Pelliccione, P., Tivoli, M.: Automatic generation of detailed flight plans from high-level mission descriptions. In: Proceedings of the ACM/IEEE 19th International Conference on Model Driven Engineering Languages and Systems, pp. 45–55 (2016)
23. Salimifard, K., Wright, M.: Petri net-based modelling of workflow systems: an overview. Eur. J. Oper. Res. **134**(3), 664–676 (2001)
24. Silva, D.C., Abreu, P.H., Reis, L.P., Oliveira, E.: Development of a flexible language for mission description for multi-robot missions. Inf. Sci. **288**, 27–44 (2014)
25. Tagliaferro, A., Lestingi, L., Rossi, M.: Towards verifiable multi-agent interaction pattern specification. In: International Conference on Formal Methods in Software Engineering, pp. 122–126. ACM (2024)
26. Tumova, J., Dimarogonas, D.V.: Multi-agent planning under local ltl specifications and event-based synchronization. Automatica **70**, 239–248 (2016)
27. Van, T.N., Fredivianus, N., Tran, H.T., Geihs, K., Huynh, T.T.B.: Formal verification of ALICA multi-agent plans using model checking. In: International Symposium on Information and Communication Technology, pp. 351–358 (2018)
28. Van Der Aalst, W.M., Ter Hofstede, A.H.: YAWL: yet another workflow language. Inf. Syst. **30**(4), 245–275 (2005)

Evaluation of Human Interaction with Fleets of Automated Vehicles in Dynamic Underground Mining Environments

Olga Mironenko(✉), Hadi Banaee, and Amy Loutfi

Center for Applied Autonomous Sensor Systems (AASS), Örebro University,
Fakultetsgatan 1, 70182 Örebro, Sweden
{olga.mironenko,hadi.banaee,amy.loutfi}@oru.se

Abstract. This study investigates the complexities of Mixed Traffic with Fleets of Automated Vehicles (MTF-AVs) in underground mining environments characterized by confined spaces, limited visibility, and strict navigation requirements. The research focuses on integrating human-controlled vehicles into coordinated AV fleets, addressing the unpredictable interactions that arise from human behaviour. The ORU coordination framework, originally designed for a fully autonomous system, is adapted for mixed traffic scenarios to evaluate the impact of human behaviour on system efficiency and safety. Through a series of simulations, the study explores how fleet coordination algorithms adapt to human driver behaviour. These simulations demonstrate that human error and rule violations significantly reduce performance, increasing safety risks and decreasing efficiency. Findings emphasize the need for advanced coordination algorithms that dynamically adapt to unpredictable human behaviour in MTF-AVs. Such algorithms would optimize interactions between automated and human-controlled vehicles, enhancing both safety and efficiency in these complex and dynamic environments. Future research will further explore the influence of human behaviour on the coordination system and develop advanced coordination algorithms with methods to evaluate these interactions effectively.

Keywords: Human behaviour in driving · Mixed traffic with fleets of automated vehicles · Centralised coordination · Underground mining

1 Introduction

In the context of driverless vehicle fleets, seamless coordination systems often assume a controlled environment with automated vehicles (AVs) adhering to predefined routes and executing pre-programmed tasks. However, when entities, such as human-driven vehicles or pedestrians, enter this idealized system, their unpredictable behaviour can lead to unforeseen traffic scenarios within the system. Such a situation which we refer to as Mixed Traffic with Fleets of AVs (MTF-AVs), poses a significant challenge for fleet coordination algorithms.

The complexity of MTF-AVs scenarios becomes even more challenging in the unique environment of underground mines. Traffic control in such mines presents distinctive challenges due to the environment's constraints, limited visibility, confined spaces with narrow tunnels, noise from mining operations. Further complicating the scenario is the issue of integrating new infrastructure like sensors or traffic control systems within these restrictive spaces. The dynamic nature of underground tunnel systems requires regular updates to mine maps, which further complicates the installation and maintenance of such systems.

Modern mines operate with a mix of human-driven, remotely operated, and partially automated large hauler truck fleets. The initial stages of ore transportation, crucial for the mining process, involve coordinating these fleets to navigate narrow tunnels and intersections (see an example of an underground mine map Fig. 1). A typical issue of regulating such traffic is the size of vehicles. The machines are usually almost as wide as the corridor and there is no room for two machines to pass each other, increasing the likelihood of traffic conflicts and potential deadlocks.

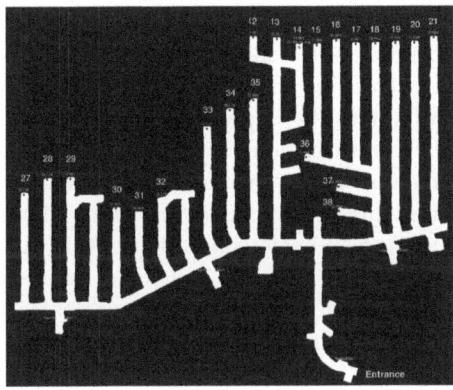

Fig. 1. Example of an underground mine map, illustrating an environment with narrow tunnels and intersections.

These partially automated machines can localise in the environment and move around in automated mode along a predefined path. However, the mining industry is struggling to manage fleets of these vehicles. Previous research [11, 18, 19, 21, 23] has advanced the control of such fleets, enabling the implementation of algorithms for fleet management. However, what has not been developed yet is the ability to mix fleets of AVs with manually controlled vehicles (MVs) or machines operated remotely by humans on the surface. This integration is crucial as full autonomy in underground mines may not be achievable. The complexity of mixing AVs and MVs arises from several factors. Ensuring deadlock-free operation, collision avoidance, and overall safety is feasible when all vehicles are controllable by algorithms. The introduction of an MV disrupts this system due to the lack of established interaction protocols and appropriate traffic regulations to facilitate such integration.

Despite the capability of AV fleet coordinators to identify MVs through sensor data, these human-controlled vehicles remain beyond the coordinator's control. Even with known positions, predicting human actions remains challenging. Considering the unique challenges of underground mines, poor visibility and environmental complexity, the risk of human drivers making errors and deviating from performing driving tasks properly significantly increases. To mitigate risks associated with MVs deviating from traffic regulations, it is crucial to address potential dangerous interactions. Identifying the human behaviour that influences fleets of AVs and modelling it within the coordination systems, can help to detect the potential dangerous or inefficient interactions. This requires advanced simulation of human driving behaviours that consider variations in driver skills, decision-making, and responses to traffic situations.

Implementing adaptive coordination models that respond to human driver behaviour in real-time can improve the robustness and resilience of AV fleet operations, ensuring both enhanced safety and optimal traffic flow. Such models, however, require advanced algorithms for human-aware AV fleet coordination, as well as simulation-based evaluation. Therefore, it is essential to first identify scenarios in which MVs might affect the efficiency and safety of interactions with AV fleets. Subsequently, strategies must be developed to adapt the coordination of these fleets to accommodate the unpredictable behaviour of MVs.

This paper presents a contribution towards our overarching goal to develop AV fleet coordination algorithms that integrate human behavioural insights within a coordination framework that can accommodate human unpredictability, ensuring enhanced efficiency and safer operation within the MTF-AVs system. Using an approach where human driving behaviour research is integrated with a simulation scenario-based study, this paper demonstrates that there is indeed a need for current coordination frameworks to better incorporate human drivers as part of fleet coordination.

The rest of the paper is organised as follows. Section 2 provides an overview of existing coordination systems for AVs and tells about human diver behaviour adaptation in the context of AVs. Section 3 describes the ORU framework used for the integration of human behaviour into the MTF-AVs environment. Section 4 outlines the proposed methodology, for this integration and the construction and evaluation of scenarios. Section 5 presents the outcomes of the experiments. Section 6 contains conclusions and provides answers to research questions.

2 Related Work

This section provides a review of relevant literature focusing on two critical aspects: coordination systems for AVs and studies on human driving behaviour.

2.1 Coordination Systems for AVs

Advancements in Artificial Intelligence and Autonomous Systems have succeeded in providing highly efficient approaches for AVs, ensuring conflict-free movement among vehicles. The literature reveals two primary strategies for multi-robot planning and coordination, grounded in techniques such as constrained optimization and heuristic search [2,14,37], which provide methods for automated multi-robot motion planning and coordination.

Centralised Approach. This approach employs a central system that oversees all vehicles' current and future movements. The system is tasked with calculating adjustments necessary for seamless operation, although it usually works well only for a limited number of robots which is one of its limitations. Despite the need for flawless communication [35], several studies, such as those by Pecora et al. [17,23], demonstrate that perfect communication is not essential and propose a more flexible approach that can manage medium-sized fleets by continuously monitoring and adjusting to significant deviations from the planned traffic flow.

Decentralised Approach. This approach highlights the importance of localized decision-making and capabilities within an external traffic management and control framework that both automated robots and human operators must adhere to. Each participant is presumed to have sensors or information enabling them to recognize potential conflicts between two vehicles that are not resolved by controller instructions [3].

Mixed Traffic Simulation Frameworks. Numerous simulation platforms have been developed for primarily urban traffic environments, for example, CARLA, LGSVL, SUMO, and Microsoft's AirSim [7,16]. While some platforms such as VISSIM and MATSim are engineered to incorporate the integration of driving behaviour models and simulate a wide range of traffic scenarios, including interactions between AVs and MVs [1,13], these systems are fundamentally designed for more open environments. Despite their extensive adaptability and customization features, significant adaptations are required to accurately represent the specialized conditions typical of underground mines, such as confined spaces, specific traffic regulations, and unique safety requirements. Such frameworks also pose limitations in simulating a fleet of vehicles due to their focus on the local perspective of individual agents, thereby only allowing for the design of singular agent behaviours.

2.2 Human Behaviour in Driving

In this work, we focus on human driver behaviour (the observable actions and reactions of a driver in response to stimuli during the driving process) as one of the major human factors that affect traffic [5]. Originally the terms 'driving style' and 'driving skill' as two components of 'driving behaviour' were described in [9]. Driving skill relates to technical competencies and refers to a driver's capability to manage specific driving tasks, such as steering accurately and reacting to hazards quickly, which generally improve with practice. In contrast, driving style describes the unique way a person drives, shaped by long-term habits.

Predicting how a human driver will react in a particular situation is a big challenge [25,29]. Human drivers may exhibit behaviours such as noncompliance with rules or instructions, misinterpretation of control signals, and communication inefficiencies. Humans may have a problem with focus of attention, leading to vehicles stopping incorrectly, failing to stop, or making unexpected speed changes. This list of issues may not be complete but it makes the behaviour modelling and integration of human decision-making towards a coherently coordinated fleet of vehicles challenging [10,25,29]. However, one also needs to consider that underground mines are highly regulated environments. Detected noncompliance with traffic and safety regulations - although happening [8,31] - may have dramatic consequences for the driver due to the severity of traffic penalties - in the worst case the driver might be relieved of their duties. Thus, we may assume that variations in driving behaviour may be limited.

As human drivers interact with AVs, their behavioural responses evolve, influenced by the perceived reliability and capabilities of these systems. The concept of behavioural adaptation in the context of AVs describes it as any change in driver behaviour following interaction with changes in the road traffic system [20,28]. Critical insights have been drawn from simulator studies and real-world driving data, illustrating how drivers adjust their driving behaviours - such as car-following distances, gap acceptance, reaction times and lane-changing behaviours in response to the presence and actions of AVs. *Car-following behaviour* is often studied in terms of *distance* and *time headways*. Distance headway refers to the bumper-to-bumper distance between the lead and the following vehicles, while time headway considers both distance and the speed of the following vehicle [33]. Another key aspect of traffic flow analysis is the *gap acceptance* behaviour, especially at uncontrolled intersections. The critical gap refers to the smallest gap a driver is willing to accept to merge into traffic [27].

Studies highlight that human drivers tend to accept smaller critical gaps when interacting with AVs [26,27,30]. They also maintain shorter headways after overtaking AVs and follow more closely when behind AVs [6,12,15,26,30,34] influenced by their expectations of AVs' cautious driving strategies [32]. Such behaviour intensifies if drivers are informed beforehand about the AVs' defensive programming, which can lead to a false sense of security known as automation complacency [22,36]. The increasing penetration rate of AVs influences these adaptations, leading to human drivers adopting behaviours more similar to AVs, including shorter time headways and smaller following distances [6].

3 ORU Coordination Framework

For our experiments, we selected the ORU coordination framework[1] - a centralised multi-robot coordination framework and methods developed by Pecora

---

[1] https://github.com/FedericoPecora/coordination_oru

et al. [18,23,24]. Based on our examination of various multi-agent simulation frameworks discussed in the related work section, we concluded that extending the ORU coordination framework presents the optimal approach for simulation purposes in our study. This framework is already tailored for the simulation and coordination of vehicle interactions within fleets. It is particularly well-suited to address the unique environmental and operational challenges of underground mines, where precise and coordinated actions are essential due to strict spatial and operational limitations. Furthermore, we verified its ability to effectively integrate a human-controlled agent and evaluate the impact of human driver behaviour on the system's overall performance. The framework has already been used in industrial projects related to underground mining [18], tested with real robots [17] and is publicly available as an open-source platform. It comes with a simple default 2D browser 'simulator'.

The operational algorithm within the ORU coordination framework is composed of several sequential steps. The system aggregates data as each vehicle transmits its computed trajectory to the central coordinator. The coordinator then performs a pairwise analysis to identify potential intersections among the specified trajectories. By considering the paths of vehicles and constraints on speed, it calculates synchronizations that avoid collisions with other vehicles and prevent deadlocks. Based on this analysis, it issues directives to the vehicles, identifying which should halt to prevent collisions, and dictates the sequence in which vehicles are to proceed. The framework encompasses several critical functions: i) *Task allocation* computes destinations and schedules for vehicles based on predetermined drivable areas, assigned tasks, and temporal constraints such as deadlines; ii) *Motion planning* calculates paths for vehicles within drivable areas, aligned with location objectives and the vehicles' kinematic models; iii) *Coordination* determines synchronization strategies to prevent collisions and avoid deadlocks, considering the bounds on vehicle speeds; iv) *Temporal reasoning* establishes vehicle speeds and traversal times based on the synchronization strategies, vehicle paths, and temporal constraints such as deadlines and precedence rules; v) *Control* implements the actual vehicle motions based on reference paths, speeds, and drivable areas [23].

A Meta-CSP (Constraint Satisfaction Problem)[2] based approach underpins this multi-robot coordination system, employing a trajectory envelope representation. The key concept in such envelopes involves imposing an increasingly tight set of constraints on trajectories to exclude paths that are either kinematically unfeasible or would result in collisions or deadlocks. The selected set of trajectories is then revised online as vehicles execute their missions [24].

4 Integration of an Interactively Human-Controlled Vehicle Into the Coordinated Fleet of AVs

We introduced a human-controlled vehicle into the ORU coordination framework to evaluate the impact of human behaviour on the system. In the current

---

[2] https://github.com/FedericoPecora/meta-csp-framework

implementation, the integration functions as follows: a human operator manages a simulated vehicle, selecting destinations via a mouse and adjusting speed using keyboard inputs for acceleration and deceleration. Additionally, the operator has the capability to disregard certain traffic rules, such as failing to yield to an AV designated by the coordinator to proceed first.

This direct human control facilitates the modelling of various human driving behaviours, including unpredictable changes in speed and route, or deliberate non-compliance with traffic laws. Such behaviour can pose challenges to the central coordination system of an AV fleet. If the vehicle deviates from the system's algorithms, it forces the coordinator to make real-time adjustments in response to unforeseen changes, requiring the system to dynamically adapt its instructions to the AVs. The impact of an MV on the functionality of the ORU coordination framework is depicted in Fig. 2. The introduction of an MV affects all aspects of the ORU framework, from task allocation to control, introducing elements of unpredictability into the system's dynamics. This requires on-the-fly recalculations of trajectory envelopes by the coordinator and confronts scenarios where vehicles cannot adjust their speed and stop in time, ultimately leading to collisions. To assess the impact of human behaviour on system performance, specifically focusing on efficiency and safety metrics, we conducted investigations and simulations across various scenarios.

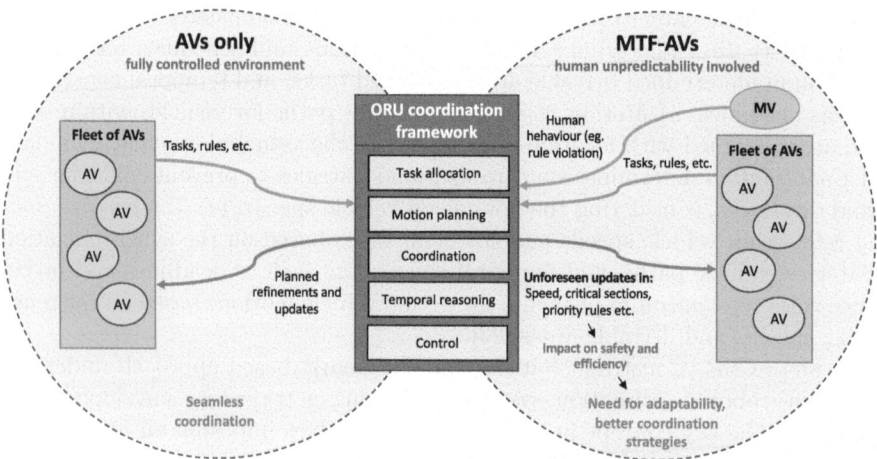

Fig. 2. Impact of an MV on ORU coordination framework. The diagram illustrates how human behaviour affects the functionality of the system, requiring unforeseen on-the-fly recalculations that impact safety and efficiency.

4.1 Simulation Setup

The purpose of the experiments is to explore how safety can be affected and the extent to which efficiency might be compromised to accommodate human driving behaviour, as well as to determine if the AV system can still operate effectively under these conditions.

For the experimental setup, we utilise a map configuration that is a grid-based layout consisting of corridors, each 52 m in length, arranged vertically and horizontally, as illustrated in Fig. 3. The grid configuration was selected based on its resemblance to the constraints of underground mine maps, characterized by narrow corridors intersecting at crossroads. All vehicles in the experiments are modelled as trucks. The types of vehicles considered include an MV designated as V0 (yellow), and AVs identified as V0, V1, V2, and V3 (blue). The identifiers and respective trajectories of the vehicles are displayed in the simulations. The movement direction of the vehicles is depicted by small arrows originating from each vehicle (Fig. 3).

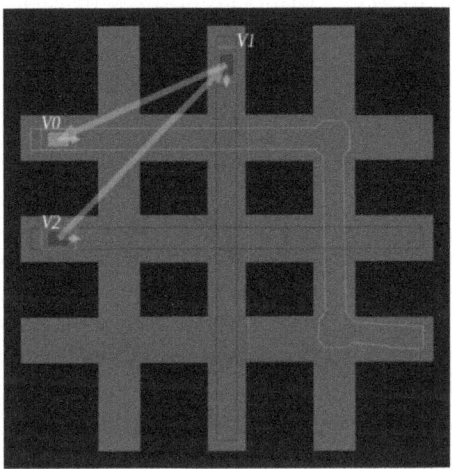

Fig. 3. A grid-based layout with two vehicle types, identified by IDs and colour-coded: MV (V0, yellow) and AVs (V1-V2, blue). Small arrows indicate the directional movement and large arrows illustrate the intended sequence in which the vehicles will proceed. (Color figure online)

To define the scenarios involving human behaviour, the following traffic regulation and compliance factors are developed in the proposed framework.

– Speed regulation. Maximum speed is set individually for each vehicle. If the distance allows and there are no obstacles on the way, vehicles aim to reach their maximum speed. The highest speed a vehicle can reach within a corridor distance of $52m$ is 5 m/s, which is set as the maximum speed limit in the experimental scenarios. Acceleration and deceleration parameters, correlated with the maximum speed, are determined according to the characteristics of diverse vehicle types as described in [4]. Both vehicle types share the same acceleration rate of 0.3 m/s^2 and deceleration rate of 0.5 m/s^2.

- Vehicles maintain a minimum distance from their front bumper to the preceding vehicle's safety distance (inter-vehicle distance). This also includes the proximity to intersections, which is the required distance from a vehicle's front bumper to an intersection. In simulations, the vehicle's safety distance is depicted as a white frame around vehicles (Fig. 3). In its current implementation, the safety distance is set at 1 m for all vehicles.
- The framework employs specific rules to prioritize interactions between AVs and the MV. The rules specify 'Closest-first', 'AV-first' or 'MV-first' priorities to effectively manage traffic flow. The 'Closest-first' priority rule dictates that the right of way is granted based on the order of vehicle arrivals at intersections. By adhering to predefined trajectories, each vehicle in the fleet is programmed to reach these intersections at scheduled times. The prioritisation protocol 'AV-first' permits AVs to proceed first, while the 'MV-first' rule grants this priority to MVs. Arrows are utilized to visualize the sequence in which vehicles are to proceed (Fig. 3).

4.2 Design of Scenarios

The scenarios are defined based on two main cases of the violation of traffic regulations and rules caused by human behaviour. One case concerns non-compliance with established priority rules at intersections, failing to yield the right of way as required by the traffic control system. The other case involves operating at speeds significantly below the average traffic flow, which can disrupt the traffic system. These violations pose risks to both traffic efficiency and safety.

Developing scenarios across these two cases was structured into three distinct phases: i) baseline scenarios with exclusively AVs to set a controlled benchmark; ii) scenarios where one AV is replaced by a human-controlled vehicle (MV), granted priority in the traffic flow thereby eliminating the influence of human driving behaviours; iii) scenarios incorporating human driving behaviours, featuring deviations from standard driving patterns expected in a fully automated environment (i.e., rule violations).

Maintaining a consistent number of vehicles, their routes, and intersection points across all scenarios of each case was essential to ensure that any observed effects were attributable to the intended experimental modifications, specifically the introduction of an MV. The controlled environment helped isolate the impact of human behaviour from other variables, such as increased traffic density. The introduction of new variables in the scenarios, including the replacement of one AV with an MV and the alteration of priority rules, was done incrementally.

Case I Priority Rule Violation: This case evaluates the efficiency and potential traffic risks associated with complacency in automation, specifically when human drivers of MVs overestimate the capabilities of AVs. This overestimation often results from a false or perceived sense of security and may lead to violations of the 'AV-first' priority rule. To address these risks and categorize their impacts, it is essential to understand the specific types of safety-critical events that can arise from these priority rule violations. Safety-critical events are categorized into two main types. One type includes near misses, which occur when the safety distance between vehicles is compromised (overlapping) (Fig. 4a). The other type consists of collisions, which are incidents where the physical bodies of two or more vehicles come into contact (Fig. 4b).

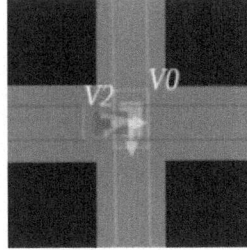

(a) Near-miss.   (b) Collision.

Fig. 4. Illustration of Safety-critical events. a) Near-miss: an occurrence where the safety distance between vehicles is compromised; b) Collision: an incident where the physical bodies of two or more vehicles come into contact.

Scenario 1.1: Baseline Scenario (AVs Only). This scenario presents a perfectly coordinated system in which a fleet of AVs (identified as V0, V1, V2) adheres to predefined trajectories, as illustrated in Fig. 5. V0 moves horizontally from left to right, then vertically down and back, completing a loop. V1 follows a vertical trajectory, moving from top to bottom and reversing its path to return to the origin. V2 operates in a horizontal loop, moving from left to right, followed by a return along the same route to the starting point. Each vehicle consistently repeats its designated loop. The area is strictly controlled and is free from human interference, allowing for seamless traffic flow with minimal stops and maximum efficiency. This scenario is guided by the 'Closest-first' priority rule.

Scenario 1.2: Human Driver Prioritisation. In this scenario, one AV (V0) is replaced by an MV (V0) following the same trajectory as in Scenario 1.1. The MV intersects the paths of other AVs (V1 and V2) at intersections, but without AV's intervention, due to the prioritisation protocol 'MV-first'. Figure 6 illustrates this setup. This scenario exemplifies the elimination of human driving behaviour influences within the traffic system.

Scenario 1.3: Misbehaving Human Driver ('Closest-first' Priority Rule Violation). This scenario maintains the environmental conditions established in Scenario 1.2 but substitutes the 'MV-first' prioritisation protocol with the 'Closest-first' priority rule used in the baseline scenario. Additionally, the MV is programmed to consistently violate this priority rule by failing to yield to an AV when required. This setup is designed to examine the effects of deliberate human-induced priority violations within the traffic system.

Fig. 5. Case I – Scenario 1.1: Baseline configuration with AVs only, following the Closest-first rule.

Fig. 6. Case I – Scenario 1.2: Human driver prioritisation under the MV-first rule.

Scenario 1.4: Misbehaving Human Driver ('AV-first' Priority Rule Violation). This scenario retains the environmental settings of Scenario 1.3 but replaces the 'Closest-first' prioritisation protocol with the 'AV-first' rule. It investigates the consequences of an MV that systematically violates the 'AV-first' rule at all critical intersections by not yielding to AVs. This scenario aims to evaluate the potential increase in near misses and collisions resulting from the MV's non-compliance with traffic priorities, thus providing insights into the safety implications. This experimental setup is crafted to quantify the maximum impact of human misbehaviour on the traffic system.

Case II Speed Violation: This case aims to evaluate the efficiency implications associated with speed rule violations, focusing on a scenario where the MV vehicle travels significantly below the mandated speed limit. Such behaviour can create a traffic hazard by unnecessarily obstructing or disrupting the normal flow of other road users.

Scenario 2.1: Baseline Scenario (AVs Only). This scenario presents a perfectly coordinated system in which a fleet of AVs (identified as V0, V1, V2, V3) adheres to predefined trajectories, as illustrated in Fig. 7a. V0 initially travels vertically from top to bottom before aligning with the trajectory of V1. V1, V2 and V3 consistently navigate similar horizontal routes, proceeding from left to right. The simulation terminates when V2 and V3, which do not intersect with any other vehicles and are unaffected by interactions, complete their designated paths (Fig. 7b). The designated area is strictly controlled and is free from human interference, allowing for seamless traffic flow with minimal stops and maximum efficiency. This scenario is guided by the 'Closest-first' priority rule.

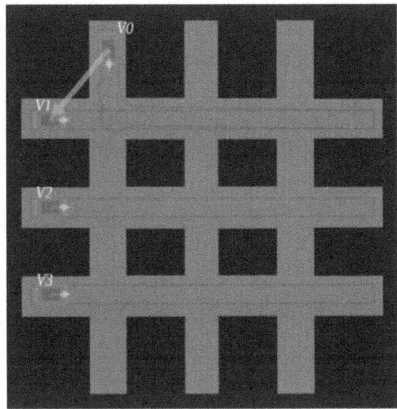

(a) Start of the route. (b) End of the route.

Fig. 7. Case II – Scenario 2.1: Baseline configuration with AVs only, following the Closest-first rule, a) starting point of the route; b) end of the route, where V2 and V3 complete their designated paths.

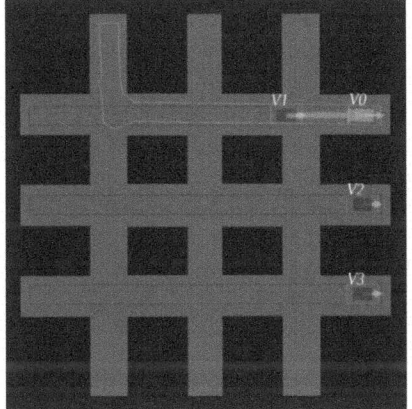
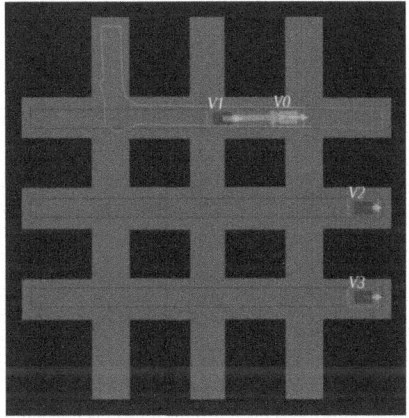

Fig. 8. Case II – Scenario 2.2: Human driver follows traffic rules. MV-first rule. End of the route.

Fig. 9. Case II – Scenario 2.3: Misbehaving human driver. MV-first rule. End of the route.

Scenario 2.2: Human Driver Prioritisation (MV Follows Traffic Rules). In this scenario, one AV (V0) is replaced by an MV (V0) following the same trajectory as in Scenario 2.1. The 'Closest-first' priority rule is altered with the 'MV-first' rule, where all AVs must yield to the MV intersecting their paths. V1 follows the MV along the same trajectory, with all vehicles adhering to a maximum speed limit of 5 m/s. The MV complies with traffic regulations and does not display any typical human driving behaviours (Fig. 8).

Scenario 2.3: Misbehaving Human Driver (Speed Limit Rule Violation). This scenario maintains the environmental settings of Scenario 2.2 while introducing the dynamics of a non-compliant human driver. While V1 trails the MV along the same trajectory, the MV breaks the traffic rule and drives with a speed of 2 m/s (well below the maximum speed of 5 m/s) (Fig. 9). This configuration is designed to assess the impact of reduced MV speeds on traffic flow.

5 Results

5.1 Case I Priority Rule Violation

The summary of the results highlights the impact of the presence or absence of the MV on two critical parameters: efficiency, as measured by the distance travelled by AVs, and safety, assessed through the occurrence of collisions and near misses in relation to violations. The analysis compares the total distance travelled by the two AVs (AV1 and AV2) present across all scenarios and the combined count of safety-critical events (collisions and near misses) experienced by V1 and V2. This method provides a clearer insight into how the presence of an MV affects the performance of the remaining AVs, isolating the influence of human intervention. Table 1 summarises efficiency and safety metrics for all vehicles for priority violation in Case I scenarios. Figure 10 provides an overview of the distances travelled (Fig. 10a) and safety-critical events experienced (Fig. 10b) by V1 and V2 across different scenarios (Scenarios 1.1 to 1.4 are labelled as s1 to s4, respectively). The simulation duration for each scenario is 1 h.

Scenario 1.1: Baseline Scenario (AVs Only). In the absence of human driver interference, this scenario records no violations, collisions, or near misses, indicative of optimal safety performance. With regard to efficiency, this scenario allows to observe the system's performance at its theoretically optimal state.

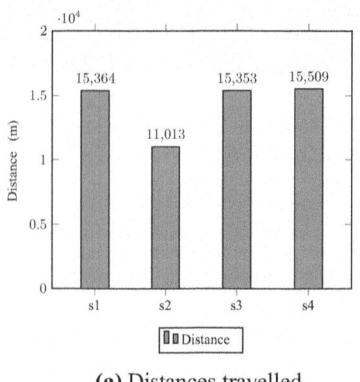
(a) Distances travelled.

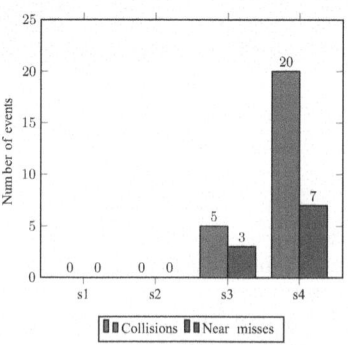
(b) Safety-critical events.

Fig. 10. Case I – Scenarios 1.1 to 1.4 (s1–s4): Comparison of a) the travelled distances and b) the number of safety-critical events in each scenario. Results consolidated for V1 and V2.

Table 1. Summary of results in Case I, considering priority rule violations.

Vehicle ID (Type) max speed (m/s)	V0 (MV) 5	V0 (AV) 5	V1 (AV) 5	V2 (AV) 5	Total (V1+V2)
Scenario 1.1: Baseline (AVs only)					
Priority Rule: Closest-first					
no. violations		-	-	-	-
no. collisions		-	-	-	-
no. near misses		-	-	-	-
distance travelled (m)		7732	7673	7691	15364
Scenario 1.2: Human Driver Prioritisation					
Priority Rule: MV-first					
no. violations	0		-	-	-
no. collisions	0		-	-	-
no. near misses	0		-	-	-
distance travelled (m)	8351		5511	5502	11013
Scenario 1.3: Misbehaving Human Driver (Priority Rule Violation)					
Priority Rule: Closest-first					
no. violations	114		-	-	-
no. collisions	5		3	2	5
no. near misses	3		0	3	3
distance travelled (m)	7870		7656	7697	15353
Scenario 1.4: Misbehaving Human Driver (Priority Rule Violation)					
Priority Rule: AV-first					
no. violations	114		-	-	-
no. collisions	20		11	9	20
no. near misses	7		3	4	7
distance travelled (m)	7575		7748	7761	15509

Scenario 1.2: Human Driver Prioritisation. Consistent with the baseline, there are no collisions or near misses, attributable to the protocol that prevents the MV from violating priority rules. Nevertheless, the distances covered by AV1 and AV2 are shorter than those in the baseline scenario (11013 m vs 15364 m) (Fig. 10a), indicating a decrease in efficiency as a result of prioritizing the MV.

Scenario 1.3: Misbehaving Human Driver ('Closest-First' Priority Rule Violation). The results show a marked decrease in safety when the MV violates priority rules resulting in 114 violations. Furthermore, this scenario recorded 5 collisions and 3 near misses, involving both V1 and V2 (Fig. 10b). These incidents account for 7% of the total violations, highlighting a significant compromise in safety.

Scenario 1.4: Misbehaving Human Driver ('AV-First' Priority Rule Violation). Similar to Scenario 1.3, this scenario records a marked decrease in safety due to

114 violations by the MV as a result of priority rule violations. This scenario is further characterized by 20 collisions and 7 near misses involving both V1 and V2 (Fig. 10b). These incidents account for 24% of the total violations, indicating an even greater compromise in safety. In terms of efficiency, both Scenarios 1.3 and 1.4 demonstrate a similar enhanced performance relative to Scenario 1.2, where the MV is prioritized. The distances travelled in these scenarios align closely with those recorded in the baseline scenario (Fig. 10a).

5.2 Case II Speed Violation

This analysis evaluates the effects of speed violation on the performance metrics of an AV, focusing on instances where the AV encounters delays due to following an AM that maintains its predefined speed limit of 5 m/s vs trailing a slower-moving MV with the speed of 2 m/s. The primary analysis compares the total distance travelled by the three AVs (AV1, AV2 and AV3) present across all scenarios. Table 2 provides a comprehensive summary of the efficiency outcomes for Case II – Speed Violation, showing the distance travelled over a 28-second simulation interval, observed across three distinct scenarios. Figure 7b illustrates the final position of V1's assigned route in the Baseline scenario. The final position of V1 in other configurations includes scenarios where the MV adheres to speed regulations (Fig. 8) and a scenario featuring a slow-moving MV (Fig. 9).

Table 2. Summary of results in Case II, considering speed violation.

Vehicle ID (Type)	V0 (MV)	V0 (AV)	V1 (AV)	V2 (AV)	V3 (AV)
Scenario 2.1: Baseline (AVs only)					
Priority Rule: Closest-first					
max speed (m/s)		5	5	5	5
distance travelled (m)		38.6	52	52	52
Scenario 2.2: Human driver prioritisation (MV Follows Traffic Rules)					
Priority Rule: MV-first					
max speed (m/s)	5		5	5	5
distance travelled (m)	51.6		43.9	52	52
Scenario 2.3: Misbehaving Human Driver (Speed Rule Violation)					
Priority Rule: MV-first					
max speed (m/s)	2*		2**	5	5
distance travelled (m)	43.3		33.2	52	52

* MV drives well below the speed limit of 5 m/s.
** The AV is unable to maintain its potential maximum speed of 5 m/s.

Scenario 2.1: Baseline Scenario (AVs Only). In a fully automated environment, where three AVs (AV1, AV2 and AV3) were tasked with identical missions, all vehicles successfully navigated a distance of 52m within 28s (Table 2), adhering to the preset speed limit of 5 m/s.

Scenario 2.2: Human Driver Prioritisation (MV Follows Traffic Rules). The integration of a compliant MV slightly modified traffic dynamics. V1, influenced by the MV's compliant behaviour, covered a slightly reduced distance of 43.9m, while V2 and V3 maintained a consistent distance of 52 m (Table 2). The decreased distance is the result of maintaining a safe inter-vehicle distance.

Scenario 2.3: Misbehaving Human Driver (Speed Limit Rule Violation). This scenario presents significant deviations due to the MV travelling considerably below the 5 m/s speed limit. Comparatively, V1 maintains a shorter trajectory when assessed against other AVs executing similar tasks under identical maximum speed constraints. V1, directly behind the slow-moving MV, was substantially impacted, travelling only 33.2m, while V2 and V3 were unaffected, each covering 52m (Table 2).

Overall, the results indicate that AV efficiency and safety are heavily influenced by the behaviour of human drivers. Non-compliance from the MV leads to reduced efficiency and significant safety risks.

6 Discussion and Conclusion

This study investigated two key research questions related to human driving behaviour in a coordination system for Mixed Traffic with Fleets of Automated Vehicles (MTF-AVs) simulated in a controlled environment. First, how can we model human driving behaviour within these systems? Second, what elements of human behaviour are essential to model for simulations that assess the impact on MTF-AV performance? To address these questions, we focused on two types of human *misbehaviour* - priority rule violations and speed limit violations - and found significant degrade in the system's efficiency and safety, leading to collisions and near misses. These findings highlight the need for a novel coordination framework specifically designed for the complex, dynamic environments with MVs encountered in specialised settings like underground mines. Such a framework is crucial for enhancing safety and efficiency in these challenging environments.

A limitation of the current study is the focus on relatively simple scenarios. To address this, future research should explore a wider range of parameter complexities within the simulation environment. This could involve introducing a variety of maps, examining different numbers of vehicles, and considering diverse priority rules. Additionally, future studies can broaden the scope of rule violations beyond the two examined in Cases I and II to include other human-specific rule violations. Analyzing such violations connects directly to the field of *human factors* in driving. Ultimately, a robust coordination system should consider these human factors to adapt the coordination systems to the unpredictable human behaviour within MTF-AV systems.

Our research questions centred on modelling human driving behaviour within MTF-AV coordination systems and the impact of such behaviour on system performance. This focus underscores the importance of understanding human factors in this context. In further exploration, developing an enhanced coordination framework requires not only robust algorithms but also methods to evaluate interactions among diverse traffic participants, including both AVs and MVs.

Acknowledgments. This work has been supported by Sustainable Underground Mining (SUM) Academy, Project SP-12 2021-2024, and the Industrial Graduate School Collaborative AI & Robotics funded by the Swedish Knowledge Foundation Dnr:20190128.

Disclosure of Interests. The authors have no competing interests to declare that are relevant to the content of this article.

References

1. Al-Msari, H., Koting, S., Ali Najah Ahmed, A.M., El-Shafie, A.: Review of driving-behaviour simulation: vissim and artificial intelligence approach. Heliyon **10**, 1–32 (2024). https://doi.org/10.1016/j.heliyon.2024.e25936
2. Atzmon, D., Stern, R., Felner, A., Sturtevant, N.R., Koenig, S.: Probabilistic robust multi-agent path finding. In: Proceedings of the International Conference on Automated Planning and Scheduling 30(1), pp. 29–37 (2020). https://doi.org/10.1609/icaps.v30i1.6642
3. Bazzan, A.L.C.: A distributed approach for coordination of traffic signal agents. Autonomous Agents Multi-Agent Syst. **10**, 131–164 (2004). https://api.semanticscholar.org/CorpusID:42505249
4. Bokare, P., Maurya, A.: Acceleration-deceleration behaviour of various vehicle types. Transp. Res. Procedia **25**, 4737–4753 (2017). https://doi.org/10.1016/j.trpro.2017.05.486
5. Bucchi, A., Sangiorgi, C., Vignali, V.: Traffic psychology and driver behavior. Procedia - Soc. Behav. Sci. **53**, 972–979 (2012). https://doi.org/10.1016/j.sbspro.2012.09.946, sIIV-5th International Congress - Sustainability of Road Infrastructures 2012
6. de Zwart, R., Kamphuis, K., Cleij, D.: Driver behavioural adaptations to simulated automated vehicles, potential implications for traffic microsimulation. Transp. Res. Part F: Traffic Psychol. Behav. **92**, 255–265 (2023). https://doi.org/10.1016/j.trf.2022.11.012
7. Dian Khumara, M.A., Fauziyyah, L., Kristalina, P.: Estimation of urban traffic state using simulation of urban mobility (sumo) to optimize intelligent transport system in smart city. In: 2018 International Electronics Symposium on Engineering Technology and Applications (IES-ETA), pp. 163–169 (2018). https://doi.org/10.1109/ELECSYM.2018.8615508
8. Duarte, J., Marques, A., Baptista, J.: Occupational accidents related to heavy machinery: a systematic review. Safety **7**(21), 21 (2021). https://doi.org/10.3390/safety7010021
9. Elander, J., West, R., French, D.: Behavioral correlates of individual differences in road-traffic crash risk: an examination of methods and findings. Psychol. Bull. **113**, 279–94 (1993). https://doi.org/10.1037/0033-2909.113.2.279

10. Engström, J., Wei, R., Mcdonald, A., Garcia, A., O'Kelly, M., Johnson, L.: Resolving uncertainty on the fly: modeling adaptive driving behavior as active inference. Front. Neurorobotics **18**, 1341750 (2024). https://doi.org/10.3389/fnbot.2024.1341750
11. Forte, P., Mannucci, A., Andreasson, H., Pecora, F.: Online task assignment and coordination in multi-robot fleets. IEEE Robot. Automation Lett. **6**(3), 4584–4591 (2021). https://doi.org/10.1109/LRA.2021.3068918
12. Gouy, M., Wiedemann, K., Stevens, A., Brunett, G., Reed, N.: Driving next to automated vehicle platoons: how do short time headways influence non-platoon drivers' longitudinal control? Transp. Res. Part F: Traffic Psychol. Behav. **27**, 264–273 (2014). https://doi.org/10.1016/j.trf.2014.03.003, vehicle Automation and Driver Behaviour
13. Horni, A., Nagel, K., Axhausen, K.: The Multi-Agent Transport Simulation MATSim, April 2016.https://doi.org/10.5334/baw
14. Korsah, G., Stentz, A., Dias, M.: A comprehensive taxonomy for multi-robot task allocation. Int. J. Robot. Res. **32**(12), 1495–1512 (2013). https://doi.org/10.1177/0278364913496484
15. Li, X., You, Z., Ma, X., Pang, X., Min, X., Cui, H.: Effect of autonomous vehicles on car-following behavior of human drivers: Analysis based on structural equation models. Phys. A Stat. Mech. Appl. **633**, 129360 (2024). https://doi.org/10.1016/j.physa.2023.129360
16. Malik, S., Khan, M., El-Sayed, H.: Carla: car learning to act - an inside out. Procedia Comput. Sci. **198**, 742–749 (2022). https://doi.org/10.1016/j.procs.2021.12.316
17. Mannucci, A., Pallottino, L., Pecora, F.: Provably safe multi-robot coordination with unreliable communication. IEEE Robot. Autom. Lett. **4**(4), 3232–3239 (2019). https://doi.org/10.1109/LRA.2019.2924849
18. Mannucci, A., Pallottino, L., Pecora, F.: On provably safe and live multi-robot coordination with online goal posting. IEEE Trans. Robot., 1–19 (2021). https://doi.org/10.1109/TRO.2021.3075371
19. Mansouri, M., Lacerda, B., Hawes, N., Pecora, F.: Multi-robot planning under uncertain travel times and safety constraints, pp. 478–484, August 2019. https://doi.org/10.24963/ijcai.2019/68
20. Organisation for Economic Co-operation and Development: Behavioural Adaptations to Changes in the Road Transport System: Report. Road transport research, Organisation for Economic Co-Operation and Development (1990). https://books.google.se/books?id=1D-LQgAACAAJ
21. Palleschi, A., Mannucci, A., Caporale, D., Pecora, F., Pallottino, L.: Toward distributed solutions for heterogeneous fleet coordination, December 2020
22. Parasuraman, R., Manzey, D.: Complacency and bias in human use of automation: an attentional integration. Hum. Factors **52**, 381–410 (2010). https://doi.org/10.1177/0018720810376055
23. Pecora, F., Andreasson, H., Mansouri, M., Petkov, V.: A loosely-coupled approach for multi-robot coordination, motion planning and control. In: Proceedings of the International Conference on Automated Planning and Scheduling **28**, 485–493, June 2018. https://doi.org/10.1609/icaps.v28i1.13923
24. Pecora, F., Cirillo, M., Dimitrov, D.: On mission-dependent coordination of multiple vehicles under spatial and temporal constraints. In: IEEE International Conference on Intelligent Robots and Systems, October 2012. https://doi.org/10.1109/IROS.2012.6385862

25. Raiyn, J., Weidl, G.: Predicting autonomous driving behavior through human factor considerations in safety-critical events. Smart Cities **7**(1), 460–474 (2024). https://doi.org/10.3390/smartcities7010018
26. Razmi Rad, S., Farah, H., Taale, H., van Arem, B., Hoogendoorn, S.P.: The impact of a dedicated lane for connected and automated vehicles on the behaviour of drivers of manual vehicles. Transp. Res. Part F: Traffic Psychol. Behav. **82**, 141–153 (2021). https://doi.org/10.1016/j.trf.2021.08.010
27. Reddy, N., Hoogendoorn, S.P., Farah, H.: How do the recognizability and driving styles of automated vehicles affect human drivers' gap acceptance at t- intersections? Transportation Research Part F: Traffic Psychol. Behav. **90**, 451–465 (2022). https://doi.org/10.1016/j.trf.2022.09.018
28. Rudin-Brown, C., Jamson, S.: Behavioural Adaptation and Road Safety: Theory, Evidence and Action, April 2013. https://doi.org/10.1201/b14931
29. Schwarting, W., Pierson, A., Alonso-Mora, J., Karaman, S., Rus, D.: Social behavior for autonomous vehicles. Proc. Nat. Acad. Sci. **116**(50), 24972–24978 (2019). https://doi.org/10.1073/pnas.1820676116
30. Soni, S., Reddy, N., Tsapi, A., van Arem, B., Farah, H.: Behavioral adaptations of human drivers interacting with automated vehicles. Transp. Res. Part F: Traffic Psychol. Behav. **86**, 48–64 (2022). https://doi.org/10.1016/j.trf.2022.02.002
31. Sudiyanto, J.H., Susilowati, I.H.: Causes of fatal accidents involving coal hauling trucks at a coal mining company in indonesia. KnE Life Sci. **4**(5), 59–70 (2018). https://doi.org/10.18502/kls.v4i5.2539
32. Trende, A., Unni, A., Weber, L., Rieger, J.W., Luedtke, A.: An investigation into human-autonomous vs. human-human vehicle interaction in time-critical situations. In: Proceedings of the 12th ACM International Conference on PErvasive Technologies Related to Assistive Environments, PETRA 2019, pp. 303–304. Association for Computing Machinery, New York (2019). https://doi.org/10.1145/3316782.3321544
33. Van Winsum, W., Heino, A.: Choice of time-headway in car-following and the role of time-to-collision information in braking. Ergonomics **39**, 579–92 (1996). https://doi.org/10.1080/00140139608964482
34. Wang, Y., Farah, H., Yu, R., Qiu, S., van Arem, B.: Characterizing behavioral differences of autonomous vehicles and human-driven vehicles at signalized intersections based on waymo open dataset. Transp. Res. Rec. **2677**(11), 324–337 (2023). https://doi.org/10.1177/03611981231165783
35. Yan, Z., Jouandeau, N., Cherif, A.: A survey and analysis of multi-robot coordination. Int. J. Adv. Robot. Syst. **10**, 1 (2013). https://doi.org/10.5772/57313
36. Zhao, X., Wang, Z., Xu, Z., Wang, Y., Li, X., Qu, X.: Field experiments on longitudinal characteristics of human driver behavior following an autonomous vehicle. Transp. Res. Part C Emerging Technol. **114**, 205–224 (2020). https://doi.org/10.1016/j.trc.2020.02.018
37. Čáp, M., Novák, P., Kleiner, A., Selecky, M.: Prioritized planning algorithms for trajectory coordination of multiple mobile robots. IEEE Trans. Automation Sci. Eng. **12**(3), 835–849 (2014). https://doi.org/10.1109/TASE.2015.2445780

Signal Sparsity Considerations for Using VAE with Non-visual Data: Case Study of Proximity Sensors on a Mobile Robot

Oksana Hagen[1](✉) and Swen Gaudl[2]

[1] University of Plymouth, Plymouth, Drake Circus, Plymouth PL4 8AA, UK
oksana.hagen@plymouth.ac.uk
[2] University of Gothenburg, 41296 Göteborg, Sweden
swen.gaudl@ait.gu.se

Abstract. This paper explores the application of Variational Autoencoders (VAEs) to sparse non-visual data, focusing on a case study involving proximity sensors on a mobile robot. Traditionally effective in dense, high-dimensional domains like image processing, VAEs face unique challenges when adapted to sparse, low-dimensional sensory data. This paper contributes to broader efforts to tailor deep generative models to the complexities of robotic sensory data, offering insights that could enhance machine perception in robotic applications. Our study demonstrates that conventional VAE settings, particularly the weighting of the KL divergence ($\beta = 1$), lead to suboptimal sparse representations for proximity sensor data with limited expressivity of learned latent space in the proposed case study of a mobile robot with proximity sensors. By systematically adjusting the β parameter and evaluating reconstruction quality and latent space utilization, we find that lower β values yield better results in sparse data scenarios. These findings suggest that adaptive or dynamic approaches to setting model parameters may be necessary to optimize VAE performance across varying data types, or finding alternative reconstruction loss formulations.

Keywords: VAE · sparse data · proximity sensors · disentangled representations · mobile robot

1 Introduction

Variational autoencoders [7] and its variants are used broadly in robotics; for learning space representations and localisation [2], locomotion [11] and even in human-robot interaction for generation of emotional body language [10,13]. It has an important role in anomaly detection in robotics [3,6,15]. VAE stands out as a lightweight model, that is particularly useful for sensor-fusion and handling multi-modal sensory input [5,8]. This paper aims to demonstrate how sparsity of the source data can impact the resulting VAE latent space, and serve as a pointer for future VAE use to model multi-modal sensory inputs in robotics or other sparse signal domains.

Problem of applying VAE to sparse data was mainly addressed in context of recommended systems in connection to discrete large-dimensional data [9,16,17]. Notably, this work shares similar questions with [9], where the authors propose techniques to enhance VAE performance on high-dimensional sparse data, common in recommended systems. In line with [9], we observe VAE underfitting on sparse data. In our work, due to the inherent interpretability of low-dimensional data, we were able to isolate a singular cause of VAE underfitting and subsequently propose and test a solution.

While attempting to obtain representations using data from *Thymio* robot, it became clear that the formulation of the loss function for VAE, as devised for encoding visual information, does not produce expected results when applied to the sparse low-dimensional proximity data of *Thymio*. Due to the nature of the data, the relative magnitude of the reconstruction loss to the latent loss is too small, thus leading to model to converge to unusable reconstructions. Using this case study the paper demonstrates how sparsity influences the resulting representations, highlighting an important consideration for the practical applications of VAE.

2 VAE Loss Function and Beta Value

The ideas behind generative models are closely connected to the assumption that data is generated by a small amount of factors of variation, that can be expressed as latent variables. At its core, the VAE operates by encoding input data x into a latent representation z through an encoder network and then reconstructing the input from this latent representation using a decoder network.

VAE is trained to minimize a loss function comprising two parts: the reconstruction error and the Kullback-Leibler (KL) divergence (latent loss). The reconstruction error ensures that the output is similar to the input, while the KL divergence measures the deviation of the learned latent distribution from a prior distribution, usually assumed to be Gaussian. VAE's loss function could be modified by introducing a hyperparameter β that weights the KL divergence term. Thus, the loss function is:

$$\text{Loss} = \text{Reconstruction Error} + \beta \times \text{KL Divergence} \quad (1)$$

For visual data [4], $\beta > 1$ prioritizes learning statistically independent latent factors over reconstructing the input accurately. Conversely, $\beta < 1$ can lead to more emphasis on reconstruction. When there is no latent loss term in the loss function ($\beta = 0$), the VAE is turned into a simple autoencoder (AE).

It has been documented that $\beta > 1$ could produce disentangled representations in visual data [4]. Bengio [1] defines a disentangled representation as one where "single latent variables are sensitive to changes in single generative factors while being relatively invariant to changes in other factors". In general, it is a desirable property, as such representation indicates that the model has discovered the structure behind sensory input, thus likely being useful in downstream tasks, but more importantly aiding interpretability [18]. As disentangled representations often come at a cost of lost nuance in the modelled data, it can be a counter-productive quality.

3 Robot Platform and Data

The *Thymio* robot is an educational open-source mobile robot [12,14]. It is equipped with a set of 5 frontal IR sensors with an operating range of around 10 cm and two motors connected to wheels to move around. At each time-step t the robot receives a 5-dimensional vector x_t from its frontal proximity sensors. When the sensor is close to the object, the proximity sensor reading equals 0, gradually linearly increasing with the distance. It will eventually saturate, as the maximum sensing range is reached, with the value of ≈ 17.5. The experimental setup involved the robot moving randomly in a rectangular box of approximately 50 by 60 cm. 10 000 interactions were collected in total.

There are 3 different cases of possible observations (see Fig. 1): (1) the robot is too far from any wall and the sensors are maxed out (2) the robot is next to the wall (3) the robot is in the corner. The first case always yields the same result; the second one can be parameterised according to the orientation of the robot to the wall θ and the distance of the robot to the wall d; the third one can be described with 3-dimensional vectors, such as relative displacement of the robot with respect to the corner and its relative orientation. As the robot moves to the centre of the box the proximity sensors are saturated. While in principle this describes main types of data, as it was collected in real robotic setting, there was some nuance. For example, some of the readings were imprecise due to the corner reflection pattern, properties of the material and changes in the lighting conditions.

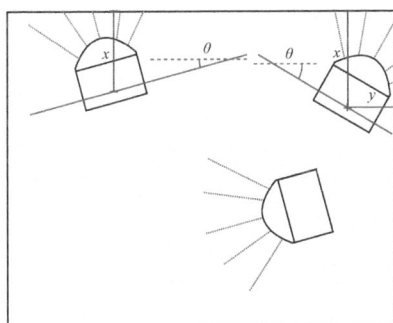

Fig. 1. Examples of the three possible modes of observations of *Thymio* within the rectangular box.

Thymio proximity sensors in our box environment generate mostly maxed-out values, as most of the time there is no obstacle within the operational distance of the sensor (see Fig. 1). After the normalisation procedure, most of the values from all of the sensors are equal to zero, as demonstrated in the Fig. 2.

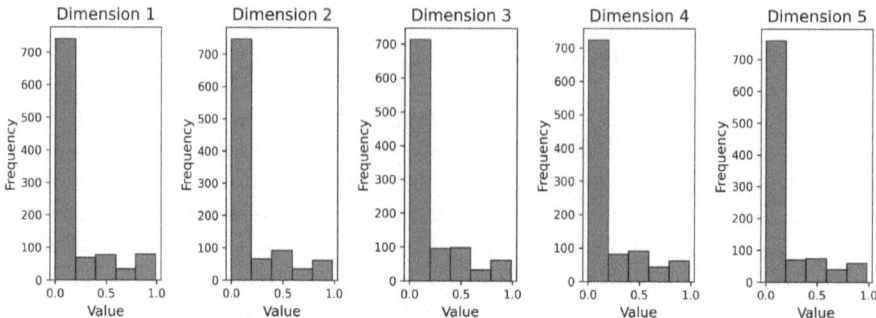

Fig. 2. Data inspection of 1000 random samples from the dataset of *Thymio* observations after normalisation. Each of the histograms corresponds to a different proximity sensor value distribution. As the robot spends the majority of the time in the middle of the box with all the walls outside of the operating range of the proximity sensors, most of the readings are equal to zero.

4 VAE Implementation and Training

The network is adapted from the version used in the paper by [4] to suit the present sensory modality; convolutional neural networks were substituted with fully connected units. There are two fully connected layers in the architecture's encoder and decoder parts: one fully connected layer with 20 units and another one with 10 units. The architecture contains 5 latent variables defined as Gaussian distribution through μ and σ^2. z is sampled from the distribution and used to be decoded back through the decoder. Softplus was used throughout the neural network. There is no information bottleneck defined in the architecture; in principle, the system has enough capacity to assign the latent variables to the five input variables for perfect reconstruction.

The reconstruction loss is calculated as a binary cross-entropy (BCE): it calculates the negative log probability of the input data under the reconstructed distribution induced by the decoder. The addition of a small constant $\epsilon = 1 \times 10^{-10}$ is a numerical stability trick to prevent taking the logarithm of zero. The reconstruction loss, calculated as a mean for the whole batch, is formulated as:

$$\text{BCE} = -\sum_i \Big(x_i \cdot \log(\epsilon + \hat{x}_i) + (1 - x_i) \cdot \log(\epsilon + 1 - \hat{x}_i) \Big),$$

where i is an observation index from the batch, x_i is an observation and $\hat{x}_i$ is a reconstructed observation.

Latent loss can be expressed as:

$$\text{KL Divergence} = -\frac{1}{2}\sum_{j}\left(1 + \log(\sigma_j^2) - \mu_j^2 - \sigma_j^2\right), \tag{2}$$

where j is a latent variable index in the range [1..5], and μ_j, σ_j are estimated mean and standard deviation for latent variable j over all of the observations from the batch.

As previously outlined, the total loss is a weighted sum of the reconstruction error and the KL divergence, with weights α and β, respectively:

$$\text{Loss} = \text{BCE} + \beta \cdot \text{KL Divergence} \tag{3}$$

The training is performed over 500 epochs over 1000 randomly sampled observations per epoch. The learning rate was set to 10^{-3}.

5 Results

The results are compared between different values of β. At $\beta=0$, the architecture is effectively an AE with the same structure and training procedure as VAE, but without the KL divergence term in the loss function.

5.1 Reconstruction

Due to increasing relative importance of the reconstruction loss in the training, reconstructions are more precise with decreasing β, and the most precise in the AE condition, when $\beta = 0$.

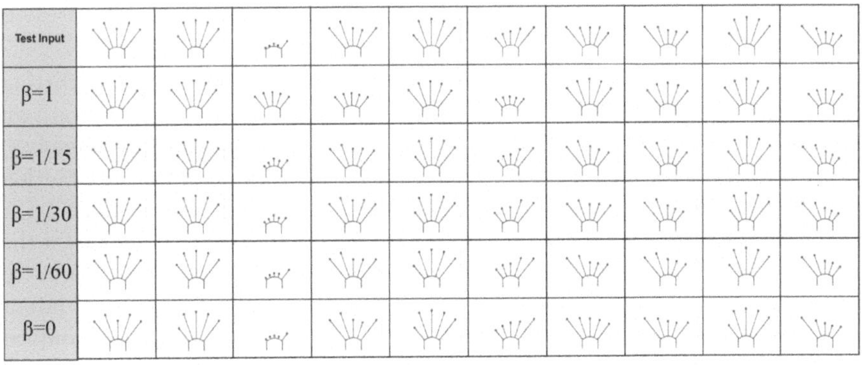

Fig. 3. The summary of randomly selected tests showing input observation reconstructions. As the ratio of β to α decreases, the reconstructions become more precise.

In the Fig. 3, the reconstructions of a few random samples from data are presented. The first line represents the input to the encoder side of the VAE network, and the next rows are the reconstructions performed by the different VAE models with varying β. At a glance, the precision of the samples is increasing. These qualitative impressions are supported by the reconstruction mean-square error (MSE) in the Table 1.

Table 1. Reconstruction MSE for VAE trained with different β for 1000 randomly selected normalised observation samples. The results in rows 2 to 5 demonstrate increased reconstruction quality. The last row corresponds to the $\beta = 0$ condition. As the cost function only has the reconstruction objective, the reconstructions are, as expected, almost exact.

β values	Reconstruction MSE
$\beta = 1$	0.0256
$\beta = 1/15$	0.0030
$\beta = 1/30$	0.0022
$\beta = 1/60$	0.0012
$\beta = 0$	0.0006

The second line in the Table 1 represents the results for the typical VAE cost function as in [7], where $\beta = 1$. However, the quality of the reconstructions is not in line with the expectations for a VAE performance. The sparsity incentivised by β has restricted the signal to be represented by only one of the five latent variables z. Thus, the reconstructions only respond to the input's main component that somewhat corresponds to the "distance to the wall" measure. We are observing an extreme case of disentanglement and only at a standard $\beta = 1$, which goes against the expectation established with visual data.

5.2 Ablation of the Latent Variables

Reconstructions provide a good reference point on the decreased underfitting performance of VAE, as the value of β is reduced. To further demonstrate an increasing utilisation of the latent dimensions by the model as a function of $1/\beta$, and consequently, the degree of disentanglement effect, we perform an ablation study. For this purpose, a set of randomly selected training data samples ($n = 1000$) is encoded to their corresponding latent values. The values of some of the latent dimensions are preserved, while others are assigned random values. To ensure that these manipulations still lie within the meaningful range of latent space values, and can be decoded adequately, the random values are sampled from Gaussian distributions characterized by the corresponding mean (μ) and standard deviation (σ).

The Table 2 summarises the MSE for 1000 randomly sampled data points. The first set of tests estimates the MSE obtained when only one of the latent

Table 2. Ablation study: MSE for combinations of meaningful variables. The rest of the variables were assigned to randomly generated values from the latent distribution. This table demonstrates, how much each of the variables contributes to the reconstruction. Even for a relatively low values of $\beta < 1$, VAE demonstrates strong disentanglement properties, when trained on sparse data.

Meaningful Variables	$\beta = 1$	$\beta = 1/15$	$\beta = 1/30$	$\beta = 1/60$	$\beta = 0$
(0)	0.1059	0.1431	0.1412	0.1322	0.1560
(1)	0.1046	0.1429	0.1385	0.1341	0.2047
(2)	0.1089	0.1393	0.1385	0.1318	0.1824
(3)	**0.0256**	**0.0341**	**0.0381**	**0.0416**	**0.1195**
(4)	0.1038	0.1241	0.1229	0.1208	0.1781
(0, 3)	0.0256	0.0336	0.0396	0.0366	**0.0877**
(1, 3)	0.0256	0.0338	0.0375	0.0419	0.1109
(2, 3)	0.0256	0.0355	0.0353	0.0406	0.1099
(3, 4)	0.0256	**0.0030**	**0.0026**	**0.0032**	0.1099
(0, 1, 3)	0.0256	0.0335	0.0404	0.0415	0.0891
(0, 2, 3)	0.0256	0.0359	0.0381	0.0346	0.0519
(0, 3, 4)	0.0256	**0.0030**	**0.0024**	**0.0012**	0.0747
(1, 2, 3)	0.0256	0.0325	0.0429	0.0398	0.0979
(1, 3, 4)	0.0256	**0.0030**	**0.0026**	**0.0034**	0.1015
(2, 3, 4)	0.0256	**0.0030**	**0.0024**	**0.0033**	0.0754
(0, 1, 2, 3)	0.0256	0.0304	0.0356	0.0386	0.0353
(0, 1, 2, 4)	0.1011	0.1213	0.1275	0.1117	0.1069
(0, 1, 3, 4)	0.0256	**0.0030**	**0.0024**	**0.0012**	0.0717
(0, 2, 3, 4)	0.0256	**0.0030**	**0.0022**	**0.0012**	0.0220
(1, 2, 3, 4)	0.0256	**0.0030**	**0.0024**	**0.0033**	0.0812

dimensions is preserved in the reconstruction process. In all the cases, z_3 is identified as the most significant dimension. The last column, corresponding to the AE condition, demonstrates distributed encoding properties where all the individual dimensions of latent space produce almost the same MSE.

For the $\beta = 1$ condition, corresponding to the original formulation of the VAE loss function, the MSE effectively saturates once z_3 is preserved and is not improved any further with the addition of any other variables to the pair. This indicates that the model has learned to encode all the information that is used for reconstruction within z_3. It is consistent with the results demonstrated in the Figs. 3 and 4, where all of the observations x both reconstructed and generated are only responding to the mean length of the signal, without any further detail. This does not align with the expected performance of VAE, but corresponds to a much higher level of sparsity in the latent space, that would be produced at much higher $\beta > 1$ values.

Test Input										
$\beta=1$										
$\beta=1/15$										
$\beta=1/30$										
$\beta=1/60$										
$\beta=0$										

Fig. 4. Reconstructions of the test input based on z_3 and z_4 values. The other dimensions were sampled randomly.

6 Conclusion

When applying machine learning algorithms, it is important to learn from failures. This study has identified challenges, when applying VAE to sparse, non-visual data, using the case study of proximity sensors on a mobile robot. Unlike applications in visual data processing where standard VAE settings generally perform well, we found that sparse sensory data can lead to excessive sparsity (or disentanglement) in the learned representations when using typical VAE configurations. Standard VAE implementation with $\beta = 1$ led to overly sparse representations that inadequately captured the nuances of the sensory data, potentially rendering the models less effective for downstream tasks. This suggests a departure from the behaviors typically observed in high-dimensional, dense data scenarios commonly found in image processing tasks.

To address these challenges, the β parameter can be modified, which balances the reconstruction loss against the KL divergence in the VAE loss function. The results indicate that lower values of β are more suitable for training VAEs on sparse data, as they help to mitigate the model's tendency toward excessive latent space sparsity and improve reconstruction accuracy. The findings suggest that future work should explore adaptive or dynamic approaches to setting the β parameter based on the characteristics of the data and the specific learning objectives. Additionally, incorporating techniques that directly address the challenges posed by data sparsity, such as modified loss functions or enhanced data preprocessing methods, could further improve model performance. Aside from modification of β parameter, future investigations should consider alternative versions of the reconstruction error that prioritise meaningful features.

While VAEs are already used in broad range of applications, their efficacy in scenarios involving sparse, non-visual data depends heavily on careful choice of training strategies. This study's insights into the unique challenges posed by such data contribute to the ongoing discussion on how best to leverage established models in diverse applications beyond the realm of image processing.

Acknowledgments. This paper is presented on behalf of the Intergenerational Co-design of Novel Technologies In Coastal Communities (ICONIC) project. The ICONIC project was awarded funding (March 2022) from UKRI/EPSRC grant reference EP/W024357/1. The researchers comprised (i) a core team of Ray Jones, Amir Aly, Alejandro Veliz Reyes, Dena Bazazian, Swen Gaudl (University of Gothenburg), (ii) Research Fellows Rory Baxter, Oksana Hagen, Marius Varga (iii) Chunxu Li (Ho Hai University), Katharine Willis, Daniel Maudlin, Sheena Asthana, Kerry Howell, Emmanuel Ifeachor, Shangming Zhou, Arunangsu Chatterjee (Leeds University), Hannah Bradwell. All listed are University of Plymouth except some who have since moved (new affiliations shown). The academic team worked closely with many partner organisations as listed on the ICONIC website. We thank our partners and participants. We thank Dr. M. G. Ortiz for his help with data collection and initial discussions. This work originally began during the first author's tenure at Aldebaran, supported by Horizon 2020 APRIL ITN funding.

References

1. Bengio, Y., Courville, A.C., Vincent, P.: Unsupervised feature learning and deep learning: a review and new perspectives. CoRR **abs/1206.5538** (2012). http://arxiv.org/abs/1206.5538
2. Bianco, M.J., Gannot, S., Gerstoft, P.: Semi-supervised source localization with deep generative modeling. In: 2020 IEEE 30th International Workshop on Machine Learning for Signal Processing (MLSP), pp. 1–6 (2020). https://doi.org/10.1109/MLSP49062.2020.9231825
3. Chen, T., Liu, X., Xia, B., Wang, W., Lai, Y.: Unsupervised anomaly detection of industrial robots using sliding-window convolutional variational autoencoder. IEEE Access **8**, 47072–47081 (2020). https://doi.org/10.1109/ACCESS.2020.2977892
4. Higgins, I., et al.: beta-VAE: learning basic visual concepts with a constrained variational framework. In: ICLR (2017)
5. van Hoof, H., Chen, N., Karl, M., van der Smagt, P., Peters, J.: Stable reinforcement learning with autoencoders for tactile and visual data. In: 2016 IEEE/RSJ International Conference on Intelligent Robots and Systems (IROS), pp. 3928–3934 (2016). https://doi.org/10.1109/IROS.2016.7759578
6. Ji, T., Vuppala, S.T., Chowdhary, G., Driggs-Campbell, K.: Multi-modal anomaly detection for unstructured and uncertain environments. In: Kober, J., Ramos, F., Tomlin, C. (eds.) Proceedings of the 2020 Conference on Robot Learning. Proceedings of Machine Learning Research, vol. 155, pp. 1443–1455. PMLR (16–18 Nov 2021). https://proceedings.mlr.press/v155/ji21a.html
7. Kingma, D.P., Welling, M.: Auto-encoding variational Bayes. In: 2nd International Conference on Learning Representations, ICLR 2014, Banff, AB, Canada, April 14-16, 2014, Conference Track Proceedings (2014)
8. Korthals, T., Hesse, M., Leitner, J., Melnik, A., Rückert, U.: Jointly trained variational autoencoder for multi-modal sensor fusion. In: 2019 22th International Conference on Information Fusion (FUSION). pp. 1–8 (2019). https://doi.org/10.23919/FUSION43075.2019.9011314
9. Krishnan, R.G., Liang, D., Hoffman, M.D.: On the challenges of learning with inference networks on sparse, high-dimensional data. In: Storkey, A.J., Pérez-Cruz, F. (eds.) AISTATS. Proceedings of Machine Learning Research, vol. 84, pp. 143–151. PMLR (2018)

10. Marmpena, M., Lim, A., Dahl, T.S., Hemion, N.: Generating robotic emotional body language with variational autoencoders. In: 2019 8th International Conference on Affective Computing and Intelligent Interaction (ACII), pp. 545–551 (2019). https://doi.org/10.1109/ACII.2019.8925459
11. Mitchell, A.L., et al.: VAE-Loco: versatile quadruped locomotion by learning a disentangled gait representation. IEEE Trans. Rob. **39**(5), 3805–3820 (2023). https://doi.org/10.1109/TRO.2023.3297015
12. Mondada, F., et al.: Bringing robotics to formal education: the Thymio open-source hardware robot. IEEE Robot. Autom. Mag. **24**(1), 77–85 (2017)
13. Osorio, P., Sagawa, R., Abe, N., Venture, G.: A generative model to embed human expressivity into robot motions. Sensors **24**(2) (2024). https://doi.org/10.3390/s24020569, https://www.mdpi.com/1424-8220/24/2/569
14. Riedo, F., Chevalier, M., Magnenat, S., Mondada, F.: Thymio II, a robot that grows wiser with children. In: 2013 IEEE Workshop on Advanced Robotics and its Social Impacts, pp. 187–193 (2013). https://doi.org/10.1109/ARSO.2013.6705527
15. Slavic, G., Baydoun, M., Campo, D., Marcenaro, L., Regazzoni, C.: Multilevel anomaly detection through variational autoencoders and Bayesian models for self-aware embodied agents. IEEE Trans. Multimedia **24**, 1399–1414 (2022). https://doi.org/10.1109/TMM.2021.3065232
16. Zhang, T., Chen, C., Wang, D., Guo, J., Song, B.: A VAE-based user preference learning and transfer framework for cross-domain recommendation. IEEE Trans. Knowl. Data Eng. **35**(10), 10383–10396 (2023). https://doi.org/10.1109/TKDE.2023.3253168
17. Zhao, H., Rai, P., Du, L., Buntine, W., Phung, D., Zhou, M.: Variational autoencoders for sparse and overdispersed discrete data. In: Chiappa, S., Calandra, R. (eds.) Proceedings of the Twenty Third International Conference on Artificial Intelligence and Statistics. Proceedings of Machine Learning Research, vol. 108, pp. 1684–1694. PMLR (26–28 Aug 2020). https://proceedings.mlr.press/v108/zhao20c.html
18. Zhu, X., Xu, C., Tao, D.: Where and what? Examining interpretable disentangled representations. In: Proceedings of the IEEE/CVF Conference on Computer Vision and Pattern Recognition, pp. 5861–5870 (2021)

Planning with Non-deterministic Actions in Jason

Josh Blondin(✉) and Babak Esfandiari

Carleton University, Ottawa, ON K1S 5B6, Canada
joshblondin@cmail.carleton.ca

Abstract. This paper proposes a planner which can take non-deterministic actions and generate AgentSpeak plans, based on an existing linear planner. It uses a pipeline transforming the initial specification of the non-deterministic planning problem into an AND-OR tree, which is then used to solve for non-deterministic post conditions and generate a contingency plan in AgentSpeak.

Keywords: BDI · AgentSpeak · Agents · Planning · Non-Determinism · AND-OR Tree · FOND

1 Introduction

Belief Desire Intention (BDI) [10] is a model that describes the actions taken by an autonomous agent. Beliefs roughly stand for what the agent knows and perceives, Desires stand for its goals, and Intentions stand for the plans that it commits to in order to achieve goals that are consistent with its beliefs. When using BDI in a dedicated programming language such as Jason [1] (which implements the AgentSpeak [9] syntax and semantics), plans are programmed and stored in a plan library. Given an agent's current perceptions and goals, the AgentSpeak interpreter selects a suitable plan to be executed (the plan may already be the one that the agent was previously committed to, in which case the next action in the plan is chosen to be executed), and may suspend or abort a current plan if it is no longer feasible or consistent with the goals.

However, there may be cases where no hand-written plans are available for the task at hand, and so it may be useful to have an automatic planner generate such plans during runtime, based on the specifications of the goals of the agent and the actions at its disposal. The state of the art example of such a planner for Jason is Peleus [6], which creates a deterministic backup plan for the agent to reach its goal. The created linear plan is a chain of deterministic actions, where the preconditions and post-conditions are predetermined and predictable. That will not always be the case, as the world is non-deterministic and effects of actions are not always predictable. This paper aims to extend Peleus in order to be able to create contingency plans that can handle unpredictable outcomes.

When generating plans, all of the actions the agent can take are described in operators. These operators state the preconditions and post-conditions an action

© The Author(s), under exclusive license to Springer Nature Switzerland AG 2025
A. Ferrando and R. C. Cardoso (Eds.): AREA 2024, CCIS 2230, pp. 83–98, 2025.
https://doi.org/10.1007/978-3-031-73180-8_6

can have. In Peleus, these are assumed to be deterministic, but it is possible for them to be uncertain. They can have two different types of uncertainty:

1. Uncertainty on the Preconditions: This covers the cases where the agent is uncertain about their environment. This could be due to sensors being faulty, or just not having being able to know the full state of the environment. For example, a cleaning robot may be tasked with cleaning wet and dry messes and will not know until they reach the mess, and so will need to be prepared for either possibility.
2. Uncertainty on the Post-Conditions: This covers the cases where when taking an action the agent is uncertain about what will happen as a result of it. For example, a cleaning robot may have a faulty vacuum which when turned on will only work half the time, and will not know if it will work until it is on.

This paper covers uncertainty on the post-conditions, and how non-deterministic backup plans can be generated when an agent fails to find a plan they are able to act on. Our insight is that since AgentSpeak handles contingencies by dropping a current intention and choosing a different plan if necessary, non-determinism can be captured by a set of linear plans that the interpreter can "jump between" given the (uncertain) effect of the previous action on the environment. We use AND-OR trees in order to generate a solution, and then convert that solution into AgentSpeak syntax in Jason.

2 Background

2.1 AND-OR Trees

An AND-OR tree is a type of search tree which is used to make decisions in a non-deterministic environment, containing AND nodes and OR nodes [11]. An OR node and its branches refer to an agent's possible choices, while an AND Node and its branches refers to the environment's choice of each outcome for each action [11]. In the context of software agents, these can be seen as nodes controlled by the environment and where any of the paths leading from it could be valid. OR nodes can be seen as nodes controlled by the agent where they will be able to select the most optimal path to take [11]. An example of an AND-OR tree can be seen as part of the Erratic Vacuum World, shown in Fig. 1.

In this example, the vacuum has the goal of removing all of the dirt. The vacuum is able to take one of three separate actions. The *Left* and *Right* actions will result in the vacuum moving in that direction if possible. The *Suck* action is uncertain on the results after it is performed: if the *Suck* action is taken on a dirty space, it will always remove the mess and has a chance to remove the mess on the other tile as well. If the *Suck* action is taken on a clean space, there is a chance it will leave some dirt as well as leave the space clean. The bold paths show the tree's solution, which is classified as a path from the root node where every terminal node is considered to be part of the goal state [11]. This solution is a contingency solution, meaning that the actions it takes depend on

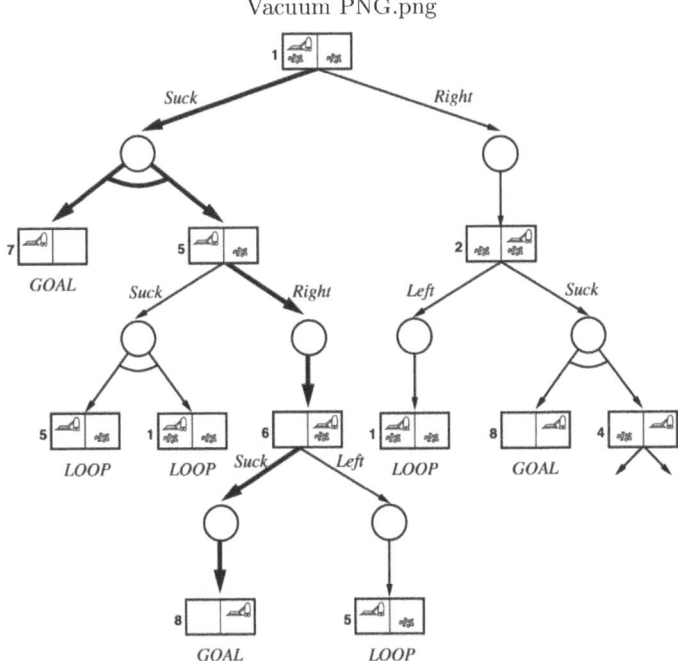

Fig. 1. AND-OR tree for the Erratic Vacuum World as seen in [11]

the uncertain outcome of the previous action, and so it must be able to reach the goal state no matter what outcome each action has.

There is a possibility that a tree could be cyclic, where a path from a node could lead to a node that was already traversed. This is represented in the Erratic Vacuum World Example by the "LOOP" keyword under some of the nodes, and is able to be solved with modern AND-OR tree solving techniques [5].

STRIPS operators are a way of describing the actions an agent can take, which include their name and inputs, their preconditions, the beliefs they add to what the agent knows and the beliefs they remove from what the agent knows [4]. The STRIPS operators which correlate to the possible actions in Fig. 1 available are shown below:

```
operator: left()
pre: [on(c2)]
add: [on(c1)]
del: [on(c2)]

operator: right()
pre: [on(c1)]
add: [on(c2)]
del: [on(c1)]
```

```
operator: suck()
pre: [on(X) & dirty(X)]
add: []
del: [(dirty(X)) XOR (dirty(X) & dirty(next(X)))]

operator: suck()
pre: [on(X) & not dirty(X)]
add: [(dirty(X)) XOR ()]
del: []
```

Note how there are two different *suck* operators with two different preconditions: one is for the case where the cell being sucked is dirty, and the other is for when it is not. The variable used by both of them, X, denotes one of the two possible cells. It is required in the operator's preconditions and post-conditions, but is notably not required as an input, as the agent does not inherently need to know where it is in order to perform the action, but it still needs to know it in order to add/delete the proper beliefs. The *next(X)* function returns the adjacent cell. In order to implement these internally, we have added Y to the operator, which represents the adjacent cell instead of using *next(X)*. In order to denote uncertainty in the operators, we are using an XOR, which denotes each possible outcome of the operator.

Next, we will move on to how these and our software agents in general run and are implemented.

2.2 BDI, AgentSpeak and Jason

As mentioned earlier, we are operating under a Belief Desire Intention (BDI) framework. AgentSpeak is a BDI language and a framework which describes an agent and its potential actions [9] [10]. It complies to all the BDI specifications and is the current standard for describing BDI agents. Jason is a popular implementation of AgentSpeak [1].

Plans in AgentSpeak take on the following form (this is a simplified case, sufficient for our purpose):

```
+!goal : guards <-
    action_1;
    action_2.
```

This plan will be considered when the achievement goal (denoted by an exclamation mark) `goal` is added (denoted by the + symbol). Then the guards (a boolean expression) are checked, and if multiple plans satisfy them, the intention selection function will select one and the actions will start to be executed.

2.3 State of the Art: Linear Planning and STRIPS with AgentSpeak

Currently the only planner which interfaces with Jason which we are aware of is the linear planner Peleus [6]. Linear planners take initial information about the problem such the initial state, the goal state and the operators and use them in order to find a chain of operators which will get from the initial state to the goal state [4]. The operators in this case are deterministic, meaning when they are executed the outcome will always be the same. These are typically formulated according to the STRIPS formulation described earlier.

When a Jason [1] agent has no valid plan to execute, Peleus [6] steps in and invokes a planner in order to generate a plan which will then be placed into the intention queue.

Our solution allows the handling of non-determinism in the post-conditions of the operators. Instead of a linear plan, a contingency plan is created, which is expressed in terms of multiple Agentspeak plans. Then, based on the non-deterministic outcomes, the Jason [1] interpreter will select the correct plan in order to reach the goal state.

2.4 Start of the Art: FOND Planning

We are working within the Fully Observable Non-Deterministic (FOND) Planning context [2], which has a wide array of existing methods. Examples include an iterative depth-first approach [8], an approach utilizing Explicit Fairness Assumptions [3], and an approach which exploits state relevance [7]. We have chosen AND-OR trees due to the simplicity and availability of implementations; it is our future work to investigate alternate approaches.

3 Overall Pipeline

In order to generate a contingency plan from a description of the problem in Jason, the following steps are performed:

1. Creating the Non-Deterministic Problem
2. Applying the Non-Deterministic Problem to an AND-OR Tree Generator
3. Generating the AgentSpeak plans from the AND-OR Tree Solution

3.1 Creating the Non-deterministic Problem

For a planning problem, the following information about the problem is given as an input [11]:

1. The Initial State $s_i \in S$
2. The Goal State $s_g \in S$
3. The Objects Used
4. The Operators

The initial state s_i is a set of beliefs pertaining to the information known by the agent. The goal state s_g is a set of beliefs which all must exist for the planning problem to terminate. The objects used are definitions of the types of variables which exist in the problem. This will typically involve their name and their possible range of values. The Operators are comprised of:

- The operator's name
- The operator's variables
- The operator's preconditions
- The operator's post-conditions

The operator's preconditions are a logical formula which dictate if the operator is able to be performed for a given state. The operator's post-conditions are how the operator affects the state. Since we are working with non-deterministic post-conditions as opposed to the standard deterministic post-conditions, they contain OR statements. In order to easily identify and work with an operator, we have limited post-conditions to be in Algebraic Normal Form (ANF). This allows us to easily work with each possible future an operator can create.

For the Erratic Vacuum Example, here is an example of an input:

```
objects:
cell(0)
cell(1)

init:
pos(0) & dirty(0) & dirty(1)

goal:
clean(0) & clean(1)

operators:

suck() {
Preconditions: pos(X) && dirty(X) && X!=Y
Effects: [not dirty(X) && clean(X) && clean(Y) && not dirty(Y)]
         XOR [not dirty(X) && clean(X)]
}

suck() {
Preconditions: pos(X) && clean(X)
Effects: [dirty(X) && not clean(X)] XOR []
}

left() {
Preconditions: pos(1)
Effects: pos(0) & not pos(1)
}

right() {
Preconditions: pos(0)
Effects: pos(1) & not pos(0)
}
```

In order to generate a non-deterministic problem which can be used in the AND-OR tree algorithm specified by [11], the following are required:

1. The Initial State $s_i \in S$
2. The Action Space A
3. The Goal State $s_g \in S$
4. A Results Function $S \times A \to 2^S$

The initial state and goal state are the same as what was given in the initial specifications. For the Action Space and the Results Function:

- A is a set of Actions containing all possible actions the agent can take, including which variable values are used in those actions.
- S_c is a set of beliefs containing the current State
- 2^S is the powerset of states: this captures that many states may result from taking non-deterministic Action $a \in A$ when in a given state $s \in S$

We define each action as a combination of its name and the values it assigns its variables. Each action represents an operator, so we can get the names from the operators. Each operator also defines its variables, so from these we can find the range of possible values for each of them, and find every unique combination of variables, which are then each assigned to an action. Taking the erratic vacuum as an example, there are three total actions in its action space:

```
left;
right;
suck;
```

Algorithm 1 transforms operators into the Results function that we require for our AND-OR tree algorithm.

Algorithm 1 can be broken into two sections; the first half, which is checking the context of the operator to make sure it matches the state, and the second half, which applies the operator's additions and deletions to the state. If we take the erratic vacuum from Fig. 1 as an example, there would be 3 total operators; *suck*, *left* and *right*. The *suck* operator changes based on the preconditions, so it will have 2 representations in the system, each with a different context checking for its specific preconditions. We will focus on the *suck* operators, since they are the ones with non-deterministic post-conditions:

```
suck_dirty()
preconditions: pos(X) && dirty(X) && X!=Y
Effects: [not dirty(X) && clean(X) && clean(Y) && not dirty(Y)]
         XOR [not dirty(X) && clean(X)]

suck_clean()
preconditions: pos(X) && clean(X)
Effects: [dirty(X) && not clean(X)] XOR []
```

Algorithm 1: Algorithm for Transforming initial operators into a results function

```
 1  function Results (operators) Input  : The initial operators operators
    Output: A ResultsFunction which maps a given state and action to a set of
             states results
 2  return (state, action) ⟹
 3  viableOperators ← operators with name matching action
 4  validValues ← ∅
 5  returnSet ← ∅
 6  forall the op ∈ viableOperators do
 7      unifiedContext ← action.variableValues applied to op.context
 8      forall the otherVariableValues ∈ allPossibleCombinations do
 9          unifiedContext ← otherVariableValues applied to op.context
10          if all terms in unifiedContext hold for state then
11              validValues ← variableArrangement
12              contextPassed ← TRUE
13          end
14      end
15      if !contextPassed then
16          break
17      end
18      forall the possibleOutcome ∈ op.body do
19          unifiedWorld ← validValues applied to possibleOutcome to unify
           their values
20          newWorld ← state
21          forall the belief ∈ unifiedWorld do
22              newWorld ← belief
23          end
24          returnSet ← newWorld
25      end
26      return returnSet
27  end
```

These operators have 2 variables representing different cells in the example. They are both of type *cell*, and have the possible values 0, 1.

The operators are used to create the *results* function. This maps how the state will change when a certain action is taken, and returns a set of all possible states which can result from taking the action. For this example, we can assume that the given state is the inital state [pos(0), dirty(0), dirty(1)], and we are attempting the *suck* action.

First, on line 3, the operators are filtered so we only look at the *suck* operators. Then, for each of these, we get the values for the variable from the action description. *Suck* does not have any variables which are denoted in the action, but it does have variables which are used to perform the post conditions. These can be found by looping through all of the possible options for them, which will be one of: 0,0, 0,1, 1,0, 1,1. Looking at the first *suck* operator, its context looks like

```
pos(X) && dirty(X) && X!=Y
```

which is then unified with the given combination of values from the action, so X = 0 and Y = 0, X = 0 and Y = 1 and so on. The unified context is then checked against the state, where we check that each belief in the unified context is in the state and that each of the relative expressions holds true.

After this process, if the unified context did not hold true, the algorithm breaks and checks the other operators. If it did hold true, then we assume this operator must be the correct one and move on to applying its body to the current state.

In the operator's body, each possibility of how the state could change are looped through. The requirements for the body are that they are in Algebraic Normal Form, which is groups of ANDs seperated by XORs. Each grouping of ANDs is considered a different possible output which could occur. These possible outputs are unified with the values we got before, so X = 0 and Y = 1.

The unified possible output then has all of its beliefs looped through, and applied to a temporary copy of the state, where each belief in the unified possible output is either added or removed from the state. That temporary copy is then stored in the return set.

For our example there are 2 possible outputs. Each of them would follow the following process:

```
[not dirty(X) && clean(X) && clean(Y) && not dirty(Y)] ->
[not dirty(0) && clean(0) && clean(1) && not dirty(1)]

new state = [pos(0), dirty(0), dirty(1)] ->
[pos(0), dirty(1)] ->
[pos(0), dirty(1), clean(0)] ->
[pos(0), dirty(1), clean(0), clean(1)] ->
[pos(0), clean(0), clean(1)]

[not dirty(X) && clean(X)] ->
[not dirty(0) && clean(0)]

new state = [pos(0), dirty(0), dirty(1)] ->
[pos(0), dirty(1)] ->
[pos(0), dirty(1), clean(0)]

Possible Outputs:
[pos(0), clean(0), clean(1)]
[pos(0), dirty(1), clean(0)]
```

These possible outputs are then returned as part of the mapping for the results function.

3.2 Applying the Non-deterministic Problem to an AND-OR Tree Generator

Now that we have all of the necessary components, we can feed that information as a non-deterministic problem into an AND-OR tree solver. The output will be an AND-OR tree solution, which will be in the form of a branching tree with a branch when there is a non-deterministic post-condition. In Erratic Vacuum example, the tree created looks the same as in Fig. 1. The root of this tree, as well as the initial state from the initial operators, are then fed into the AgentSpeak generation algorithm.

3.3 Applying the AND-OR Tree Solution to the AgentSpeak Plan Generation Algorithm

The algorithm for generating the AgentSpeak plans can be found in Algorithm 2. It passes through every node in the tree, creating a unique Jason plan for each one in-case it needs to be referenced to, as well as adding that node to the parent node's plan if there were no non-deterministic branches between them.

The Generate function has the root AND-OR tree plan and the initial state as its inputs. It returns a PlanLibrary, which is comprised of the new Jason plans the agent will be able to use. This function is only used to call recursiveGenerate. It returns the value which is returned from recursive Generate. The second function, recursiveGenerate, has 4 parameters:

1. plan: The current AND-OR Plan which is being output P_{AO}
2. state: The current state s_c
3. planLibrary: The library which is to be updated and returned $\{P_J\}$, which contains Jason Plans.
4. parent: The current AND-OR plan's parent P_{parent}, only passed when the parent does not have multiple conditionals.

This function also returns planLibrary. This function passes through each plan, and if it not empty, adds the state it is in and the action it takes as a new plan in the plan Library.

The AND-OR Plan Data Structure is made up of 2 Parts: The Action and the Conditional. The action represents the chosen action at the OR Node. The conditional is the subsequent AND Node, and is a list of IF statements, which have state conditions tied to which AND-OR plans could be enacted based on the non-deterministic nature of the selected action. If there is only one IF statement, then that means there is no relevant AND Node at that junction. Together the action and the conditional are considered to be the Steps which comprise the Plan.

For the erratic vacuum, the following set of plans is created:

```
+!act: [dirty(1), pos(0), dirty(0)] <-
    .suck;
    !act.
```

```
+!act: [pos(0), dirty(1), clean(0)] <-
    .right;
    .suck;
    !act.

+!act: [dirty(1), pos(1), clean(0)] <-
    .suck;
    !act.
```

It should be noted that there are many ways to internally store each plan's guards. The way we are storing them are as a set of beliefs which all must be true in order for the plan to be enacted. For our use case the guards will always be in this shape so this is the most efficient way of storing and representing them.

For these plans, the agent will check the beliefs to see which action it should take, however if there are multiple actions which can be taken in a row with no non-determinism in between them, they will trigger one directly after the other in the same plan.

This algorithm still has some limitations. First of all, it has a requirement where the agent needs to be able to see every state as disjunct. For example, consider the output for the erratic vacuum. If there was no "clean" beliefs, and there was only dirty, then it is possible the agent could call *right* instead of *suck*, if it had a higher priority in the intention selection function. Since the algorithm does not call for a specific ordering of plans, if the *right* plan had a higher priority in the intention selection function, it would be incorrectly enacted.

In order to solve this, every state needs to be disjunct, such that one state could not be confused for another. This means that for every identifier (for example 'pos' and 'dirty') they always need to be represented in the state. This is can be done by either having separate identifiers for when they do not exist (such as for the vacuum example, when a cell is not dirty it will always be clean and vice versa), or by always checking whether or not it exists and asserting when it does not (so instead of having 'clean(0)', it would assert 'not dirty(0)'). The latter would require knowing all of the possible states ahead of time, so they can be asserted that they do not exist in the current context of the agent. Also, if the agent does not perceive the state it can still be checked, and assuming it is not a broken sensor and the agent is working as intended, the fact that it does not exist will not affect the outcome, as it would have been taken into account when the tree was generated.

Algorithm 2: Algorithm for Generating AgentSpeak Plans from an AND-OR tree

1 function Generate (*root, initialState*);
   Input : The root plan *root*, A Collection acting as the initial State *initialState*
   Output: A Jason Plan Library *planLibrary*
2 **return RecursiveGenerate**(*root, initialState*, ∅, ∅);
3 ───
4 function RecursiveGenerate (*plan, state, planLibrary*);
   Input : An AND-OR Tree Plan *plan*, A Collection acting as the state *state*, A Jason Plan Library *planLibrary*, The plan's parent *parent*
   Output: A Jason Plan Library *planLibrary*
5 **if** *plan.isEmpty()* **then**
6 | **return** *planLibrary*
7 **end**
8 *trigger* ← +!*act*
9 *context* ← *state*
10 *body* ← *plan.action*; !*act*;
11 *planLibrary.add*(*trigger, body, context*)
12 **if** *parent* **then**
13 | *planLibrary.get*(*parent*) ← *body*
14 **end**
15 **if** *plan.conditionals.size* = 1 **then**
16 | **return RecursiveGenerate**(*plan.conditionls*[0].*plan*, *plan.conditionls*[0].*state, planLibrary, parent?parent* : ∅)
17 **end**
18 **forall the** *conditional* ∈ *plan.conditionals* **do**
19 | *planLibrary* ←**RecursiveGenerate**(*conditional.plan, conditional.state, planLibrary*, ∅)
20 **end**
21 **return** *planLibrary*

4 Results

Our evaluation and results are based on two case studies:

1. Since we want to compare performance to Peleus, which is non-deterministic, we need to use an example which it is able to solve. As such we have chosen to use the basic block world example included in Peleus.
2. The Erratic Vacuum World example, which we used as a running example for a FOND problem throughout the paper.

The basic example included in Peleus involves an agent stacking blocks on a table. The initial state has block 1 on top of block 2, block 2 on the table, and block 3 on the table. The goal is to move the blocks such that they are stacked with block 1 on top and block 3 on the bottom. In order to achieve this, there are two operators; moveToTable, which places a block from somewhere other than on the table onto the table, and move, which moves one block from anywhere onto another block. This problem was chosen as it is simple and the default problem included in Peleus.

When running Peleus for this problem, gives the following actions within the plan of its output:

```
moveToTable( b1, b2 )
move( b2, table, b3 )
move( b1, table, b2 )
```

Our solution has the following output:

```
+!act : [clear("table"), on("b2","table"), clear("b3"),
        on("b1","b2"), clear("b1"), on("b3","table")] <-
    moveToTable("b1","b2");
    move("b2","table","b1");
    move("b2","b1","b3");
    move("b1","table","b2");
    !act.

+!act : [clear("b2"), on("b2","table"), clear("b3"),
        clear("table"), clear("b1"), on("b1","table"),
        on("b3","table")] <-
    move("b2","table","b1");
    !act.

+!act : [clear("b2"), on("b2","b1"), clear("b3"),
        clear("table"), on("b1","table"), on("b3","table")] <-
    move("b2","b1","b3");
    !act.

+!act : [clear("b2"), clear("table"), clear("b1"),
        on("b1","table"), on("b3","table"), on("b2","b3")] <-
    move("b1","table","b2");
    !act.
```

The solution mimics the original outputs plan in the first plan generated, solving the problem in a different way. There are also extra plans generated as a backup in case those states are ever somehow reached, there will be a clear path to follow.

Comparing performance to Peleus, it runs its planner in an average of 59.3 milliseconds (measured over 10 attempts). The solution we propose runs the pipeline in an average of 41.5 milliseconds (measured over 10 attempts). However if the creation of the planning problem is included, which includes generating the results and action functions, the time our solution takes rises to 131.0 milliseconds (measured over 10 attempts). This shows that if the creation of the problem is ignored, which can be done ahead of time, our solution is slightly faster, however it is much slower if the creation of the plan is taken into account.

The difference in timings is shown in Fig. 2. The sample size was small, however it showed that at runtime, our solution is more efficient than Peleus.

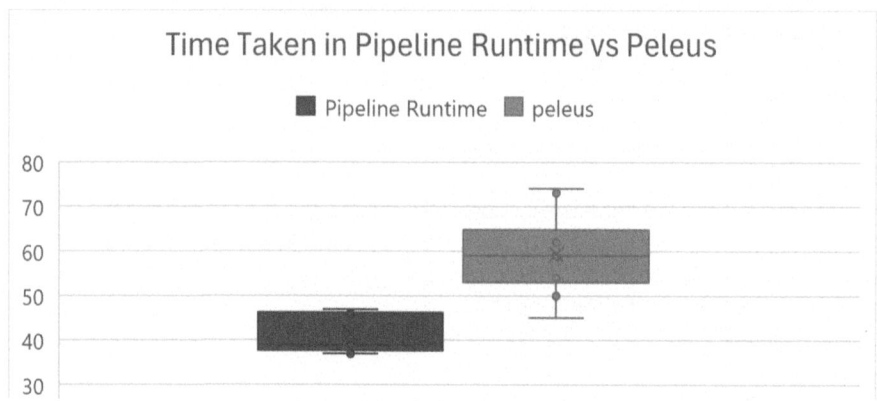

Fig. 2. Performance of our solution with respect to Peleus (milliseconds)

In order to stress test the system, an example was created modelled after the Erratic Vacuum World [11], which has any number of cells in a row. Like this original Erratic Vacuum World, the agents begins in the left most cell and all of the cells start dirty. When performing the *suck* action, there is a chance that both of the adjacent cells can become clean when the action is performed. This example cleans up the old Erratic Vacuum Example as well, by having only 1 variable required for the *suck* action, and just taking the value above it and below it for the cells which could potentially be cleaned, with special cases for the edges. Using this example, we were able to test how scaling a problem up linearly would affect the performance.

The addition of cells are not values which can be applied to a more broad scope, so we can translate them into the number of total possible states, which will better show how our solution could scale against them. The number of states in the case of the Enhanced Erratic Vacuum World is equal to

$$N * 2^N$$

where N is the number of cells. This means the number of states scaled exponentially as we linearly increase the problem, and since this is a very simple example, one could expect more complex examples to have much higher complexities.

After initially running this example it was found that it could consistently run up to 140 cells before exceeding the memory limitations of the IDE (which was set to 6GB). As such, we ran all of the examples through the pipeline (excluding step 4) 5 times, and then took the average timings of each run for each number

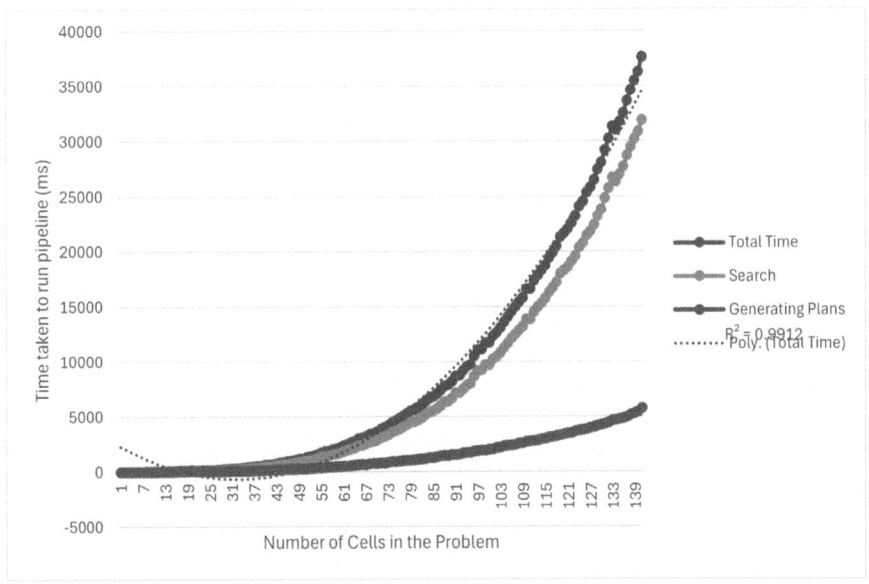

Fig. 3. The time taken to execute the pipeline for an increasing number of cells in the Enhanced Vacuum World

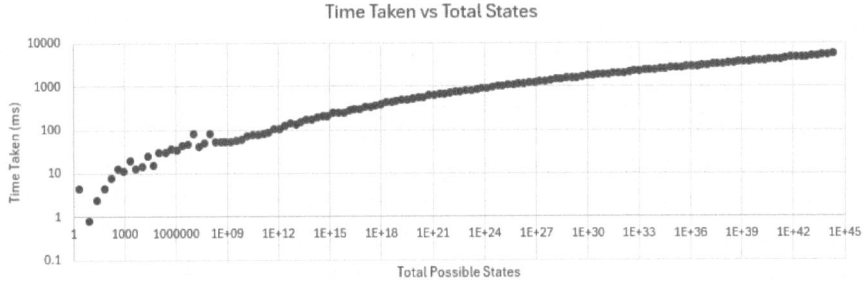

Fig. 4. Log-Log Plot of the time to execute the pipeline for an increasing number of states in the Enhanced Vacuum World

of cells and displayed them in Fig. 3. The setup and the problem generation averaged to 0, so they were not included. The majority of the processing time was taken up by the AND-OR tree generation and search, with the remainder being taken up by AgentSpeak plan generation. Looking at the trend of the total time, the closest match is a quadratic with an R-squared value of 0.9912.

The increase in the total possible number of states can be viewed in Fig. 4. The plots look to have a positive correlation, but are not fully linearly correlated.

5 Conclusion

This paper discussed an extension of Peleus, a linear planner which interfaces with Jason, which would be capable of handling operators which have non-deterministic post-conditions. It takes the same inputs as Peleus and uses a pipeline to transform them into a contingent plan which takes the form of multiple AgentSpeak plans.

In the future, more work can be done on cleaning up the guards, as they require an exact state and are not reusable. This can be done by using variable literals instead of ground literals. What can also be done is merging plans that have the same body by combining their guards. More work can also be done on non-deterministic preconditions, when the world is partially known. Larger examples should also be explored, to determine the scalability of our solution, and to look for possible optimizations. More work can also be done on incorporating and comparing/contrasting different FOND techniques into the pipeline instead of using the AND-OR Tree method.

References

1. Bordini, R.H., Hübner, J.F., Wooldridge, M.: Programming multi-agent systems in AgentSpeak using Jason. John Wiley & Sons (2007)
2. Cimatti, A., Pistore, M., Roveri, M., Traverso, P.: Weak, strong, and strong cyclic planning via symbolic model checking. Artif. Intell. **147**(1–2), 35–84 (2003)
3. Engesser, T., Miller, T.: Implicit coordination using fond planning. In: Proceedings of the AAAI Conference on Artificial Intelligence, vol. 34, pp. 7151–7159 (2020)
4. Fikes, R.E., Hart, P.E., Nilsson, N.J.: Learning and executing generalized robot plans. Artif. Intell. **3**, 251–288 (1972)
5. Hansen, E.A., Zilberstein, S.: LAO: a heuristic search algorithm that finds solutions with loops. Artif. Intell. **129**(1), 35–62 (2001). https://doi.org/10.1016/S0004-3702(01)00106-0
6. Meneguzzi, F., Luck, M.: Leveraging new plans in agentspeak(pl). In: Baldoni, M., Son, T.C., van Riemsdijk, M.B., Winikoff, M. (eds.) Declarative Agent Languages and Technologies VI, pp. 111–127. Springer, Berlin Heidelberg (2009)
7. Muise, C., McIlraith, S., Beck, C.: Improved non-deterministic planning by exploiting state relevance. In: Proceedings of the International Conference on Automated Planning and Scheduling, vol. 22, pp. 172–180 (2012)
8. Pereira, R.F., Pereira, A.G., Messa, F., De Giacomo, G.: Iterative depth-first search for fond planning. In: Proceedings of the International Conference on Automated Planning and Scheduling, vol. 32, pp. 90–99 (2022)
9. Rao, A.S.: AgentSpeak(L): BDI agents speak out in a logical computable language. In: Van de Velde, W., Perram, J.W. (eds.) MAAMAW 1996. LNCS, vol. 1038, pp. 42–55. Springer, Heidelberg (1996). https://doi.org/10.1007/BFb0031845
10. Rao, A.S., Georgeff, M.P.: Modeling rational agents within a BDI-architecture. Readings in agents, pp. 317–328 (1997)
11. Russell, S.J., Norvig, P.: Artificial intelligence a modern approach. London (2010)

Bid Intercession to Unlock Human Control in Decentralized Consensus-Based Multi-robot Task Allocation Algorithms

Victor Guillet[(✉)], Christophe Grand, Charles Lesire, and Gauthier Picard

DTIS, ONERA, Université de Toulouse, Toulouse, France
{victor.guillet,christophe.grand,charles.lesire,gauthier.picard}@onera.fr

Abstract. We investigate the introduction of novel intercession mechanisms in consensus-based decentralized task allocation within a heterogeneous multi-agent fleet. Intercession refers to the principle of agents biding on behalf of other agents or imposing certain allocations in decision-making architectures leveraging auction-based decision strategies. This is particularly relevant in settings where human operators, having more precise knowledge of the system situation, want to steer or force the multi-robot task allocation (MRTA). We thus extend an existing consensus framework, consensus-based auction algorithm (CBAA), while offering a simple generic method that operates independently of the underlying reasons, enabling interventions in a decentralized coordination process by humans at the agent and task levels. These interventions, whether systematic or occasional, have the added benefit of incurring minimal computational costs for field agents while maintaining the underlying algorithm's convergence and performance properties. We experimentally evaluate the proposed algorithm, I-CBAA, on synthetic MRTA scenarios implemented using the ROS framework.

Keywords: Consensus-Based Auctions · Mixed Initiative · Multi-Robot Task Allocation

1 Introduction

Multi-robot systems offer significant potential for various applications across diverse sectors, such as search and rescue operations, environmental monitoring and infrastructure inspection. In fact, their ability to execute tasks efficiently and autonomously proves invaluable. Multi-robot task allocation (MRTA) tackles the challenge of efficiently assigning a set of tasks to a team of robots [4]. MRTA aims to achieve optimal system performance, often measured by minimizing completion time or maximizing task coverage, whilst considering various operational constraints like robot capabilities, task dependencies, and environmental factors. MRTA encompasses a range of techniques, from centralized algorithms that make global decisions to distributed approaches where robots collaborate to determine task assignments [8,12]. Its successful implementation is crucial for enabling effective teamwork in multi-robot systems and unlocking their full potential in various applications.

However, achieving optimal performance in these scenarios often necessitates a delicate balance between automated task allocation and human control [6]. While automated task allocation algorithms have demonstrably achieved impressive results, concerns remain regarding the relinquishing of complete control to centralized or decentralized decision-making processes, such as auction-based [7] and consensus-based [2] task allocation algorithms. Human operators, equipped with domain expertise and real-time awareness, can offer invaluable insights and adapt to unforeseen circumstances that algorithms might struggle with [13], as initially identified in a mixed-initiative context [1,5].

This paper addresses the challenge of incorporating human control into the multi-robot task allocation framework. We present a novel approach, *intercession* in consensus-based auction mechanisms (namely the consensus-based auction algorithm, CBAA), that strives to strike this crucial balance, empowering human operators with greater control over the task allocation process without compromising on the efficiency and performance achieved by the underlying methods.

This paper is structured as follows. Section 2 provides background on MRTA and consensus-based task allocation, along with related works. Section 3 expounds the core contribution of the paper, I-CBAA, an extension to CBAA [2] with intercession, for which we provide convergence analysis in Sect. 4. We experimentally evaluate I-CBAA on synthetic scenarios using a ROS implementation in Sect. 5. Section 6 concludes the paper with some perspectives.

2 Background and Related Works

This section identifies the core problem and related consensus-based methods from the literature, before discussing works related to human participation in such settings.

2.1 Multi-robot Assignment Problem (MRTA)

The multi-robot assignment problem, also known as the Multi-Robot Task Allocation [4] (MRTA) problem, refers to the challenge of assigning N_t tasks to N_u agents, to obtain a conflict-free distribution of tasks to agents that maximize some overall reward (or minimize some overall cost). An allocation is qualified as "conflict-free" if each distinct task is assigned to at most one agent. A maximum of L_t tasks can be assigned to each agent, and the assignment is considered as completed once $N_{\min} \triangleq \min\{N_t, N_u L_t\}$ tasks have been assigned. This problem has been extensively studied and for the sake of maintaining consistency with the existing literature, the following integer (possibly non-linear) program formulation proposed in [2] will be adopted to formalize the problem.

$$\max \quad \sum_{i=1}^{N_u} \left(\sum_{j=1}^{N_t} c_{ij}\left(\mathbf{x}_i, \mathbf{p}_i\right) x_{ij} \right) \tag{1}$$

$$\text{s.t.} \quad \sum_{j=1}^{N_t} x_{ij} \leq L_t \quad \forall i \in \mathcal{I} \tag{2}$$

$$\sum_{i=1}^{N_u} x_{ij} \leq 1 \quad \forall j \in \mathcal{J} \tag{3}$$

$$\sum_{i=1}^{N_u} \sum_{j=1}^{N_i} x_{ij} = N_{\min} \triangleq \min\{N_t, N_u L_t\} \tag{4}$$

$$x_{ij} \in \{0,1\} \quad \forall (i,j) \in \mathcal{I} \times \mathcal{J} \tag{5}$$

Here, decision variable $x_{ij} = 1$ if task i is assigned to agent j, and is set to 0 otherwise. $\mathbf{x}_i \in \{0,1\}^{N_t}$ is then a vector with x_{ij} as jth element. Index sets are defined as $\mathcal{I} \triangleq \{1, \ldots, N_u\}$ for the agents, and $\mathcal{J} \triangleq \{1, \ldots, N_t\}$ for the tasks. Vector $\mathbf{p}_i \in (\mathcal{J} \cup \{\emptyset\})^{L_t}$ then represents an ordered sequence of tasks for agent i; its kth element is $j \in \mathcal{J}$ if agent i conducts j at the kth point along the path, and becomes $\emptyset$ (denoting an empty task) if agent i conducts less than k tasks. The local reward for agent i is therefore represented by the summation term in Eq. 1. It should be noted that in this formalization, the allocation operates around a reward function, resulting in a maximization problem. This score function is usually assumed to satisfy $c_{ij}(\mathbf{x}_i, \mathbf{p}_i) \geq 0$ and can be any (usually non-negative) function of either assignment $\mathbf{x}_i$ and/or path $\mathbf{p}_i$. In the case of mobile autonomous vehicles and robots, scoring/cost functions usually exploit path-dependent properties to represent the cost/reward of taking on various tasks (e.g. path length, mission completion time).

2.2 Consensus-Based MRTA Algorithms

Consensus-based methods, a subset of market-based methods, leverage peer-to-peer exchanges of information combined with auction logic to determine an allocation in a decentralized and distributed fashion. Two methods form the basis of most of this category, namely CBAA and CBBA [2]. Contrary to conventional auctions, consensus-based methods decentralize the winner determination problem, and thereby avoid a central single point of failure. CBAA and CBBA determine the task allocation through each agent locally determining bids, sharing them with their neighbors, and determining the assignment locally from all the information received. Such algorithms therefore alternate between two phases; an auction phase (during which bids are computed locally), and a consensus phase (during which the results of the auction phase, referred to as the winning bids lists, are shared and conflict resolution is performed to converge to a global allocation of tasks). CBAA and CBBA differ in the fact that CBAA considers each task independently, whereas in CBBA, tasks are evaluated on the basis of their respective added value in a local plan constructed by each agent.

In this paper, we will focus on CBAA as it is the simplest algorithm, CBBA being an extension of CBAA. It will allow to clearly evaluate the benefit of our intercession mechanism. CBAA auction and consensus phases are detailed below.

Phase 1: Auction. Initially, two vectors of length N_t are created (initialized as zero vectors) and maintained by each agent locally throughout the assignment process. $\mathbf{x}_i$ is the agent's task list, where $x_{ij} = 1$ if agent i has been assigned to task j, and 0 otherwise. $\mathbf{y}_i$ then represents the list of the winning bids, which is assumed to be the most up-to-date estimation of the current highest bids made across all agents so far. In other words, y_{ij} is the largest bid known by agent i to have been placed for task j across the fleet.

The complete original algorithm logic from the CBAA paper [2] is provided in Algorithm 1. Each agent places bids on the different tasks asynchronously with the rest of the fleet:

Step 1—Compute a Local Bid: Agent i computes a local bid $c_{ij} \geq 0$ for each task j. This step is performed whenever a new task is found. It is done before calling procedure SELECT TASK in Algorithm 1.

Step 2—If Free, Determine The List of Valid Tasks: *Valid tasks are tasks for which the local bid c_{ij} outbids the winning bid y_{ij}.* CBAA being a single-task allocation process, agents only perform the auction process when being currently unassigned ($\sum_j x_{ij}(t) = 0$, line 5, with t being time). The list of valid tasks $\mathbf{h}_i$ is generated using the winning bids list using $h_{ij} = \mathbb{I}(c_{ij} > y_{ij}) \, \forall j \in \mathcal{J}$ (line 6), where $\mathbb{I}(\cdot)$ is the indicator function that is unity if the argument is true and zero otherwise.

Step 3—Select and Assign a Task to Self: Check if there are valid tasks (line 7). If so, select the task J_i in the valid tasks list $\mathbf{h}_i$ with the highest local bid c_{ij} (line 8), update winning bids to match the task's local bid ($y_{i,J_i}(t) = c_{i,J_i}$, line 9), and assign it to self ($x_{i,J_i}(t) = 1$, line 10). $\mathbf{y_i}$ and $\mathbf{x_i}$ matrices are updated every time the agent wins a task, i.e. $\mathbf{h}_i \neq \mathbf{0}$. The chosen task J_i is selected using $J_i = \mathrm{argmax} \; h_{ij} \cdot c_{ij}$.

Algorithm 1: CBAA Auction Phase for agent i at iteration t

```
1  Procedure SELECT TASK
2      (c_i, x_i(t-1), y_i(t-1))
3      x_i(t) = x_i(t-1)
4      y_i(t) = y_i(t-1)
5      if ∑_j x_ij(t) = 0 then                         // Step 2: if free
6          h_ij = 𝕀(c_ij > y_ij(t)),  ∀j ∈ 𝒥           // determine valid tasks
7          if h_i ≠ 0 then                             // Step 3: if there are valid tasks
8              J_i ← argmax_j h_ij · c_ij              // select v.task with largest local bid
9              y_{i,J_i}(t) ← c_{i,J_i}                // update winning bids
10             x_{i,J_i}(t) ← 1                        // assign task to self
```

Phase 2: Consensus. The purpose of this phase is to converge to a consensus on a single list of winning bids across the agent collective, which is in turn used to determine the winners and subsequent task allocation. The original algorithm

[2] can be seen in Algorithm 2. CBAA defines $\mathbb{G}(\tau)$ to be the undirected communication network at time τ with symmetric adjacency matrix $G(\tau)$, which models the existence of links between agents in such a way that $g_{ij}(\tau) = 1$ if a link exists between agents i and j, and 0 otherwise. Agents i and j are qualified as neighbors if linked. Additionally, every agent has a self-connected edge ($g_{ii}(\tau) = 1, \forall i$ by convention). At each time step τ, the consensus phase performed by each agent is decomposed into the following steps:

Step 1—Share and Receive Local States with Neighbors: Each agent i sends its local winning bids list $\mathbf{y_i}$ to its neighbors (line 1) and receives a winning bids list from its neighbors (line 2).

Step 2—Update Local States Using Ones Received: The consensus process is performed for each received bid list $\mathbf{y_k}$ for all agents k for which $g_{ik}(\tau) = 1$. Agent i replaces y_{ij} values with the largest value observed in the $\mathbf{y_k}$ obtained from all its neighbors as seen in line 5.

Step 3—Lose Assignment if Outbid by Neighbors: Each agent loses its assignment if it finds itself outbid by another agent for the task it currently has selected. For each task, the winning agent is determined by line 6. If this agent is agent is not self (line 7), the local task assignment is set to zero (the task is dropped, line 8).

Note that in the event of a tie in determining J_i in the auction phase or z_{i,J_i} in the consensus phase are resolved systematically, through lexicographic tie-breaking heuristics based on agent and/or task ids.

Algorithm 2: CBAA Consensus Phase for agent i at iteration t

---

1 SEND $\mathbf{y}_i$ to k with $g_{ik}(\tau) = 1$ // Step 1: share local states
2 RECEIVE $\mathbf{y}_k$ from k with $g_{ik}(\tau) = 1$ // receive neighbors local states
3 **Procedure** *UPDATE TASK*
4     $\left(\mathbf{g}_i(\tau), \mathbf{y}_{k \in \{k | g_{ik}(\tau) = 1\}}(t), J_i\right)$
5     $y_{ij}(t) = \max_k g_{ik}(\tau) \cdot y_{kj}(t), \forall j \in \mathcal{J}$ // Step 2: update winning bids
6     $z_{i,J_i} = \mathrm{argmax}_k\, g_{ik}(\tau) \cdot y_{k,J_i}(t)$ // Step 3: find winning agent for J_i
7   **if** $z_{i,J_i} \neq i$ **then**   // if self is not winning agent
8        $x_{i,J_i}(t) = 0$ // drop task J_i

2.3 Related Works

Our direction is close to the notion of *shared autonomy* which is defined as "the autonomous control of the majority of degrees of freedom in a system, while designing a control interface for human operators to control a reduced number of parameters defining the global behavior of the system" [11]. This may be done to enable controlling robots through packaging complex action sequences into abstract task sequences [14], or controlling a large number of robots with few operators [15]. Additionally, a lot of research may be found on autonomous allocation of tasks for a team made up of both humans and robots [9,16], and on human monitoring of mission execution [3].

Human-robot interaction may furthermore be broken down into two key paradigms [10]: *complementary interaction* (where the human and the robots control different subsets of tasks, and the robots plan "around" the human instructions), and *overlapping interaction* (where both the human and robots control the same set of tasks). While a number of approaches exist for the former [10], little work has been done on the later, which our work seeks to address.

We therefore propose a solution for the challenge of combining human and autonomous control in a task allocation problem through the introduction of a novel mechanism in decentralised auction-based methods: bid intercession. We seeks to retain underlying convergence and robustness guarantees while enabling the injection of additional expertise in the allocation process to optimise desired metrics.

3 Consensus-Based Algorithms with Intercession

To install control in consensus-based algorithms, we introduce a novel mechanism, *bid intercession*. It refers to the process of bidding on behalf of target agents in an auction process by leveraging a prioritization mechanism. Bid intercession enables to influence an auction outcome without modifying the fundamental allocation protocol. While consensus is steered in a specific direction, it effectively retains full freedom and control over the allocation. This may be performed by any agent, it will be leveraged here specifically for human control and intervention in the coordination process.

To enable intercession, an additional information vector must be introduced, N_ρ, defining a fixed hierarchy between agents in N_u. N_ρ is therefore a vector of length N_u containing integers representing the priority level associated with each agent u. This vector is used to decide which bids are used in the allocation process in the event of an intercession.

3.1 Phase 1: Auction Process

In order to enable bid intercession in decentralised methods, the standard CBAA algorithm need to be extended as follows. The task vectors $\mathbf{x}_i$ and $\mathbf{y}_i$ remain the same as the ones described in Sect. 2.2, and the new "current bids" matrix $\mathbf{b}_i$ of size $N_t \times N_u$ is defined. It is the most up-to-date estimation of the *current highest priority/value bids made across the fleet for each task and each agent*. In other words, b_{ijr} is the highest priority/value bid known by agent i to have been placed for task j for agent r across the fleet. Additionally, the β_i matrix also of size $N_t \times N_u$ is introduced. This matrix corresponds to the *priority levels associated with each bid in* $\mathbf{b}_i$. It is used in priority merging processes (Algorithm 3) to decide which values to keep when updating the $\mathbf{b}_i$ matrix. Note that similarly

Algorithm 3: Merging two values (v and w) depending on their priorities (p and q)

1 **Procedure** merge(v, w, p, q)

2 $\quad v \leftarrow \begin{cases} w & \text{if } q > p, w \neq 0 \\ v & \text{if } q < p \\ \text{apply tie-breaker} & \text{if } q = p \end{cases}$

3 $\quad p \leftarrow \begin{cases} q & \text{if } q > p, w \neq 0 \\ p & \text{if } q < p \\ \text{apply tie-breaker} & \text{if } q = p \end{cases}$

to the original CBAA algorithm, it is assumed that all ties (such as when the priority levels are not sufficient to determine the winner ($N_\rho(i) = \beta_{ijr}$)) are resolved systematically. The auction phase of I-CBAA operates as follows:

Step 1a—Computes Local Bids for Each Task, for Self and Each Agent Self Intercedes On Behalf Of: We redefine $c_{ijr} \geq 0$ to be the bid that agent i places for task j, *for agent r*. This results in a matrix c_i of size $N_t \times N_u$, initialized to 0 to allow for discerning whether a bid has been calculated or not (it is assumed that the bids resulting from the bid estimation process are always greater than zero). Here, $r \neq i$ and $c_{ijr} \neq 0$ only when agents perform intercessions. The rest of the time the only indexes yielding non-zero values are the ones where $r = i$. The choice of which agent performs intercessions and when is dependent on the choice of architecture and agent hierarchy adopted. It is done before calling procedure SELECT TASK in Algorithm 4.

Step 1b—Update Local States: The current bids matrix $\mathbf{b}_i$ is updated where relevant based on said bids' corresponding priority β_i, the agent's own priority level $N_\rho(i)$, and the local bids c_{ijr} following the *prioritization* process (lines 5-7).

Step 2—If Free, Determine the List of Valid Tasks: If free (line 8), the valid tasks $\mathbf{h}_i$ are generated using $h_{ij} = \mathbb{I}(b_{iji} > y_{ij}) \quad \forall j \in \mathcal{J}$ (??). It is important to note here that b_{iji} is considered and not c_{ij}. This is necessary to ensure that the bid intercessions with larger priorities (than that of agent i) are the ones considered in the auction process.

Step 3—Lose Assignment if Outbid by Neighbors: A valid task is selected, assigned, and the winning bids list is updated the same way as it is done in the base CBAA algorithm (lines 11-14).

The updated auction phase is provided in Algorithm 4.

3.2 Phase 2: Consensus Process

Only one modification is necessary here to adapt the consensus phase to support bid intercession. The updating process must be extended to also merge the

Algorithm 4: I-CBAA Auction Phase for agent i at iteration t

1 **Procedure** *SELECT TASK*
2     $(\mathbf{c}_i, \mathbf{x}_i(t-1), \mathbf{y}_i(t-1), \mathbf{b}_i(t-1), \beta_i(t-1))$
3     $\mathbf{x}_i(t) = \mathbf{x}_i(t-1); \mathbf{y}_i(t) = \mathbf{y}_i(t-1)$
4     $\mathbf{b}_i(t) = \mathbf{b}_i(t-1); \beta_i(t) = \beta_i(t-1)$
5   **for** $j \in N_t, r \in N_u$ **do**   // Step 1b: update local states
6   **if** $c_{ijr} \neq 0$ **then**
7   merge$(b_{ijr}(t), c_{ijr}, \beta_{ijr}(t), N_\rho(i))$
8   **if** $\sum_j x_{ij}(t) = 0$ **then**   // Step 2: if free
9        $h_{ij} = \mathbb{I}(b_{iji}(t) > y_{ij}(t)), \quad \forall j \in \mathcal{J}$ // determine valid tasks
10   **if** $\mathbf{h}_i \neq 0$ **then**   // Step 3: if there are valid tasks
11         $J_i \leftarrow \text{argmax}_j\, h_{ij} \cdot b_{iji}(t)$ // get v.task with largest local bid
12         $y_{iJ_i}(t) \leftarrow b_{iJ_ii}(t)$ // update winning bids
13         $x_{iJ_i}(t) \leftarrow 1$ // assign task to self

received $\mathbf{b}_k$ and β_k matrices with local $\mathbf{b}_i$ and β_i matrices following the prioritization logic (mentioned previously in the auction phase section). Note that unlike in the base merge function (Algorithm 3), an agent here also loses its assignment x_{ij} if its local current bids matrix $\mathbf{b}_i$ is updated for a task j. This is necessary to ensure that in the event of an intercession with a smaller bid, the agent correctly releases the task. This procedure is referred to as merge_r (see Algorithm 5). The complete updated consensus phase is provided in Algorithm 6.

Algorithm 5: Merging *with reset* two values (v and w) depending on their priorities (p and q)

1 **Procedure** merge_r(x, v, w, p, q)
2     $v \leftarrow \begin{cases} w & \text{if } q > p, w \neq 0 \\ v & \text{if } q < p \\ \text{apply tie-breaker} & \text{if } q = p \end{cases}$
3     $p \leftarrow \begin{cases} q & \text{if } q > p, w \neq 0 \\ p & \text{if } q < p \\ \text{apply tie-breaker} & \text{if } q = p \end{cases}$
4     $x \leftarrow 0$ if $q > p$ and $q \neq 0$

4 Convergence

The algorithm's convergence refers to its ability to produce a conflict-free assignment in a finite amount of time. Two key aspects are considered here: the ability to converge, referred to as *convergence termination*, the *convergence iteration*

Algorithm 6: I-CBAA Consensus Phase for agent i at iteration t

1. SEND $\mathbf{y}_i, \mathbf{b}_i, \beta_i$ to k with $g_{ik}(\tau) = 1$ // Step 1: share local states
2. RECEIVE $\mathbf{y}_k, \mathbf{b}_k, \beta_k$ from k with $g_{ik}(\tau) = 1$ // receive neighbors local states
3. **Procedure** *UPDATE LOCAL STATES*
4. $(\mathbf{g}_i(\tau), \mathbf{x}_i(t))$,
5. $\mathbf{b}_i(t), \mathbf{b}_{k \in \{k|g_{ik}(\tau)=1\}}(t), \beta_i(t), \beta_{k \in \{k|g_{ik}(\tau)=1\}}(t)$,
6.   **if** $g_{ik}(\tau) = 1$ **then**
7.   **for** $j \in N_t$ AND $r \in N_u$ **do**
8.   **if** $b_{kjr} \neq 0$ **then**
9.   merge_r$(x_{ij}(t), b_{ijr}(t), b_{kjr}(t), \beta_{ijr}(t), \beta_{kjr}(t))$

10. **Procedure** *UPDATE TASK*
11. $(\mathbf{g}_i(\tau), \mathbf{y}_{k \in \{k|g_{ik}(\tau)=1\}}(t), J_i)$;
12. $y_{ij}(t) = \max_k g_{ik}(\tau) \cdot y_{kj}(t), \forall j \in \mathcal{J}$ // Step 2: update winning bids
13. $z_{i,J_i} = \arg\max_k g_{ik}(\tau) \cdot y_{k,J_i}(t)$ // Step 3: find winning agent for J_i
14.   **if** $z_{i,J_i} \neq i$ **then**   // if self is not winning agent
15. $x_{i,J_i}(t) \leftarrow 0$ // drop task J_i

complexity i.e. the number of logical steps necessary to converge to a solution, and *time complexity*, the time required to converge to a solution. In order to evaluate those properties, we demonstrate that it is possible to inherit the convergence guarantees of the underlying decentralized algorithm (Proposition 1). Furthermore, I-CBAA was implemented to verify experimentally the correctness of the proposed approach and its convergence properties.

Before evaluating the hypotheses proposed for this analysis, the following must first be defined:

Property 1 (Deterministic and consistent prioritization). The prioritization logic always yields the same results given the same inputs across the whole fleet.

Property 2 (Global priority state). The prioritization mechanism used by each agent leverages a prioritization state globalized across the entire fleet of agents participating.

Failing to possess any of the above-mentioned properties will result in agents obtaining different results in the prioritization process and in turn locally determining the winning bids inconsistently, preventing the algorithm from converging correctly to a global consensus on the allocation.

Lemma 1 (Unambiguous source of truth). *The prioritization process yields consistent results across all agents when performed on the basis of the same information.*

Proof. In the above-defined problem and algorithm, the deterministic and constant nature of the prioritization mechanism (Property 1), the globalised nature of the agent's priority levels (Property 2), and the assumed systematic resolution of conflicts allows for asserting the deterministic and unambiguous nature of the source of truth at all times.

Proposition 1. *The process of intercession does not have any impact on the convergence of the underlying distributed method of a given auction, given that the source of truth is unambiguously defined at all times. More specifically,* convergence termination *and* convergence iteration complexity *are not impacted.*

Proof. As specified in [2, section V-D]: *"[...] whatever knowledge each agent scoring scheme is based on, the only needed information for resolving conflicts among agents are the winning bid list, winning agent list, and the time stamp. If these three pieces of information are communicated error-free,* **the conflict resolution process [...] is insensitive to the details of each agent's scoring scheme**.*"*

Bid intercession solely introduces additional logic and conditions adjusting the source of information in the process of winning bid determination and exchange of information (intercession requiring slightly more already existing information to be passed around). These modifications in turn allow for intelligently managing different scoring schemes present within a single network, and "overwriting" scoring results before performing the auction process (which itself remains unchanged). The detail of the scoring process logic and/or the data used in it is therefore abstracted away in the bid value. Intercession thus fundamentally only effectively modifies the agents' scoring scheme. Accordingly, the consensus process as defined by the underlying algorithm remains unaltered and unaffected.

Consequently, the above provided in conjunction with Lemma 1 makes it possible to infer that the introduction of bid intercession has no impact on the convergence properties of the underlying algorithm it uses as a baseline, thereby verifying Proposition 1.

5 Experimental Evaluation

To evaluate the validity and applicability of bid intercession, a few synthetic test cases are considered. We seek through this representation to evaluate scenarios where one human operator with higher context awareness seeks to steer the allocation process in a specific direction to ensure a more efficient outcome. More specifically, we seek to devise a simple example to demonstrate two key aspects: the concrete execution of intercession in a fleet, and its effectiveness in making additional information available during the allocation. As such, for the evaluation metrics presented below, jumps in performance are expected *given* the additional information is correctly fused and effectively leveraged in the problem resolution.

5.1 Experimental Setup

We consider 4 agents positioned in a 20x20 grid, from which we randomly removed 10% of the edges (Fig. 1).

Two different categories of *tasks* are distinguished. The goto tasks may be performed by any agent, and completing them can lead to discovering an action task. Those are either a_1, which may only be performed by agents equipped with skill s_1, or a_2, which equivalently requires the skill s_2. Note that an action task is not always discovered upon completing a goto task.

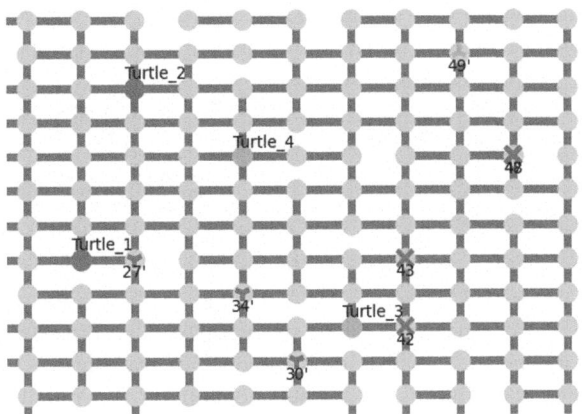

Fig. 1. Zoom of grid environment used in the experiments. The circles represent the agents, the crosses the goto tasks, and action tasks for the rest. The colors represent the skill types of the agents, the action tasks located at a goto destination for the crosses, and the action task types for the rest.

Two different categories of *agents* are considered; *robots*, and (a single) *human operator*, also referred to here as the *interceding agent*.

- The *robots* are created with different skill sets (common goto skill, plus a combination of skills from $\{a_1, a_2\}$). They all possess a priority $N_\rho = 0$, and evaluate their own bids c_{iji} as the inverse of the distance between their current locations and a given task's location. Note that if any agent is not equipped with the required skill for performing a task, its bid defaults to 0, to ensure only agents capable of performing a task bid.
- The *interceding agent* possesses a priority $N_\rho = 1$, and unlike robots, it is capable of anticipating action tasks at a given goto task destination. For a given task, the interceding agent i will bid for all robots r capable of performing a task and its subsequent action task (if any), and produce bids c_{ijr} magnitude larger than the largest possible ones computed by all other agents ($\times 40$ for a 20×20 grid). This agent represents a human operator injecting higher situation awareness into the allocation process.

During each run, all robots start at the same location (bottom left of the grid), and after an initial announcement of 10 goto tasks, the 40 others goto are announced gradually throughout the run, from closest to farthest from the starting point. Upon having reached a consensus on an allocation, robots move to the corresponding tasks' locations (taking the shortest path), where they possibly discover an action task. The simulation runs in epochs, with tasks having a specific release epoch, and agents being able to perform one move per epoch (take a step towards a goto task destination, or complete an action task).

We consider scenario configurations with different task schedules, task requirements, and different fleet compositions (generated randomly): task requirements are defined by the number $\overline{a_1}$ (resp. $\overline{a_2}$) of a_1 (resp. a_2) tasks; fleet compositions are defined by the number $\overline{s_1}$ of robots equipped with s_1 and the number of $\overline{s_2}$ robots equipped with s_2.

We evaluate the following algorithms: CBAA, our implementation of CBAA [2] (no interceding agent); I-CBAA, our implementation of I-CBAA, where intercession is applied to bids for tasks a robot can perform, and for goto tasks followed by an action task a robot can perform. Here the human operator (represented by an interceding agent) predicts (or just acquired extra knowledge to know) which action tasks will appear after goto tasks, and thus intercedes for compatible robots. In CBAA and I-CBAA, bids are only computed when a task is discovered. We also consider versions noted CBAA$^+$ and I-CBAA$^+$ where bids are re-assessed whenever a task is discovered. This was chosen to observe the influence of intercession in a context where replanning was possible.

Finally, five key metrics are defined: total step count is the fleet's overall distance traveled, total tardiness measures the elapsed time between task discovery and completion, and total goto tardiness and total action tardiness track the accumulated delays for respective task types. Lastly, total message count is the cumulative number of messages exchanged during operations.

The % match allocation (the number of instances where an agent undertook a goto and its subsequent action task) is also tracked to better observe the influence of bid intercession on the allocation process.

5.2 Results Analysis

Table 1 summarizes the results obtained from running the simulated experiments, implemented using ROS 2, across 10 different task schedules for all algorithms and configurations mentioned (for a total of 160 individual runs). Each value represents the mean across all runs for a given configuration, and the corresponding standard deviations are also provided. Note that *gains in performance are expected under the condition that the additional information available to the interceding agent is correctly injected and leveraged by the allocation process.*

When comparing the original CBAA algorithms to their CBAA$^+$ variants, we observe significant improvements in performance in the total step count across all scenarios and test cases (the smallest difference representing a 26% reduction in total distance travelled for the (20, 20) scenario). Similar observations can be made about the total tardiness, where the smallest improvements observed were

Table 1. Average values (and standard deviation) over 10 instances of performance metrics for each configuration and algorithm

$\overline{a_1}, \overline{a_2}$	$\overline{s_1}, \overline{s_2}$	Algorithm	Total step count	Total tardiness	Total goto tardiness	Total action tardiness	% matched alloc.	Total msg count
25, 25	2, 2	CBAA	756.8 (±7.6%)	3263.7 (±16.3%)	2460.5 (±26.1%)	803.2 (±54.1%)	50.4 (±11.3%)	1449.9 (±2.0%)
25, 25	2, 2	I-CBAA	538.0 (±11.1%)	1795.0 (±19.4%)	1785.7 (±19.4%)	9.3 (±141.4%)	**98.2** (±2.6%)	**1243.1** (±1.6%)
25, 25	2, 2	CBAA⁺	487.6 (±6.6%)	1823.3 (±12.0%)	1410.2 (±11.3%)	413.1 (±40.9%)	52.6 (±12.3%)	2393.5 (±2.8%)
25, 25	2, 2	I-CBAA⁺	**423.2** (±5.8%)	**1416.8** (±10.3%)	**1353.0** (±9.8%)	63.8 (±53.5%)	89.2 (±2.8%)	2100.7 (±1.8%)
20, 20	2, 2	CBAA	611.2 (±9.5%)	2584.3 (±16.8%)	2103.1 (±20.7%)	481.2 (±28.4%)	51.8 (±11.4%)	1319.9 (±2.0%)
20, 20	2, 2	I-CBAA	519.6 (±7.7%)	1814.5 (±11.7%)	1806.2 (±11.6%)	8.3 (±173.7%)	**98.2** (±2.4%)	**1136.2** (±1.5%)
20, 20	2, 2	CBAA⁺	452.0 (±11.9%)	1730.7 (±23.1%)	1221.1 (±11.9%)	509.6 (±55.5%)	45.2 (±17.8%)	2165.6 (±2.0%)
20, 20	2, 2	I-CBAA⁺	**406.8** (±6.7%)	**1415.9** (±10.9%)	1332.6 (±10.0%)	83.3 (±54.8%)	88.5 (±4.7%)	1890.8 (±3.0%)
35, 5	2, 2	CBAA	710.4 (±11.6%)	2929.0 (±14.3%)	2085.6 (±13.5%)	843.4 (±42.7%)	38.5 (±25.3%)	1345.1 (±1.6%)
35, 5	2, 2	I-CBAA	660.0 (±12.1%)	2321.0 (±18.4%)	2022.7 (±18.1%)	298.3 (±42.0%)	66.2 (±13.2%)	**1173.5** (±1.2%)
35, 5	2, 2	CBAA⁺	467.2 (±10.1%)	1656.1 (±21.3%)	**1200.9** (±20.3%)	455.2 (±56.0%)	39.8 (±18.9%)	2141.6 (±4.3%)
35, 5	2, 2	I-CBAA⁺	**459.2** (±6.5%)	**1500.8** (±17.1%)	1279.9 (±15.2%)	220.9 (±43.3%)	69.8 (±14.1%)	1884.3 (±1.8%)
39, 1	1, 3	CBAA	1427.2 (±12.5%)	5810.2 (±10.8%)	1939.7 (±17.6%)	3870.5 (±19.4%)	7.5 (±66.7%)	1299.1 (±1.3%)
39, 1	1, 3	I-CBAA	1526.0 (±11.6%)	5805.8 (±17.2%)	2506.5 (±18.8%)	3299.3 (±33.5%)	23.8 (±24.9%)	**1255.0** (±0.6%)
39, 1	1, 3	CBAA⁺	834.3 (±12.9%)	3080.1 (±12.4%)	**1045.4** (±14.1%)	2034.7 (±19.8%)	7.0 (±32.8%)	1987.4 (±1.6%)
39, 1	1, 3	I-CBAA⁺	**809.2** (±12.4%)	3055.8 (±12.2%)	1610.5 (±17.4%)	**1445.3** (±33.3%)	25.8 (±22.0%)	1981.9 (±2.3%)

of 33% for the (25, 25) scenario. This is explained by the fact that recomputing bids allows for a more up-to-date evaluation of the system's state, in turn allowing for better optimising the sequences of tasks undertaken by each agent throughout a run. This however is achieved at the expense of a large message count, a result of the additional consensus rounds performed every time the bids are recomputed (resulting in an increase of up to 48% for the (25, 25) scenario between the CBAA and CBAA+ variants).

When comparing results by algorithm, we observe that I-CBAA (both non-+ and + variants) consistently outperform their respective counterparts base variants on all metrics except message count. The largest gains in performance are observed to be between non-+ variants, which may be explained by the inherent degradation of the estimated bids as the mission progresses. This results in the base CBAA algorithm performing poorly in a consequently less constrained problem (the sole information leveraged being the shortest path length at the time of task discovery). The addition of intercession effectively simplifies the problem significantly, and in turn allows the underlying CBAA mechanism to better allocate tasks. It is noted however that the best solutions regarding total step count and total tardiness are consistently produced by I-CBAA+. When compared with the base CBAA implementation, the smallest gain observed for the total step count is of 33.5% for the (20, 20) scenario (with the largest improvement observed being of 44.1% for the (25, 25) scenario). Similar observations can be made for the total tardiness, where the smallest improvement observed was of 47.4% for the (39, 1) scenario, and maximum improvement is of 56.6% for the (25, 25) scenario.

Finally, we can observe that in all scenarios tested, the % matched allocations constantly increased with the introduction of the action tasks knowledge through intercession. The % match allocation did not reach 100% as CBAA is a task-by-task algorithm, and the release schedule of the task does not ensure that agents always have a tasks they specialise into available to take on. In such situations, agents fall back to taking on the closest tasks, completing the goto task and revealing the action task to then be completed by another with the correct skill. This also explains why the scenario with a 1:1 ratio of tasks and agents allows for the largest % matched allocation results (resulting in up to a 98.2% matched alloc. for I-CBAA).

6 Conclusions

In this work, we propose a novel mechanism for enabling overlapping control in decentralised auction-based mechanisms while retaining the robustness and convergence guarantees of the underlying method.

The novel mechanism, referred to as *Bid Intercession*, enables agents to intervene in the allocation process by biding on behalf of others to impose their own evaluation of a given situation. This proves particularly effective in enabling human control in the process while retaining the core properties and decentralised nature of the underlying algorithms.

The results successfully demonstrate the injection of superior situational awareness through bid intercession, which allowed for consistently achieving a reduction of at least 33.5% in total distance travelled, and a reduction of 47.4 % in total tardiness of tasks across all tests at the expense of additional communication load. The results allow us to conclude that the introduction of bid intercession successfully enables the agents to integrate and leverage the additional information provided by the interceding agent (our operator) to improve their autonomous allocation process. Additionally, the results obtained for the $^+$ variants suggest that it may be desirable to investigate the integration of bid intercession into more advanced allocation mechanisms (such as the consensus-based bundle algorithm, CBBA), which may in turn further improve the performance of our reference metrics.

Finally, additional extensions may be considered, such as introducing variable priority levels and hierarchies, and/or investigating the potential intercession assemblages and compositions for varying the properties of the coordination mechanism.

Acknowledgments. Research funded by the Defence Innovation Agency of the French Ministry of Defence.

References

1. Chiou, M., Hawes, N., Stolkin, R.: Mixed-initiative variable autonomy for remotely operated mobile robots. ACM Trans. Hum.-Robot Interact. **10**(4) (2021). https://doi.org/10.1145/3472206
2. Choi, H.L., Brunet, L., How, J.P.: Consensus-based decentralized auctions for robust task allocation. IEEE Trans. Robot. **25**(4) (2009). https://doi.org/10.1109/TRO.2009.2022423
3. Dahiya, A., Cai, Y., Schneider, O., Smith, S.L.: On the impact of interruptions during multi-robot supervision tasks. In: International Conference on Robotics and Automation (ICRA), London, UK (2023). https://doi.org/10.1109/ICRA48891.2023.10160323
4. Gerkey, B.P., Matarić, M.J.: A formal analysis and taxonomy of task allocation in multi-robot systems. Int. J. Robot. Res. **23**(9) (2004). https://doi.org/10.1177/0278364904045564
5. Horvitz, E.: Mixed-initiative interaction. IEEE Intell. Syst. (1999)
6. Johnson, A.W., Oman, C.M., Sheridan, T.B., Duda, K.R.: Dynamic task allocation in operational systems: issues, gaps, and recommendations. In: IEEE Aerospace Conference, Big Sky, MT, USA (2014). https://doi.org/10.1109/aero.2014.6836205
7. Koenig, S., et al.: The power of sequential single-item auctions for agent coordination. In: AAAI Conference on Artificial Intelligence (AAAI), Boston, MA, USA (2006)
8. Korsah, G.A., Stentz, A., Dias, M.B.: A comprehensive taxonomy for multi-robot task allocation. Int. J. Robot. Res. **32**(12) (2013). https://doi.org/10.1177/0278364913496484
9. Lippi, M., Di Lillo, P., Marino, A.: A task allocation framework for human multi-robot collaborative settings. In: International Conference on Robotics and Automation (ICRA), London, UK (2023). https://doi.org/10.1109/ICRA48891.2023.10161458

10. Musić, S., Hirche, S.: Control sharing in human-robot team interaction. Ann. Rev. Control **44** (2017). https://doi.org/10.1016/j.arcontrol.2017.09.017
11. Queralta, J.P., et al.: Collaborative multi-robot search and rescue: planning, coordination, perception, and active vision. IEEE Access **8** (2020). https://doi.org/10.1109/ACCESS.2020.3030190
12. Quinton, F., Grand, C., Lesire, C.: Market approaches to the multi-robot task allocation problem: a survey. J. Intell. Robot. Syst. **107**(2) (2023). https://doi.org/10.1007/s10846-022-01803-0
13. Ramchurn, S.D., et al.: A disaster response system based on human-agent collectives. J. Artif. Intell. Res., September 2016
14. Schou, C., Andersen, R.S., Chrysostomou, D., Bøgh, S., Madsen, O.: Skill-based instruction of collaborative robots in industrial settings. Robot. Comput.-Integr. Manuf. **53** (2018). https://doi.org/10.1016/j.rcim.2018.03.008
15. Taranta II, E.M., Seiwert, A., Goeckner, A., Nguyen, K., Cherry, E.: From warfighting needs to robot actuation: a complete rapid integration swarming solution. Field Robot. **3**(1) (2023). https://doi.org/10.55417/fr.2023015
16. You, Y., Thomas, V., Colas, F., Alami, R., Buffet, O.: Robust robot planning for human-robot collaboration. In: International Conference on Robotics and Automation (ICRA), London, UK (2023). https://doi.org/10.1109/ICRA48891.2023.10161406

Reason Logically, Move Continuously

Andrea Gatti

University of Genoa, Genova, Italy
andrea.gatti@edu.unige.it

Abstract. The vacuum cleaner robot is a common didactic example in the field of multi-agent systems. Normally, the robot is placed inside a grid world and reasons directly on the step to perform. In this work, we propose a different approach where the robot body and the robot mind are separated, the body is placed in a continuous environment and the mind reasons in a more abstract way on regions instead of cells, leaving to the body the task of moving continuously. In this way, the robot is able to abstract more and focus on high-level tasks instead of low-level details. An implementation of the proposed approach is presented with JaCaMo agents and a Godot simulation, using Region Connection Calculus (RCC) as base for the agent.

Keywords: Intelligent Agents · Virtual Environment · Cleaning Robot

1 Introduction and Motivation

The scenario of the cleaning robot is often used in textbooks as an example to present intelligent agents and their basic principles; it is sufficient to cite "Artificial Intelligence: A Modern Approach" [1] by S. Russell and P. Norvig, who use it as early as the second chapter as an introduction to intelligent agents concept. The case study is simple, a robot vacuum cleaner is in a grid environment and has to clean the whole space by having motion and cleaning as actions. There are then various versions related to map knowledge that obviously influence the agent's behavior. In the most basic versions the agent has a full knowledge of the map, knows the cells where the dirt is and has to decide how to clean the entire space. In more complex versions the agent has a partial knowledge of the map, it could know where the dirt is but not how the environment is arranged or the opposite or both.

The robot vacuum cleaner in these examples reasons on a space being discretized and so it is able to perform very low-level actions, deciding what individual steps to take and in what direction. Also, this approach reduces the agents' rotational degrees of freedom to the four directions *above*, *below*, *right* and *left*, altering also the path final trajectory as shown in Fig. 1.

This discretization is certainly necessary if one thinks that an agent moving through the space has to reason not so much about *what* it has to do but more about *how* it has to do it and the individual steps that lead it to achieve its

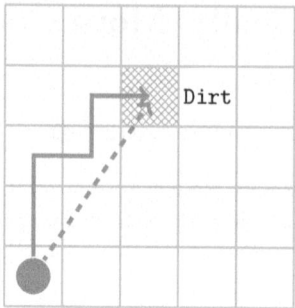

Fig. 1. The differnce between discrete and continuous path finding.

goal. While this may be true for some type of agents, it is certainly reductive for logical agents based on the Belief-Desire-Intention paradigm, which instead have their strength precisely in abstraction and in delegating the management of the environment to external artifacts. Let the agent reason about what to do and the body compute how to do it.

Moreover, in the current state of the art, most simulation software and game engines carry much more advanced path finding technologies than a simplistic discrete representation of the world. Godot [2] implements NavigationPaths, Unity [3] has an entire Navigation System that implements path finding, and even Unreal Engine [4] implements Navigation Mesh that is used by agents to move through space. All these tools also implement the handling of stair steps, ascents, descents, and other situations that in a logical implementation should be considered as separate instances and handled properly.

Even in the field of robotic research, we can find multiple approaches to finding optimal paths that consider continous space, finding detailed solutions that do not simply involve left, right steps with predetermined rotations but realistic paths to be followed with 360-degree of freedom. A complete overview of the state of the art from this point of view can be found in the survey [5] by K. Karur et al. on path planning for mobile robots. The paper makes a first major division between global algorithms in which the agent has complete knowledge of the environment and local algorithms in which, on the other hand, it knows only a neighborhood of its location and must therefore update its path as it moves. A second major division is between offline and online algorithms, the former being those that plan the entire path before starting to move, the latter being those that plan the path as they move. The algorithms presented move from discrete to continuous space, demonstrating that here, too, technology has moved beyond a grid representation of the world.

In [6] M. Psotka et al. presented a modification of the wavefront algorithm for ground mobile robots to compute global paths. They consider a known environment with obstacles and apply two modifications: the first one is the removal of redundant waypoints and the second one focuses on making the path smoother. V. Bulut presented a novel path planning algorithm that is based on clustering-obstacles and quintic trigonometric Bézier curves in [7]. The algorithm is composed of two steps: the first part finds the waypoints using clustering-obstacles and the second part uses the waypoints to compute the path using quintic trigonometric Bézier curves making the path smooth in the continous. In [8] J. Yao presented a path planning algorithm for mobile robots in unknown indoor environments that makes use of both global and local planning, using a combination of an improved version of A* with and the artificial potential field algorithm for local modifications. The resulting path is smooth and avoids obstacles in the continous space. In all these works however, there is no reasoning by the agent, the robot is simply a machine that moves following the path computed by the algorithm having a spatial destination as its final goal.

In the research branch on BDI agents, on the other hand, we find another survey by Ferrando et al. [9] exploring recent spatial reasoning techniques for BDI agents. In the approaches presented, agents reason about where they are, often discretizing, but still always deciding on individual movement directly by the agent. Some works reason directly about Cartesian coordinates, others about the four directions (front, behind, right, left), and others with structures borrowed from other areas of research (such as Entity-Relation diagrams). Of all the approaches, the most widely used is the Region Connection Calculus, which will be presented in Sect. 2 since our implementation also makes use of it.

Always in the BDI context the research about path planning is also active. Let us introduce a few examples. In [10] B. Shofer et al. presented a centralized approach to path planning with obstacle uncertainty in which the agent is able to re-plan the path in case it found out that the path is blocked. The agent in this case moves on a grid, reasoning discretly, and has a local knowledge of the environment.

M. O. Keskin et al. in [11] presented a decentralized multi-agent path finding framework and strategies based on automated negotiation. The framework tries to find a good trade-off between the single agent privacy and the effectiveness of the solutions creating a bilateral negotiation protocol. In the paper are presented two negotiation strategies. The problem is to try to manage multiple agents in the same environment that cannot lay on the same cell at the same time but all want to reach their goal. The main focus is on the collaboration between agents and not on the environment reasoning. The paper offers implementative examples of the strategies, also in this case in a grid environment.

In [12] A. Zanetti et al. presented an implementation of a BDI agent that is higly proactive and reactive capability during execution, giving the agent the main role in the decision making process. The simulation is performed in a robotic scenario that uses Robotic Operating System (ROS) as simulation software. The approach is based on temporal and spatial reasoning but also the agent is aware of the Cartesian coordinates of itself and of the other objects and does not abstract in any way, considering directly the coordinates.

Fitting within the work of VEsNA, presented at AREA in 2022 [13] (where the current challenge is to have a BDI agent interact with any virtual environment by exploring it and making use of state-of-the-art tools) this paper seeks a solution to the simpler problem of the vacuum cleaner robot. It takes into account the novelties on both simulation and robotics side, going to use state-of-the-art path planning tools in a continous environment, without limiting the robot's degrees of freedom making the agent reason on the regions to be explored using a logical agent. This makes the implementation furthermore explainable and transparent, as well as enhancing the programming paradigm. In this early work the agent has a comprehensive knowledge of the environment and where the dirt is. An exploratory version of the project is already in the works in which the agent starts without a map and has to create it from scratch.

The paper is structured as follows: Sect. 2 presents the design and implementation of our approach, detailing the environment and regions, the BDI agent, and the virtual environment. Section 3 discusses the results of our implementation, highlighting the successful separation of logical reasoning from coordinate management. Finally, Sect. 4 concludes the paper, summarizing our contributions and outlining future work directions, including plans for an exploratory version of the framework.

2 Design and Implementation

To implement an agent that reasons logically about regions and takes advantage of simulation software to do path finding, it is necessary to choose the most suitable tools. Since there is no embedded toolkit for implementing BDI agents on major game engines, it was necessary to separate the two components and create a connection between them. The first component handles the intelligent agent and the second handles the simulated body and environment. The framework must ensure an end-to-end connection between the BDI agent and its body. The architecture can be seen in Fig. 2.

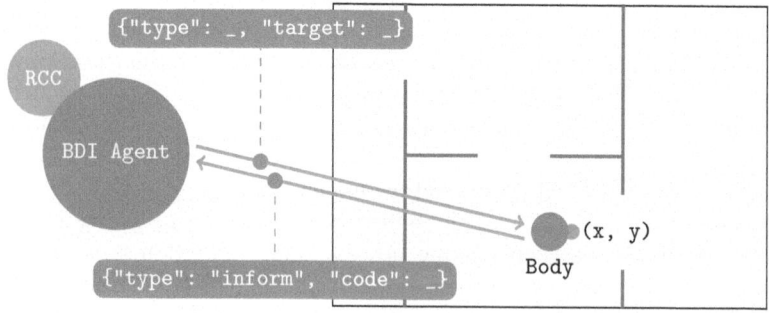

Fig. 2. The architecture of the system

The section is now subdivided into three subsections. Subsection 2.1 introduces some design fundamentals that needs to be shared by agent and environment, in particular it presents some basic concept about Region Connection

Calculus (RCC) and the chosen environment in which the simulation will take place, Subsect. 2.2 presents the design and implementation of the BDI agent, and Subsect. 2.3 follows the same path for the implemented virtual environment.

2.1 Environment and Regions

The environment and agent must properly implement the principles of Region Connection Calculus (RCC) introduced by D. A. Randell, Z. Cui and A. G. Cohn in [14]. In this paper, we will make use of RCC8 that provides some basic relationships between regions, as shown in Fig. 3. With these relationships it is possible to describe any environment qualitatively, abstracting from coordinates (x, y, z). The relations that turn out to be most used within this work are EC(A, B), PO(A, B) and NTPP(A, B), which are the essential relations to be able to find an object or a region inside an another region and know which regions touch with others in order to move between them.

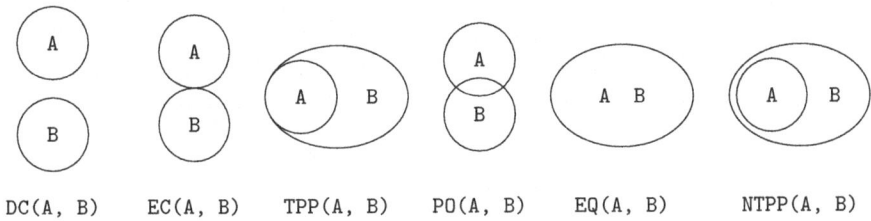

Fig. 3. RCC relations between regions: DC (A, B): disconnected; EC (A, B): externally connected; PO (A, B): partially overlaps; EQ (A, B): equal; TPP (A, B): tangential proper part; NTPP (A, B): non-tangential proper part.

The problem of robot vacuum cleaning is to remove all the dirt from the floor. The relation that carries this information is NTPP(dirt, Region) where Region is the region where the dirt is actually contained. We then decided to include another hierarchical concept to make the reasoning finer, adding the concept of room. Each region is then contained within a room with the relation NTPP(Region, Room). The rooms are then connected by doors. Doors are considered as regions that have intersection with both one room and the other (PO(door, Room1), PO(door, Room2)) but are not contained in either. Only the regions that are traversable by the robot are considered in this initial work without taking into account the objects in the room that are only handled by the simulation side of the framework for the time being. The regions within a room are all close but without overlapping, thus respecting the relation EC(Region1, Region2).

In order to give a proof of concept in an environment that was as verisimilar and nontrivial as possible, the study room of computer science PhD students at the University of Genoa was considered as a virtual environment. This environment can be seen in Fig. 4.

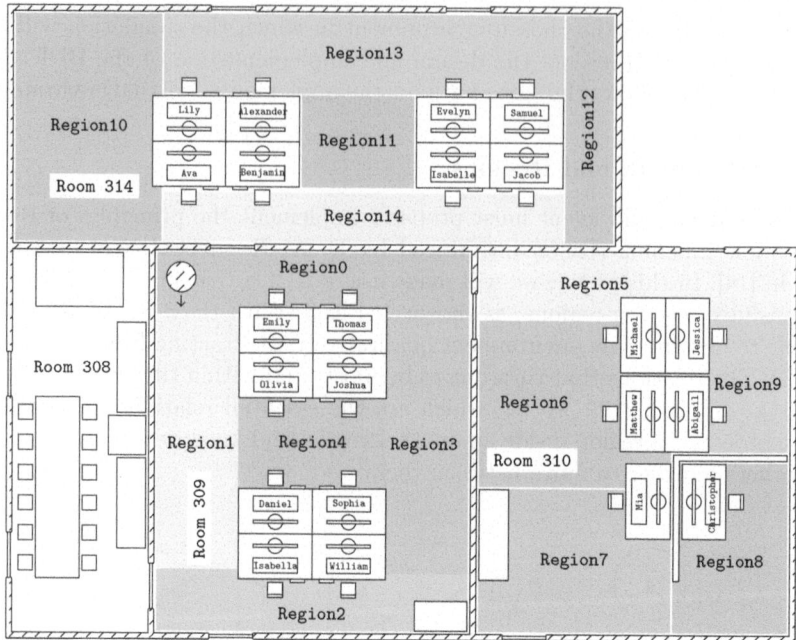

Fig. 4. The test environment

The study room is divided into 4 rooms, from left to right: the common room (not considered for the current implementation), room 309, room 310 and at the top room 314. There are workstations and cabinets in each of the rooms. They were divided into hard-coded regions based on the location of the desks, trying to find the right balance between the whole room and excessive granularity. These regions can be seen as corridors. Using the representation of a real environment makes the simulation nontrivial and verisimilar.

Regions for the moment are only areas in the environment while they are terms for the agent. Obviously, the relationships between regions considered by the agent must respect what is present in the environment and vice versa, and the agent must always have an understanding of the region it is in.

2.2 Agent: Design and Implementation

The agent is based on the BDI paradigm and knows the entire map through RCC. We want to avoid in any way that the agent has Cartesian cognition of the space it is in.

The agent aims to remove all the dirt in the room and has two plans for doing so:

1. *clean*: removes the dirt;
2. *reach*: a plan that tells the body which region it wants to reach among those adjacent to or contained in the one it is in.

The agent must know the logical map of the room as shown in Fig. 5 and updates the region it is in as it goes, always keeping the term as ground as possible (the smallest subregion occupied by the agent). Ultimately, the agent must be able to reason about the paths to be taken to reach its goal. To do this requires an additional plan to be interrogated to find a sequence of noncyclic adjacent regions from the current region to the desired one. The agent must then have a way to connect to its body to send requests and receive information.

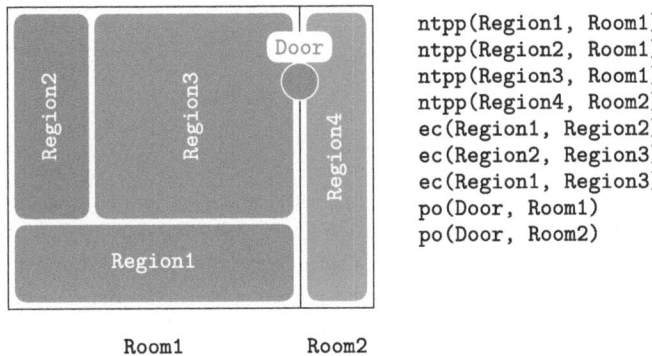

Fig. 5. A simple map with corresponding RCC8 representation.

The implementation was done using JaCaMo. JaCaMo [15,16] *"is a framework for Multi-Agent Programming that combines three separate technologies, each of them being well-known on its own and developed for a number of years so they are fairly robust and fully-fledged"* [17]. As a first step, the agent creates an artifact that establishes the connection with the physical body. An artifact is a Java class that the agent can use. The artifact then is owned by the agent, making this direct connection between agent and body without further intermediaries. The agent then executes the go_to_clean plan, which aims to remove all the dirt in the room. A plan in JaCaMo has this structure:

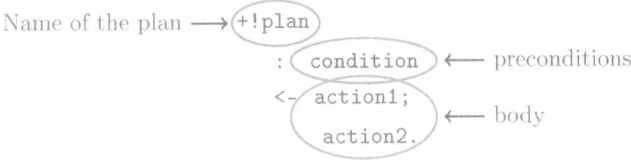

It has a name, a set of preconditions and a body. The body is executed sequentially but at each action the agent is able to change its mind if anything in the environment happened or some new knowledge is added. There can be multiple plans with the same name. In that case, the order matters and it is chosen the first plan that meets the preconditions.

The plan has three variants that are recursively referred to. The first has as preconditions that there is still at least one piece of dirt to be cleaned and that dirt is in the same region as the agent. In this case the agent must ask the body to reach the dirt subregion and once it reaches it, clean it. When it receives confirmation of the cleaning it removes that dirt from its beliefs and calls `go_to_clean` again.

```
+!go_to_clean
    :     ntpp(Dirt, Region) & my_region(Region) & dirt(Dirt)
    <-    move_to(Dirt);
          .wait({+gained});
          clean(Dirt);
          .wait({+cleaned});
          -ntpp(Dirt, Region);
          !go_to_clean.
```

The second, on the other hand, only knows that there is still dirt. If the agent uses this plan, it is because the dirt is not in the same region and therefore must move to the region where the dirt is contained. To do this, the agent has another plan `move_to` that allows it to reach the region where the dirt is.

```
+!go_to_clean
    :     ntpp(Dirt, Region) & dirt(Dirt)
    <-    !move_to(Region);
          !go_to_clean.
```

The `move_to` plan also has variations. In particular, it must take into account the room in which it is located; if in fact the target region is in another room, the agent must look for a door that will take it into it, reach it, and then once inside it find the path to the region in which the dirt is located or another door if necessary. If, on the other hand, it is in the same room, it must find and follow the sequence of regions that lead him to the desired one. The `move_to` plan, in addition to finding the path is also concerned with following it, that is, waiting until a message has arrived for each region from the body indicating that it has been reached before moving on to consider the next one with the `follow_path` plan.

```
+!move_to(region)
    :     my_region(CurrentRegion) &
          not sameroom(CurrentRegion, Region) &
          ntpp(Region, Room) & ec(Door, Room)
    <-    ?find_path(CurrentRegion, Door, Path);
          .reverse(Path, ReversePath);
          !follow_path(ReversePath);
          !move_to(Region).

+!move_to(Region)
    :     my_region(CurrentRegion)
    <-    ?find_path(CurrentRegion, Region, Path);
          .reverse(Path, ReversePath);
          !follow_path(ReversePath).
```

For the time being, no path search optimization logic is implemented but simply the agent searches for one that is walkable.

The third variant of the `go_to_clean` plan is the one that is called when there is no more dirt to clean. In this case the agent has reached its goal and can finish its task. This plan is needed because the other two always call recursively itself, this way the recursion ends.

Finally, the agent has a `clean` plan that allows it to remove dirt by communicating to its body to perform the action. This plan is called when the agent is on dirt and is the one that eliminates it. It has no preconditions, because indeed a robot vacuum cleaner can vacuum even where it is already clean, it is the `find_and_clean` plan that calls it at the right time.

Finally, communication with the environment is done within the Java artifact that implements a Websocket client and can send two types of messages:

- ''type'': "gain", "target": Target''type'': ''gain'', ''target'': Target: sent to reach a Target region;
- ''type'': "clean", "target": Target''type'': ''clean'', ''target'': Target: sent to clean the Target dirt.

2.3 Environment: Design and Implementation

The environment must represent the map presented in Fig. 4 with the due physical characteristics of the objects and walls and must handle agent displacement and dirt removal. The regions must be inserted into the scene in a physical way as invisible objects and not as abstract concepts: the robot must not reason about them, it must find path and realize it has reached the region, so they must be something the robot can virtually interact with. Note that regions also need to be inserted at doors that make it possible to pass from one room to another.

The environment was implemented with Godot. Godot is an open-source game development software that allows to place objects within a 3D virtual environment and attach scripts to some objects. The environment was built as visible in Fig. 6 respecting the features shown in Fig. 4. In this early implementation, regions have been implemented as `Marker3D`s and thus as individual points near which the agent must pass. They have the same name as logical regions. This choice was made in this preliminary version of the implementation for simplicity but will be modified in the future to actually implement a region. The points are located in the center of the region. The robot is implemented as `CharacterBody3D` and has a script attached that implements agent connection, movement, and dirt removal. Movement is allowed wherever the robot can pass, even under desks.

The `NavigationRegion3D` node was used to implement path finding. This type of node creates a map of walkable surfaces from the nodes it has as children. In our case the entire environment except the vacuum cleaner itself is instantiated as a child of this node, making everything walkable. The robot is then implemented using the `CharacterBody3D` as its main node with a `NavigationAgent3D` as its child that implements the robot's walk on the

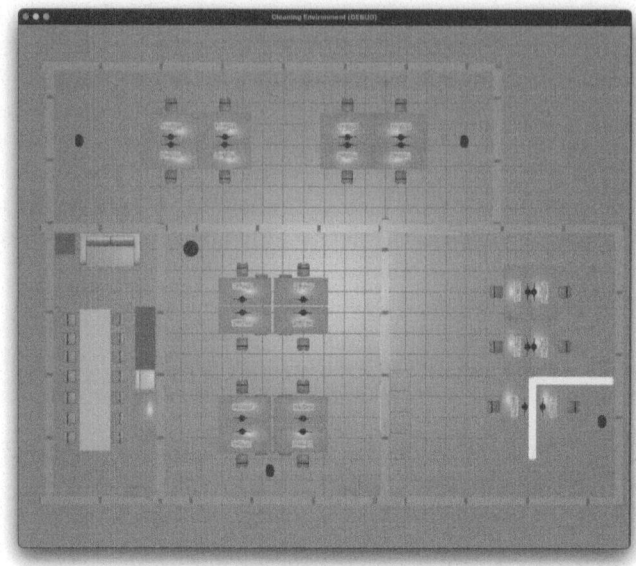

Fig. 6. The Godot environment

map given by the `NavigationRegion3D`. The algorithm that is used by the `NavigationAgent3D` to find the best path is a version of A* for a continous environment with steps of unfixed length.

The connection is implemented as a WebSocket Server directly within the script so again the robot communicates directly with its agent. This creates a end-to-end agent-robot correlation that is essential as we move from a single agent to having multiple agents and multiple robots in the same environment.

When the agent sends to the robot a message of type {"type": "gain", "target": "regionX"} the received region is entered as the target of `NavigatAgent3D`. It then calculates the shortest path to reach it and follows it step by step. The robot's degrees of rotation are not constrained in any way, nor is the length of the space it travels at each step. When it has reached the goal it sends a message {"type": "inform", "code": "gained"} to the agent informing it that it is ready to perform the next task, be it moving to another region or cleaning up. If the agent requests cleaning then the node depicting dirt from the robot is destroyed and a message {"type": "inform", "code": "cleaned"} is sent to the agent awaiting new instructions.

3 Results

In this section we briefly present the results obtained. The agent communicates correctly with the virtual robot and manages to complete its task completely. It is possible to see the operation of the framework in two videos, one in which the agent simply performs its task and one in which the debug mode is activated in which we can see the paths calculated by the robot.

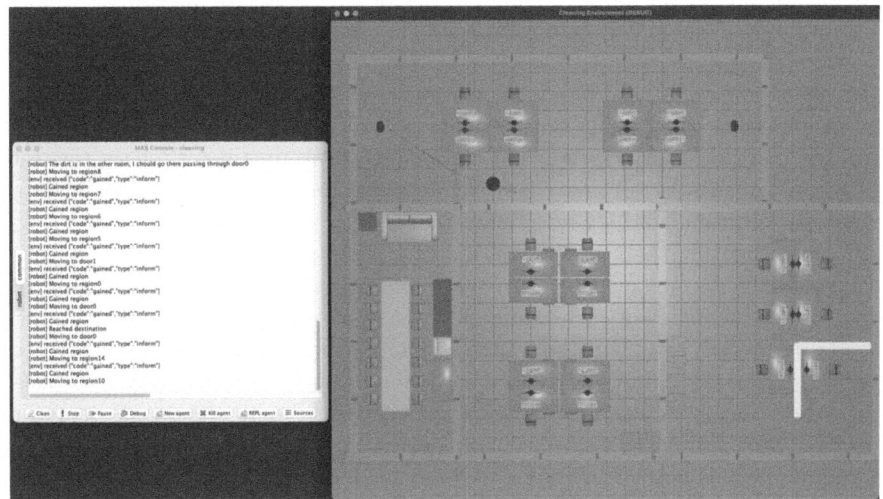

Fig. 7. The agent in action.

In the Fig. 7 you can see the framework in action with the debug path line. On the left is the JaCaMo window in which the agent is implemented while on the right is visible Godot and the robot in the room.

In the implementation we were able to completely separate the logical reasoning part from the management part. For the time being, however, the agent is still not looking for the best path but simply for a walkable path from one region to another. The results confirm that the robot in this way has full freedom of rotation by producing non-regular paths and that the ability to find paths in a continous environment is enhanced. The robot's path planning, in addition to the features already listed, also has the ability to adapt to any occlusions dynamically, recalculating the path in case something has moved without having to reason again logically on the goal.

This implementation is easily scalable from both the environment and multi-agent system perspectives. In fact, the region-based logic model makes it very easy to expand the environment both in width and depth (increasing the levels of subregions); we have already demonstrated the work of subregions by implementing rooms. The connection between agent and robot implemented end-to-end with a private artifact of the agent and a script of the robot also makes the multi-agent system scalable without the need for further major modifications.

The code used for this project is available on GitHub at the following link: https://github.com/driacats/VacuumCleaner.

4 Conclusions and Future Work

We presented a framework in which a BDI agent implemented in JaCaMo controls a robot vacuum cleaner simulated in Godot with a precise division of responsibilities, giving logical task management to the agent and physical management of movement and cleaning to the robot. Going through the key theoretical concepts, we showed how the environment must be studied and designed for this kind of approach, then going on to see the actual implementation of all components with JaCaMo and Godot. The implementation aims not to discretize the robot's movements by forcing them within some predetermined logical actions (like steps, rotations and low-level movements) but by choosing the actions logically, implementing them in the continous space.

The current implementation has many limitations, the two most important being the management of regions on the virtual environment side and the insertion of objects into the logical map. In Godot, the region should be implemented as an Area3D, looking for the nearest location without having to reach the center or a specific predetermined point. Agent side, the map should also contain objects. A new reswearch on how to implement them, if they are only regions or something more is needed, thinking of a scenario where they are most meaningful. Also, the agents may be interested in interacting with them.

Future work will therefore go in these directions. In addition to this, an exploratory version of the framework will be implemented in which the agent faces the challenge of cleaning without knowing the map at all and without knowing where the dirty areas are. The robot in Godot is already equipped with the tools needed for an exploratory version and the JaCaMo agent is already able to manage the messages containing sight information from the robot. The real challenge in this version will be to figure out how to subdivide the walkable regions, what are the criteria that make a region stand on its own or not.

References

1. Russell, S., Norvig, P.: Artificial Intelligence: A Modern Approach, 4th edn. Pearson (2020)
2. Godot Engine. https://godotengine.org/. Accessed 28 Sept 2024
3. Unity real-time development platform. https://unity.com/. Accessed 28 Sept 2024
4. Unreal Engine. https://www.unrealengine.com/. Accessed 28 Sept 2024
5. Karur, K., Sharma, N., Dharmatti, C., Siegel, J.E.: A survey of path planning algorithms for mobile robots. Vehicles (2021)
6. Psotka, M., Duchon, F., Mykhailyshyn, R., Tölgyessy, M., Dobis, M.: Global path planning method based on a modification of the wavefront algorithm for ground mobile robots. Robotics **12**(1), 25 (2023)
7. Bulut, V.: Path planning algorithm for mobile robots based on clustering-obstacles and Guintic trigonometric Bézier curve. Ann. Math. Artif. Intell. **92**(2), 235–256 (2024)
8. Yao, J.: Path planning algorithm of indoor mobile robot based on ROS system. In: 2023 IEEE International Conference on Image Processing and Computer Applications (ICIPCA), pp. 523–529 (2023)

9. Ferrando, A., Gatti, A., Mascardi, V.: Geometric and spatial reasoning in BDI agents: a survey. In: De Angelis, E., Proietti, M. (eds.) Proceedings of the 39th Italian Conference on Computational Logic (CEUR Workshop Proceedings), Rome, 26–28 June 2024, vol. 3733. CEUR-WS.org (2024)
10. Shofer, B., Shani, G., Stern, R.: Multi agent path finding under obstacle uncertainty. In Koenig, S., Stern, R., Vallati, M. (eds.) Proceedings of the Thirty-Third International Conference on Automated Planning and Scheduling, Prague, 8–13, 2023, pp. 402–410. AAAI Press (2023)
11. Keskin, M.O., Cantürk, F., Eran, C., Aydogan, R.: Decentralized multi-agent path finding framework and strategies based on automated negotiation. Auton. Agents Multi Agent Syst. **38**(1), 10 (2024)
12. Zanetti, A., Moro, D.D., Vreto, R., Robol, M., Roveri, M., Giorgini, P.: Implementing BDI continual temporal planning for robotic agents. In: IEEE International Conference on Web Intelligence and Intelligent Agent Technology, WI-IAT 2023, Venice, 26–29 October 2023, pp. 378–382. IEEE (2023)
13. Gatti, A., Mascardi, V.: Towards vesna, a framework for managing virtual environments via natural language agents. In: Cardoso, R.C., Ferrando, A., Papacchini, F., Askarpour, M., Dennis, L.A. (eds.) Proceedings of the Second Workshop on Agents and Robots for Reliable Engineered Autonomy, AREA@IJCAI-ECAI 2022, Vienna, 24th July 2022, vol. 362, pp. 65–80. EPTCS (2022)
14. Randell, D.A., Cui, Z., Cohn, A.G.: A spatial logic based on regions and connection. In: Nebel, B., Rich, C., Swartout, W.R. (eds.) Proceedings of the 3rd International Conference on Principles of Knowledge Representation and Reasoning (KR 1992), Cambridge, 25–29 October 1992, pp. 165–176. Morgan Kaufmann (1992)
15. Boissier, O., Bordini, R.H., Hübner, J.F., Ricci, A., Santi, A.: Multi-agent oriented programming with JaCaMo. Sci. Comput. Program. **78**(6), 747–761 (2013)
16. Boissier, O., Bordini, R.H., Hubner, J., Ricci, A.: Multi-agent Oriented Programming: Programming Multi-agent Systems Using JaCaMo. MIT Press (2020)
17. Jacamo. https://jacamo-lang.github.io/. Accessed 28 Sept 2024

Attentive A* for Visual Cue Based Path Planning in Complex Environments

Abhay Kumar, Kunal Verma, Armaan Garg(✉)[ID], and Shashi Shekhar Jha[ID]

Indian Institute of Technology Ropar, Rupnagar, Punjab, India
{2020eeb1144,2020eeb1182,armaan.19csz0002,shashi}@iitrpr.ac.in

Abstract. Navigating through complex environments has always been a big challenge for smart robots and AI agents. This paper focuses on a specific problem within the domain of path planning, aiming to aid agents in navigating through intricate environments using raw images as input. Data-driven path-planning algorithms have emerged as a cogent solution to such problems. These algorithms are a fusion of deep learning models for cost approximation, and differentiable versions of classical planning algorithms. While these methods excel at handling combinatorial data, their computational demands are high. These often leads to poor function approximation due to ineffective feature extraction in complex environments. Drawing from the significance of the attention mechanism in various deep learning applications, we present Attentive A*, introducing attention to data-driven path-planning algorithms. The proposed approach provides precise cost approximations by leveraging visual cues, resulting in enhanced performance across various metrics. A comprehensive assessment is conducted on diverse datasets, including MP, Tiled MP, CSM and Warcraft, to assess the effectiveness of the proposed approach compared to other baselines.

Keywords: Path Planning · Attention mechanism · Raw Images

1 Introduction

Path planning holds immense importance across various applications, from guiding autonomous vehicles through complex urban terrains [30] to facilitating navigation of spacecraft and space probes in extraterrestrial environments [23]. The problem of finding the optimal path between two points efficiently remains a crucial pursuit. There are various techniques for path planning, for example, reactive planning [5,19], where decisions are made based solely on the current sensory input without explicitly modeling the environment or considering future states. Sampling-based planning [25] works by sampling the configuration space of a system and constructing a graph and search-based planning that systematically explores the state-space to find optimal or near-optimal paths, utilizing popular algorithms like A* [14], Dijkstra [11], Greedy-best first search [18], etc. Search-based planning is a versatile approach that guarantees a solution if it exists.

A* search excels in finding the shortest path between points when provided with consistent and admissible heuristics. Dijkstra's algorithm, although potentially slower, guarantees optimality [28]. Considering the criteria of optimality and efficiency, A* emerges as a preferred solution for path-planning tasks.

Recently, there has been a growing interest in integrating deep-learning architectures with search-based planning algorithms [3,22,32]. These data-driven path-planning algorithms find optimal paths more efficiently than classical heuristics planners by leveraging deep learning architectures. These algorithms can be employed in real-world scenarios like planning on raw images, which is difficult for classical planners unless semantic pixel-wise cost labeling is provided. Manual semantic pixel-wise labeling is labor-intensive [17,24] and defeats the purpose of an autonomous system. However, the discrete nature of classical planners make it difficult to train a deep learning architecture since it involves non-differentiable operations. Thus, the development of backpropagation-ready algorithmic layers has been a topic of interest. For instance, in [2], the author enables end-to-end learning of the controller's cost and dynamics by differentiating through MPC using the KKT conditions, [1] introduced a network architecture that integrates optimization problems as layers, [6] leverages stochastically perturbed optimizers to make optimization procedures differentiable thus enabling end-to-end learning for machine learning pipelines involving discrete decisions, [22] introduces an approach that implements an efficient backward pass through black-box implementations of combinatorial solvers with linear objective functions, [31] introduces a maximum satisfiability solver to enable learning for deep learning architectures with discrete operations and [32] introduces a differentiable version of the A* algorithm.

Further, there have been notable advancements in the development of data-driven path-planning algorithms that enables planning of 2-D grid world and raw images, notably [29] proposes a differentiable approximation of the value-iteration algorithm represented as a convolution neural network, [19] reframes VINs as recurrent-convolutional networks, [16] introduces an approach to compute motion plans for complex robotic systems by learning a plannable latent representation, [22] enabled end-to-end training through combinatorial algorithms by applying black-box optimization to combinatorial solvers integrated with neural networks. [32] proposes an end-to-end trainable neural network planner by transforming A* into a differentiable model and combining it with a convolutional encoder. Some other data-driven planners are [3,8,26].

Previous studies typically employ a feature extraction stage followed by a planner module, which may or may not be differentiable. The purpose of feature extraction step is to estimate the movement cost, called guidance cost by leveraging visual information from raw image. Guidance cost is used instead of movement cost since movement cost are not explicitly available in case of raw images. While some prior works have utilized hand-crafted methods to compute guidance cost [8], recent advancements have seen the adoption of neural networks for this task [3,32]. The quality of guidance cost influences the optimality and efficiency of data-driven planners. Thus, it is empirical to employ methods that can generate high quality guidance costs. We conceptualize the generation of the guidance cost map from raw images as akin to a semantic segmentation task, since the goal is to generate improved input map representation in the form of guidance cost map. This involves assigning a cost to each region of the planner map indicating the relevancy of the region in searching the optimal path. Motivated by the success of attention mechanisms in improving the performance of deep learning models across various domains, this paper introduces Attentive A*, a novel data-driven search-based planner with an attention mechanism. The algorithm comprises an encoder module, which is a convolutional encoder with attention, and a solver module that utilizes a backpropagation-ready differentiable planner proposed in [32]. Extensive evaluations conducted on various datasets demonstrate that Attentive A* outperforms the state-of-the-art data-driven search-based planner [32], to the best of our knowledge.

2 Preliminaries

The input image is visualized as a graph with eight-grid world setting [22], where each node has at most 8 neighbors. Each pixel of the image is seen as a node of the graph and nodes are arranged in a grid-like pattern. Considering a graph $G = (V, E)$, where V is the set of vertices and E is the set of edges connecting the nodes. Let $(v_i, v_j) \in E$ be an edge between $v_i, v_j \in V$, then $\forall \ (v_i, v_j) \ \exists \ C(v_i, v_j) \in \mathbb{R}_+$. Let $N(v)$ be the set of neighbors of a vertex $v \in V$, then $N(v)$ is defined as, $N(v) = \{v' \mid (v, v') \in E, \text{ where } v \neq v'\}$. Let $v_s \in V$ be the start node and $v_g \in V$ be the end node, then the aim of a path-planning algorithm is to find the shortest path, S where, $S = \{v_i \mid v_i \in V \text{ and } (v_{i-1}, v_i) \in E\}$ constrained to,

$$\min(\sum_{i=0}^{n-1} C(v_i, v_{i+1})), \quad v_i, v_{i+1} \in S \quad (1)$$

where $v_0 = v_s$ and $v_n = v_g, n \in \mathbb{N}$.

Each node is connected to its surrounding nodes by an edge, where edge cost is

$$C(v_i, v_j) = \begin{cases} 1, & \text{if passable node} \\ \infty, & \text{if obstacle node} \end{cases} \quad (2)$$

where $v_j \in N(v_i)$.

2.1 A* Search

A* search algorithm finds the shortest path, S, by minimizing the total cost, which consists of the actual cost, $g(v)$, and heuristic cost, $h(v)$. Here, $g(v)$ is the actual cost from v_s to v, and $h(v)$ is the heuristic cost from v to v_g. This algorithm can be divided into three major steps:

Algorithm 1. Differentiable A* Algorithm [32]

Input: Y, Ω, H
Output: $\mathbf{T}, S$
1: Initialize $\mathbf{F} \leftarrow \mathbf{F} + V_s$, $\mathbf{T}$ with all values zero, G with all values as maximum and $G = G \circ (\mathbf{1} - V_s)$
2: **while** True **do**
3:    Choose V^* with least $G + H$ according to equation 6
4:    **if** $V^* == V_g$ **then**
5:      **break**
6:    **end if**
7:    Update $\mathbf{F}$ and $\mathbf{T}$ according to equation 8,9 respectively
8:    Find $\mathbf{N}(V^*)$ using equation 7
9:    **for** V in $\mathbf{N}(V^*)$ **do**
10:      Relax the edge (V^*, V) using equation 10
11:      Update G using equation 11
12:    **end for**
13: **end while**

- **Selecting the most appropriate node**: The next node is selected from F(open list containing all the candidate nodes), which is initialized with v_s (start node). This choice is based on the following equation:

$$v^* = \arg\min_{v \in F} \{g(v) + h(v)\} \qquad (3)$$

- **Exploring the neighborhood**: All the neighbors of the selected node v^* are explored, and v^* is pushed to T (closed list containing all the visited nodes). The closed list T acts as the search history of the algorithm. The following condition is used while expanding the neighborhood nodes of the selected node v^*:

$$V_{\text{nb}} = \{v' \mid v' \in N(v^*) \text{ and } v' \notin T\} \qquad (4)$$

Then, the elements of the set V_{nb} are added to F to update the candidate nodes for the next step.

- **Updating the nodes' cost**: The cost of each neighborhood node, $v' \in N(v^*)$, is updated with respect to the parent node v^* using the following relation:

$$g(v) = \min(g(v'), g(v^*) + c(v^*, v')) \qquad (5)$$

These steps are followed iteratively until $v^* = v_g$ (terminating condition).

2.2 Differentiable A*

In this subsection we discuss the Differentiable A* approach, as given by Algorithm 1 [32]. The input to the algorithm is a 2D Grid World Map/Raw Image I. X is the 8-grid world graph of the normalized input I. V_s, V_g, V^* are the one-hot indicator matrices of v_s, v_g, v^* respectively, such that $\langle V_g, \mathbf{1} \rangle = \langle V_s, \mathbf{1} \rangle = \langle V^*, \mathbf{1} \rangle = 1$, where $\langle A, B \rangle$ denotes the inner product of A and B and $\mathbf{1}$ is an all-ones matrix. Problem instance, $Y = (X, V_s, V_g)$, consists of the input graph X conditioned by start node V_s and end node V_g. Y is fed to the encoder module to generate the guidance cost map, Ω, which is the matrix version of one step guidance cost $\phi(v)$. G & H are the matrix versions of $g(v)$ and $h(v)$ respectively. Instead of accumulating the original movement cost which is not always available, here $g(v)$ represents total guidance cost for the actual path taken. $\mathbf{F}$ and $\mathbf{T}$ are matrix versions of open list F, and closed list T.

In contrast to the A* algorithm, the selection of the node is based on the following relation [9, 32]:

$$\mathbf{V}^* = \mathcal{K}_{max}\left(\frac{exp(-(G+H)/\tau) \circ \mathbf{F}}{\langle exp(-(G+H)/\tau), \mathbf{F}\rangle}\right) \tag{6}$$

where τ is a hyperparameter denoting the fraction of the input map to be explored, $A \circ B$ is the element-wise product of A and B.

The neighbors are explored by convolving a 3 X 3 filter, $D = [[111]^T [101]^T [111]^T]$, [29]. This follows the relation:

$$\mathbf{N}(\mathbf{V}^*) = \begin{cases} (\mathbf{V}^* * D)) \circ X \circ (1 - \mathbf{T}), & \text{if } X \text{ is a 2D grid map} \\ (\mathbf{V}^* * D) \circ (1 - \mathbf{T}), & \text{if } X \text{ is a raw image} \end{cases} \tag{7}$$

where $\mathbf{N}(\mathbf{V}^*)$ is the matrix version of $N(v^*)$(refer to line 8 of Algorithm 1). To update the open list, the following equation is used,

$$\mathbf{F} \leftarrow \mathbf{F} + \mathbf{N}(V^*) \tag{8}$$

and for updating the closed list, this equation is followed,

$$\mathbf{T} \leftarrow \mathbf{T} + V^* \tag{9}$$

For every $V \in \mathbf{N}(V^*)$, its total cost, G, is updated by G' using the following relation:

$$G' = \langle G, V^* \rangle \cdot \mathbf{1} + \Omega \tag{10}$$

$$G = \min(G, G') \cdot \mathbf{N}(V^*) + G \cdot (1 - \mathbf{N}(V^*)) \tag{11}$$

The algorithm strives to find the shortest path, $\mathbf{S}$, constrained to,

$$\min(\langle \mathbf{S}, \Omega \rangle) \tag{12}$$

where $\mathbf{S}$ is the one-hot encoded matrix representation of S.

3   Attentive A*

This section introduces Attentive A*, an attention based data-drive path planning algorithm on 2D Grid Map/raw image. Attentive A* has two major

Algorithm 2. Attentive A*

Input: Y (Problem Instance), H (Heuristic)
Output: Nodes explored, **T**, and Solution path, **S**
Encoder Module:
1: Feature Map $F^e \leftarrow$ Unet_Encoder(Y)
2: $F^e = \{F_1^e, F_2^e, \ldots, F_k^e, \ldots, F_t^e\}$, where F_k^e is kth encoder block output
3: Skip Connections: $S^f = F^e$
4: UNet Bottleneck: $F_0^d \leftarrow$ Bottleneck(F_t^e)
5: **for** k^{th} block in the UNet Decoder **do**
6: $\quad F_{k-1}^d \leftarrow F_{k-1}^d + S_{d-k}^f$
7: $\quad F_k^d \leftarrow$ DecoderBlock(F_{k-1}^d)
8: $\quad$ SCSE mechanism: $F_k^d \leftarrow F_{cSE}(F_k^d) + F_{sSE}(F_k^d)$
9: **end for**
10: Ω, Guidance Map $\leftarrow$ OutputLayer(F_k^d)
11: $\Omega \leftarrow$ interpolation(Ω) as discussed in 3.1
Solver Module:
1: **T, S** $\leftarrow$ Differentiable_A*(Y, Ω, H), as given in Algorithm 1

modules : a) Encoder Module, which learns the input representations, and b) Solver Module, which is the differentiable version of A* search algorithm, as proposed by [32]. Our proposed approach is an end-to-end trainable path-planning algorithm that improves semantic labelling using attention thereby improving the overall performance of the planner.

3.1 Input Representation

We follow the representations as described in Sect. 2. Let the output of the encoder be $E(Y) = \Omega$, with dimensions $n \times m$ same as that of I, we reformulate $E(Y)$ to $E'(Y)$ with dimensions $n' \times m'$ using interpolation. Here, $n' = n/g_1$ and $m' = m/g_2$, thus transforming $E(Y)$ into a grid $E'(Y)$ with cells of dimension $g_1 \times g_2$. V_s and V_g are transformed accordingly. This step ensures efficiency and noise reduction in case of large input dimensions. For further discussion $E'(Y)$ will be treated same as Ω.

3.2 Encoder Module

In this algorithm we find the path, S in accordance to Eq. 12. This condition implies that the semantic labelling, $E(Y)$ directly impacts the accuracy of our approach. The challenge is to be able to distinguish between different regions of I. The encoder module should be able to allocate costs to each region of I according to its degree of passability, thus making it necessary to capture visual cues from the input. We employ an autoencoder based architecture called U-net [27] in our

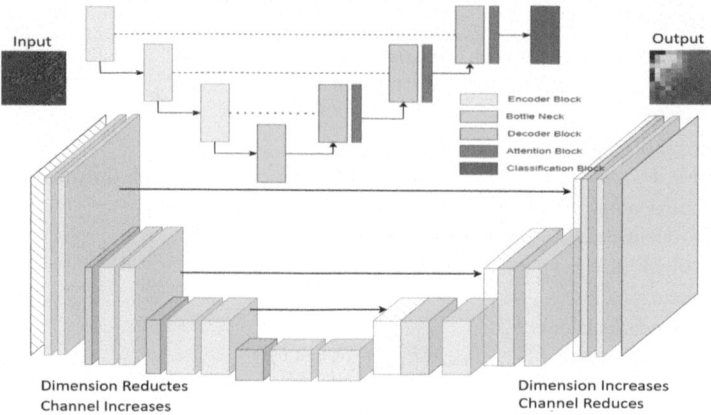

Fig. 1. Architecture of the Encoder Module representing the position of SCSE attention module in the decoder branch of U-Net.

encoder module. U-Net is a widely adopted framework for image segmentation, which comprises of an encoder, a bottleneck, a decoder, and skip connections. The encoder maps the input into a higher-level latent encoding space, and the decoder recovers the original feature space from the encoding space [20]. The encoder down-samples the input while increasing the channels and pass it to the bottleneck layer which up-samples the input. The decoder layer receives input from bottleneck layer and encoder, via skip-connections, and up-samples it to match the input dimensions (refer to Algorithm 2).

The inherent loss of spatial information in the encoder necessities a strategic enhancement to preserve both spatial details and channel information in U-Net. This compressed representation form the encoder is rich in contextual details but lacks spatial information. The challenge lies in reconstructing the spatial information while maintaining important contextual information by emphasizing on the relevant features through the decoder. We introduce the use of the attention mechanism [4] in the U-Net architecture, with VGG - 19 as its backbone, which is shown in Fig. 1. We adopted VGG-19 as the backbone owing to its efficient feature extraction approach. It contains 16 convolutional layers and 3 fully connected layers. The attention mechanism allows the addition of an additional layer of refinement in feature selection and provides the ability to dynamically focus on salient regions while suppressing less critical areas. To leverage the attention mechanism, we employed the Spatial and Channel Squeeze and Excitation Block (SCSE) framework as introduced by [13]. This framework incorporates two key components: the Spatial Squeeze and Channel Excitation (cSE) block, along with the Channel Squeeze and Spatial Excitation (sSE) block. The cSE block dynamically recalibrates channel importance, allowing the model to emphasize essential channels and disregard less informative ones. Let $Z \in \mathbb{R}^{H \times W \times C}$ be the input to the cSE block then each channel of Z will be recalibrated as follows [15]:

$$p_k = \frac{1}{H \times W} \sum_{i=1}^{H} \sum_{j=1}^{W} z_k(i,j) \qquad (13)$$

$P \in \mathbb{R}^{1 \times 1 \times C}$ is a vector of spatially squeezed channels via global average pooling. P undergoes series of transformations leading to its modified representation denoted as $\hat{P}$. After passing $\hat{P}$ through a Sigmoid activation, the resulting output is used to adjust the weights of the channels in input Z.

$$\hat{Z} = [\sigma(\hat{p_k})z_1, \sigma(\hat{p_k})z_2, \sigma(\hat{p_k})z_3, ..., \sigma(\hat{p_k})z_C] \qquad (14)$$

On the other hand, the sSE block recalibrates each spatial location based on its global importance, addressing the need for fine-grained image segmentation. Let $Z \in \mathbb{R}^{H \times W \times C}$ be the input to the sSE block. Calculate $l \in \mathbb{R}^{H \times W}$ by multiplying Z with $W_{sq} \in \mathbb{R}^{1 \times 1 \times C}$, where each element combines representations of all channels at a specific location [13]:

$$l = W_{sq} \times Z \qquad (15)$$

The l vector undergoes a Sigmoid activation to enhance the spatial features of Z. This enables the model to assign greater importance to pertinent spatial locations.

$$\hat{Z} = [\sigma(g_{1,1})z^{1,1}, ..., \sigma(g_{i,j})z^{i,j}, ..., \sigma(g_{H,W})x^{H,W}] \qquad (16)$$

To optimize the U-Net architecture, we strategically apply SCSE attention to the decoder block (refer to line 8 of Algorithm 2), which can be seen in Fig. 1. The cSE component enhances the relevance of extracted features, while the sSE component improves spatial information reconstruction. This dual-attention approach effectively boosts the model's performance, resulting in an effective segmentation accuracy and fine-grained spatial understanding. The collaboration of VGG-19 and the attention mechanism contributes to an improved semantic cell-level cost labelling. This approach refines segmentation outcomes, yielding better-defined object boundaries and improved cell-level accuracy.

3.3 Solver Module

We use differentiable A*, as discussed in Sect. 2.2, for implementing the solver module. This module takes input $E'(Y)$ from encoder module. Guidance map, $E'(Y)$, serves the purpose of movement cost in the differentiable A*. This eliminates the need of explicit movement cost maps in case of any image. The heuristic used in this module is Chebyshev Distance, which is used in Eq. 12 for node selection. The output of the algorithm is the closed list T, which serves as the search history of the solver module.

3.4 Loss Function

The purpose of making the classical planner differentiable is served in connecting the encoder module to the loss function through the guidance map. Let $\hat{S}$ be the one-hot encoded ground-truth path then, mean $L1$ loss is calculated between T and $\hat{S}$, ground-truth path map which is a binary matrix. It is calculated according to the following equation:

$$L = \frac{\|T - \hat{S}\|_1}{|V|}$$

This loss is used to update the parameters of encoder module. In the ideal case, both $\hat{S}$ and T will be equivalent, meaning that planner selects only the relevant nodes. Thus, this loss ensures that the planner selects nodes in $\hat{S}$ only and does not selects nodes that are not in $\hat{S}$. For enabling mini-batch training we use the method as described in [32].

4 Datasets

Attentive A* is evaluated on various datasets evaluating different aspects. We use 2d-grid map datasets, MP [7], Tiled MP [32] and CSM [21], to evaluate the optimality of Attentive A* algorithm. We evaluate Attentive A* on Warcraft Dataset [22] to demonstrate the robustness of the proposed approach on complex raw data. Through these datasets we demonstrate that Attentive A* produce precise guidance cost maps. The details of the datasets used are provided below.

- **Motion Planning (MP) Dataset:** This dataset is a collection of eight types of grid-world environments, each having unique obstacle shapes and complexity, created by [7]. Each environment group has 1000 samples of dimension 32×32. All the images in the dataset are binary images. Although the obstacles in each group maintain the same shape, they are placed in different arrangements, orientations, and complexity.
- **Tiled MP Dataset:** This dataset is an extension of the MP dataset, created by [32]. Each map in this dataset is a blend of four maps from the MP dataset chosen randomly. It contains 4000 samples, each with a dimension of 64×64. This dataset contains more complex and diverse obstacles.
- **City/Street Map (CSM) Dataset:** This dataset is a compilation of thirty city maps in a binary image format organized and annotated by [21]. Random patches of size 128×128 are sampled from original maps and resized to 64×64 as in [32]. This dataset contains 4000 samples, each with a dimension of 64×64.
- **Warcraft Dataset:** The Warcraft dataset, created by [22], is used for path planning on raw images formatted in RGB. Within this dataset, the images depict distinct terrains such as rocks, water bodies, trees, grass, and plain ground. Each node within the maps corresponds to a specific segment of these terrains. The model's primary objective is identifying the optimal path from

the initial start node to the designated goal node across these varied terrains. The dataset has 12000 samples, each with a map resolution of 96 × 96 and a grid shape of 12 × 12.

Ground truth data for MP, Tiled MP, and CSM dataset is generated using Dijkstra's Algorithm, while manual annotation is conducted for the Warcraft dataset. In the first three datasets, the start and goal nodes are generated randomly [32]. Whereas, in the Warcraft dataset, the starting node consistently corresponded to the top-left corner of the map, while the goal node consistently represented the bottom-right corner [12].

5 Experimentation and Results

The train-val-test split used for the MP and Tiled MP data-sets is 80:10:10, whereas, for the CSM data-set, the training and validation set consists of the first 20 maps, and the training set consists of the rest of the samples. The U-Net architecture used for each of the model was initialized with the weights pretrained on ImageNet data-set [10]. The major reasons for using transfer learning are:

- It helps in mitigating the problem of small dataset by providing an efficient starting point, enhancing the network to recognize relevant spatial features and visual cues crucial for effective path planning
- The model converges faster and requires fewer samples for fine-tuning in specific path planning tasks.

During the training process, the models are trained on the datasets with the following parametric configurations. The algorithm is trained on all the datasets with a mini batch size of 100 and learning rate of 0.001. The MP dataset is trained for 100 epochs, and the MP tiled and CSM datasets is trained for 400 epochs. The models were trained on the Warcraft dataset for 78 epochs. The tie-breaking is handled using Euclidean distance. The evaluation criteria includes the following metrics:

- **Reduction ratio of node explorations (P_Exp)**, indicating the percentage of search steps minimized by the model in comparison to standard A* search. It shows how fast the algorithm converges to find the optimal solution [32]. This can be calculated as follows:

$$P\_Exp = \max\left(\frac{U - U*}{U*}, 0\right) \qquad (17)$$

where $U*$ is the nodes explored by normal A* and U is the nodes explored by any other planner.
- **Path optimality ratio (P_Opt)**, depicting the model's ability to predict the shortest paths across various environmental maps. This is indicative of the optimality of the algorithm [22].

Table 1. Performance Metrics of NA*16, NA*19 and Attentive A*(Att A*) on all MP Datasets and Tiled MP Datasets.

Dataset Abbreviations	H_mean			P_Opt			P_Exp		
	NA*16	NA*19	Att A*	NA*16	NA*19	Att A*	NA*16	NA*19	Att A*
MP(A)	0.5854	0.5534	**0.5888**	0.98	0.94	0.92	0.4173	0.3921	**0.4329**
MP(B)	0.5439	0.6007	**0.6119**	0.92	0.93	**0.99**	0.3861	0.4436	0.4428
MP(C)	0.4117	0.4656	**0.4985**	0.81	0.85	0.81	0.2760	0.3206	**0.3600**
MP(D)	0.4827	0.4374	**0.5128**	0.89	0.82	0.87	0.3312	0.2983	**0.3635**
MP(E)	0.5582	0.5744	**0.6155**	0.86	0.93	0.91	0.4132	0.4156	**0.4650**
MP(F)	0.4706	0.4859	**0.5434**	0.82	0.85	**0.87**	0.3300	0.3402	**0.3951**
MP(G)	0.5987	0.5746	**0.6688**	0.91	0.88	**0.99**	0.4461	0.4266	**0.5050**
MP(H)	0.3539	0.3539	**0.3582**	0.91	0.91	0.87	0.2196	0.2196	**0.2255**
TiledMP(A)	0.5553	0.5483	**0.5761**	0.75	0.725	0.725	0.4419	0.4411	**0.4774**

- **The Harmonic mean (H_mean) of P_Exp and P_Opt**, showcases how well a model strikes a balance between these two contrasting objectives. It provides an indication of the model's overall performance in achieving both optimal path prediction and efficient exploration within the problem space. Achieving a higher Harmonic Mean indicates an effective trade-off between accuracy and efficiency in solving the given problem.
- **Chamfer Distance**, is used to calculate the distance between two set of points. It is used to evaluate the performance of different baselines on Warcraft dataset. We use this metric because the ground truth for this dataset is manually annotated and thus the previous metrics cannot be used to evaluate this dataset. Along with that training loss, validation loss is also used.

Table 2. Dataset abbreviations and their names

Dataset Abbreviations	Dataset Name
MP(A)	maze_032_moore_c8
MP(B)	alternating_gaps_032_moore_c8
MP(C)	bugtrap_forest_032_moore_c8
MP(D)	forest_032_moore_c8
MP(E)	gaps_and_forest_032_moore_c8
MP(F)	multiple_bugtraps_032_moore_c8
MP(G)	shifting_gaps_032_moore_c8
MP(H)	single_bugtrap_032_moore_c8
TiledMP(A)	all_064_moore_c16

Table 3. Performance Metrics on CSM Dataset

Name of the Model	H_Mean	P_Opt	P_Exp
NA*16	0.4444	0.7525	0.3155
NA*19	0.4568	**0.7875**	0.3238
Attentive A*	**0.4787**	0.7724	**0.3511**

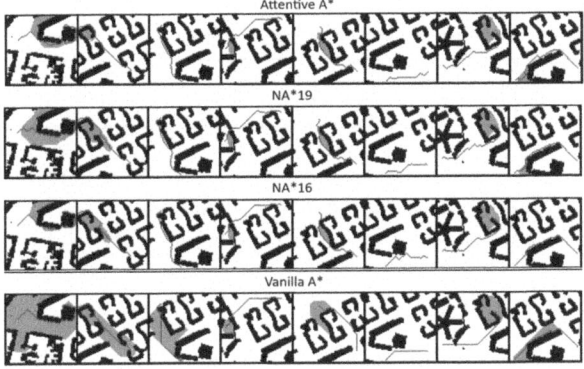

Fig. 2. This figure shows the performance of a) Attentive A*, b) NA*19, c) NA*16, d) Classical A* on a batch of 8 images from CSM Dataset. Black pixels represent the obstacles, predicted path is annotated in red, and explored nodes are annotated in green. (Color figure online)

5.1 Baselines

To evaluate the significance of Attentive A* in search-based planning, we compared it against other data-driven search-based planners. These baseline competitors were implemented by extending the authors' existing implementations. We compared Attentive A* against the following baselines:

- **NA*16** [32]: A data-driven search based path planning algorithm called Neural A*. It is the state of the art (to the best of our knowledge) in the field of data driven path-planning. It uses U-net encoder with VGG-16 as its backbone.
- **NA*19:** We used another baseline as one of the variant of Neural A* search using VGG-19 as the backbone of the encoder architecture. This is done to show the effectiveness of the attention mechanism in the encoder architecture.

5.2 Results

The results in Table 1 (Table 2 provides the dataset name to the abbreviations used in Table 1) and Table 3 compares the performance among the baselines and Attentive A* on MP - Tiled MP dataset and CSM dataset respectively.

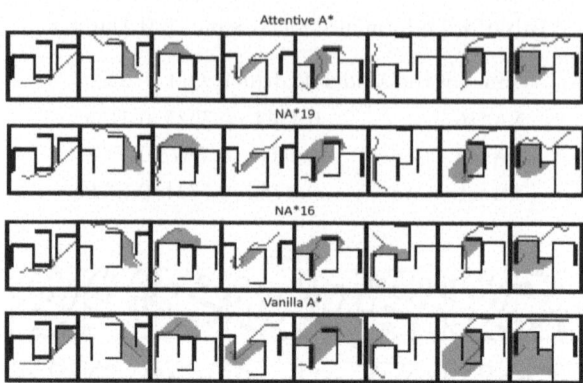

Fig. 3. The figure shows performance of a) Attentive A*, b) NA*19, c) NA*16, and d) Classical A*, from top to bottom on a batch of 8 images from the MP Dataset. Black pixels represent the obstacles, predicted path is annotated on red, and explored nodes are annotated in green. (Color figure online)

Attentive A* outperforms NA*16 and NA*19 in terms of both H-mean and P-Exp in all the groups of the said datasets proving the efficacy of our approach. It can be observed in Table 1 and Table 3 that Attentive A* shows significant improvement in P-Exp implying that the number of nodes explored for finding the optimal path reduced significantly, thus improving the efficiency. While P-Opt remains comparable to other baselines. In Table 1 we observe that Attentive A* reaches near perfect P-Opt score on alternating_gaps_032 moore and shifting gaps 032 moore indicating consistency of the algorithm. Figure 3 visualize search results on samples from the MP and tiled-MP dataset. It can be observed that in Fig. 3 a) the region explored to find the optimal path in small compared to other approaches.

Figure 2 visualizes search results on samples from the CSM dataset which is much more complex as compared to MP dataset. It can be observed that in Fig. 2 a) the region explored to find the optimal path is small compared to other approaches and the paths predicted are subtly straightforward. The experimental findings demonstrate an average enhancement of 9.19% in H_mean when utilizing Attentive A* compared to NA*16, along with a 7.89% improvement over NA*19, across both MP and Tiled MP datasets. Similarly, for the CSM Dataset, there is a 7.71% increase in H_mean with Attentive A* compared to NA*16, and a 4.79% enhancement over NA*19.

Table 4 compares the baseline results with Attentive A* on Warcraft dataset in terms of training loss, validation loss and Chamfer distance. It can be observed that Attentive A* outperforms other baselines in terms Chamfer Distance and training loss. Moreover, it demonstrates comparable results in terms of validation loss. Figure 4 shows the visual results of NA*16, Fig. 5 shows the visual results of NA*19, Fig. 6 shows the visual results of Attentive A* on Warcraft Dataset. Each of the algorithm is evaluated on a set of 10 examples. In Fig. 4(a), NA*16

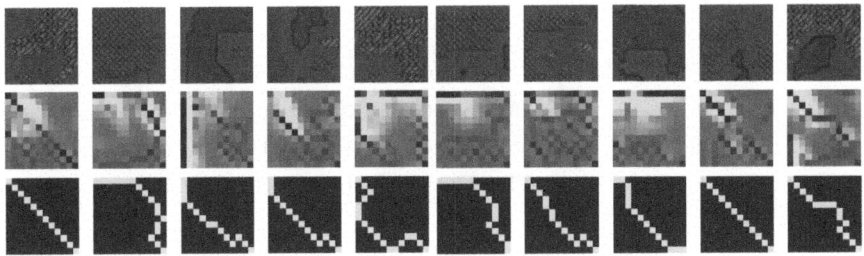

Fig. 4. The performance of NA*16 on the Warcraft dataset is presented: the first row includes the input images, the second row consists of the guidance maps of those input images, and the third row displays the predicted paths associated with those images. The figure shows performance on ten examples, denoted as (a), (b), (c), (d), (e), (f), (g), (h), (i), (j) (from left to right).

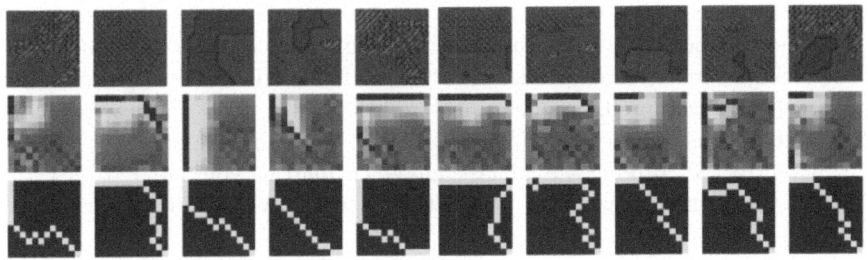

Fig. 5. The performance of NA*19 on the Warcraft dataset is presented: the first row includes the input images, the second row consists of the guidance maps of those input images, and the third row displays the predicted paths associated with those images. The figure shows performance on ten examples, denoted as (a), (b), (c), (d), (e), (f), (g), (h), (i), (j) (from left to right).

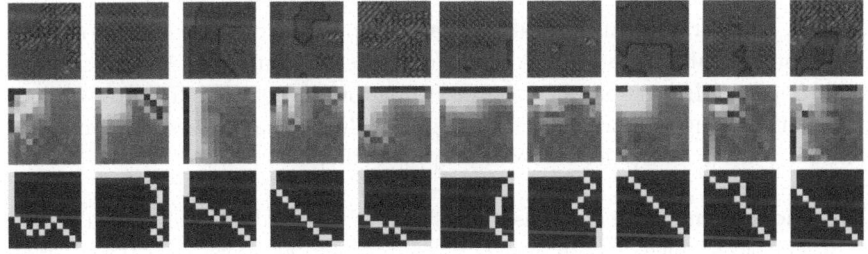

Fig. 6. The performance of Attentive A* with attention on the Warcraft dataset is presented: the first row includes the input images, the second row consists of the guidance maps of those input images, and the third row displays the predicted paths associated with those images. The figure shows performance on ten examples, denoted as (a), (b), (c), (d), (e), (f), (g), (h), (i), (j) (from left to right).

Table 4. Performance Metrics on Warcraft Dataset

Name of the Model	train_loss	val_loss	Chamfer Distance
NA*16	0.002569	0.038535	20.929 (2.828, 50.917)
NA*19	0.004792	0.024458	31.783 (0.0, 147.715)
Attentive A*	**0.001667**	0.024632	**18.469 (0.0, 45.541)**

predicts the path that intersects the rocks, which is not an optimal route. While, in Fig. 6(a), Attentive A* predicts the path to skirt along the boundary of the rocks rather than crossing them. This is because the guidance cost map produced in case of Attentive A*, in Fig. 6(a), assigns high cost to the rock region as compared to the guidance cost produced in case of NA*16, Fig. 4(a).

A similar trend is observed in Fig. 4(f) and in Fig. 6(f). From Fig. 6(j) and Fig. 5(j) we can compare the results between Attentive A* and NA*19. In Fig. 6 (j), planner predicts a path through low cost regions (such as water bodies and grass) owing to precision of Attentive A* in producing guidance maps. Whereas in Fig. 5(j) the path predicted passes through high cost regions (such as rocks) due to sub-optimal of guidance maps by NA*19. From these figures it is evident that Attentive A* produces a precise guidance map as compared to NA*19. These results demonstrates the proficiency of Attentive A* in capturing the visual cues from raw images.

6 Conclusion

This paper advances data-driven path planning techniques through an improved path-planning algorithm, Attentive A*. The empirical results highlight an overall improved performance clearly demonstrating the effectiveness of attention mechanism for visual path planning. The integration of attention mechanism enhances encoder robustness and accuracy, improving guidance and cost map generation. Notably, the study's shift from the conventional A* search algorithm to a data-driven approach signifies superior efficacy. The future work may involve integrating reinforcement learning, handling dynamic environments, and addressing uncertainties for real-world applicability.

Acknowledgments. The work has been partially supported by the National Science and Technology Council, Taiwan NSC-112-2927-I-194-001 and NSC-111-2927-I-194-001 along with SERB grant CRG/2023/002142.

References

1. Amos, B., Kolter, J.Z.: Optnet: differentiable optimization as a layer in neural networks. CoRR abs/1703.00443 (2017). http://arxiv.org/abs/1703.00443
2. Amos, B., Rodriguez, I.D.J., Sacks, J., Boots, B., Kolter, J.Z.: Differentiable MPC for end-to-end planning and control. CoRR abs/1810.13400 (2018). http://arxiv.org/abs/1810.13400

3. Archetti, A., Cannici, M., Matteucci, M.: Neural weighted a*: Learning graph costs and heuristics with differentiable anytime A. CoRR abs/2105.01480 (2021). https://arxiv.org/abs/2105.01480
4. Bahdanau, D., Cho, K., Bengio, Y.: Neural machine translation by jointly learning to align and translate. ArXiv **1409**, September 2014
5. Belkhouche, F.: Reactive path planning in a dynamic environment. IEEE Trans. Rob. **25**(4), 902–911 (2009). https://doi.org/10.1109/TRO.2009.2022441
6. Berthet, Q., Blondel, M., Teboul, O., Cuturi, M., Vert, J., Bach, F.R.: Learning with differentiable perturbed optimizers. CoRR abs/2002.08676 (2020). https://arxiv.org/abs/2002.08676
7. Bhardwaj, M., Choudhury, S., Scherer, S.: Learning heuristic search via imitation, October 2017
8. Choudhury, S., Bhardwaj, M., Arora, S., Kapoor, A., Ranade, G., Scherer, S.A., Dey, D.: Data-driven planning via imitation learning. CoRR abs/1711.06391 (2017). http://arxiv.org/abs/1711.06391
9. Courbariaux, M., Hubara, I., Soudry, D., El-Yaniv, R., Bengio, Y.: Binarized neural networks: Training deep neural networks with weights and activations constrained to +1 or -1, February 2016
10. Deng, J., Dong, W., Socher, R., Li, L.J., Li, K., Li, F.F.: Imagenet: a large-scale hierarchical image database, pp. 248–255, June 2009. https://doi.org/10.1109/CVPR.2009.5206848
11. Dijkstra, E.: A note on two problems in connexion with graphs. Numerische Mathematik **1**, 269–271 (1959). http://eudml.org/doc/131436
12. Entertainment, B.: War2/war2edit: Warcraft ii world map editor (2023). https://github.com/war2/war2edit. Accessed 27 Dec 2023
13. Guha Roy, A., Navab, N., Wachinger, C.: Concurrent Spatial and Channel 'Squeeze & Excitation' in Fully Convolutional Networks, pp. 421–429, September 2018. https://doi.org/10.1007/978-3-030-00928-1_48
14. Hart, P., Nilsson, N., Raphael, B.: A formal basis for the heuristic determination of minimum cost paths. IEEE Trans. Syst. Sci. Cybern. **4**, 100 – 107 (1968). https://doi.org/10.1109/TSSC.1968.300136
15. Hu, J., Shen, L., Sun, G., Albanie, S.: Squeeze-and-excitation networks. IEEE Trans. Pattern Anal. Mach. Intell. **PP**, September 2017. https://doi.org/10.1109/TPAMI.2019.2913372
16. Ichter, B., Pavone, M.: Robot motion planning in learned latent spaces. CoRR abs/1807.10366 (2018). http://arxiv.org/abs/1807.10366
17. Kim, B., Pineau, J.: Socially adaptive path planning in human environments using inverse reinforcement learning. Int. J. Soc. Robot. **8**, 51–66 (2015). https://api.semanticscholar.org/CorpusID:6640745
18. Korf, R.E.: Depth-first iterative-deepening: an optimal admissible tree search. Artif. Intell. **27**(1), 97–109 (1985). https://doi.org/10.1016/0004-3702(85)90084-0
19. Lee, L., Parisotto, E., Chaplot, D.S., Xing, E.P., Salakhutdinov, R.: Gated path planning networks. CoRR abs/1806.06408 (2018). http://arxiv.org/abs/1806.06408
20. Lopez Pinaya, W., Vieira, S., Garcia-dias, R., Mechelli, A.: Autoencoders, pp. 193–208. Elsevier, Netherlands, January 2019. https://doi.org/10.1016/B978-0-12-815739-8.00011-0
21. Lucas, S.: Computational intelligence and ai in games: A new ieee transactions. IEEE Trans. Comput. Intellig. AI Games **1**, 1–3 (2009). https://doi.org/10.1109/TCIAIG.2009.2021433

22. P., M.V., Paulus, A., Musil, V., Martius, G., Rolínek, M.: Differentiation of blackbox combinatorial solvers. CoRR abs/1912.02175 (2019). http://arxiv.org/abs/1912.02175
23. Parmar, K., Taheri, E., Guzzetti, D.: Comparison of learning spacecraft path-planning solutions from imitation in three-body dynamics. J. Spacecraft Rockets **60**, 1–17 (2023).https://doi.org/10.2514/1.A35458
24. Pérez-Higueras, N., Caballero, F., Merino, L.: Learning human-aware path planning with fully convolutional networks. In: 2018 IEEE International Conference on Robotics and Automation (ICRA), pp. 1–5 (2018), https://api.semanticscholar.org/CorpusID:3648591
25. Plaku, E., Hager, G.: Sampling-based motion and symbolic action planning with geometric and differential constraints, pp. 5002–5008, May 2010. https://doi.org/10.1109/ROBOT.2010.5509563
26. Qureshi, A.H., Bency, M.J., Yip, M.C.: Motion planning networks. CoRR abs/1806.05767 (2018). http://arxiv.org/abs/1806.05767
27. Ronneberger, O., Fischer, P., Brox, T.: U-net: Convolutional networks for biomedical image segmentation, vol. 9351, pp. 234–241, October 2015. https://doi.org/10.1007/978-3-319-24574-4_28
28. Russell, S., Norvig, P.: Artificial Intelligence: A Modern Approach. Prentice Hall, 3 edn. (2010)
29. Tamar, A., Levine, S., Abbeel, P.: Value iteration networks. CoRR abs/1602.02867 (2016). http://arxiv.org/abs/1602.02867
30. Teng, S., et al.: Motion planning for autonomous driving: The state of the art and future perspectives. IEEE Trans. Intell. Vehicles **PP**, 1–21 (2023). https://doi.org/10.1109/TIV.2023.3274536
31. Wang, P., Donti, P.L., Wilder, B., Kolter, J.Z.: Satnet: Bridging deep learning and logical reasoning using a differentiable satisfiability solver. CoRR abs/1905.12149 (2019). http://arxiv.org/abs/1905.12149
32. Yonetani, R., Taniai, T., Barekatain, M., Nishimura, M., Kanezaki, A.: Path planning using neural a* search, September 2020

Centralized Stochastic Multi-agent Pathfinding Under Partial Observability

Guy Shani, Roni Stern[✉], Itay Raveh, and Inon Katz

Ben Gurion University of the Negev, Be'er Sheva, Israel
shanigu@bgu.ac.il, roni.stern@gmail.com, {ravehit,inonk}@post.bgu.ac.il

Abstract. Multi-Agent Pathfinding (MAPF) is the problem of finding paths for multiple agents where each agent aims to reach a given goal location without conflicting with the other agents. In MAPF applications with physical robots, we can expect the agents to have stochastic behavior and imperfect localization. Planning for such centrally-controlled agents can be viewed as a special case of Partially Observable Markov Decision Process (POMDP), but off-the-shelf POMDP solvers cannot scale to plan for even a very small number of agents, due to the exponentially large size of the state and action spaces. Instead, we propose the Online Prioritized Planning (OPP) approach, where each agent computes and follows its individually-optimal policy until a potential conflict is detected. OPP resolves detected potential conflicts by replanning online for a subset of the agents so as to avoid positions that are potentially occupied by other agents. We describe how OPP can be implemented and propose two extensions that encourage the agents to leverage localization actions when needed. We evaluate OPP and its extensions empirically to highlight the pros and cons of our approach and show it can scale better than an offline baseline.

Keywords: Multi-agent path finding · POMDP

1 Introduction

In classical Multi-Agent Pathfinding (MAPF) agents navigate in an environment represented as a graph. Each agent must move from its current position to a given goal position without conflicting with other agents [32]. Real-world MAPF applications include automated logistic centers [22,39], airport towing [18], autonomous vehicles [40], robotics [35], and digital entertainment [15]. However, MAPF research has mainly focused on deterministic and fully observable domains, i.e., where the effects of each action are known and deterministic and agents can fully observe their environment. Both assumptions, deterministic effects and full observability, are often violated in real-world problems, especially when the agents are physical robots. This work addresses MAPF problems where both types of uncertainty exist, which we refer to as *Stochastic MAPF with Partial Observability* (SMAPF-PO). Classical MAPF solvers cannot solve SMAPF-PO problems without compromising agents' safety.

We consider SMAPF-PO problems in which the agents are controlled in a centralized manner, e.g., a warehouse management system. Such SMAPF-PO problem can be reduced to a single-agent Partially Observable Markov Decision Process (POMDP) over states and actions that represent the agents' joint positions and actions. Solving this exponentially large POMDP is only practical for extremely small problems, even with modern online POMDP solvers. Dec-POMDP solvers, which are designed for solving multi-agent problems scale to solve problems with approximately 180K states [1]. SMAPF-PO with only 4 agents on a 20 × 10 grid reaches 1G states, 625 actions, and 2K observations. Thus, popular POMDP and Dec-POMDP solvers handle only tiny SMAPF-PO problems.

Inspired by *Prioritized Planning* (PP) [27] for classical MAPF, we propose the *Online Prioritized Planning (OPP)* approach for solving SMAPF-PO problems. OPP starts by computing a single-agent policy for each agent independently, ignoring all other agents. The agents execute these policies until the belief over the agents' current location indicates a conflict may occur. At this stage, OPP attempts to resolve potential conflicts by replacing the individually-optimal policy of some agents with policies that avoid the conflict. This planning is done online, to avoid the need to plan a-priori for every contingency. Finally, OPP employs a dedicated mechanism to encourage agents to optimize their policy over time. We discuss several design choices and challenges when implementing OPP, and propose two extensions designed to encourage the agents to intelligently perform localization action when needed.

Our main contribution is a decoupling method that allows us to avoid directly solving the joint problem. The proposed method, OPP, allow us to scale to problems many orders of magnitude larger than a standard POMDP solver can handle over the joint problem. A secondary contribution is a set of problem-specific modifications for the underlying POMDP solver, that provide additional leverage in the navigation and localization task that we define. Experimental results over 12 SMAPF-PO problems show that, as expected, POMDP solvers over the joint problem cannot scale beyond tiny grids with two agents in reasonable time. OPP with our extensions can tackle non-trivial problems with up to 4 agents.

2 Background

MAPF. A classical MAPF problem is defined by a tuple $\langle k, G, \{s_1, \ldots, s_k\},\rangle$ $\langle\{g_1, \ldots, g_k\}\rangle$, where k is the number of agents, $G = (V, E)$ is an undirected graph where V represents positions agents may occupy over time; $s_i, g_i \in V$ are the initial and target position of agent i, respectively. Time is discretized into time steps. At every time step, each agent either stays in its current position or moves to a neighboring one along an edge. A single-agent plan π_i for agent i in MAPF is a path in G that starts in s_i and ends in g_i.

A *solution* to a classical MAPF problem is a set of single-agent plans $\Pi = \pi_1, \ldots, \pi_k$ that do not *conflict*. We consider two types of conflicts, *vertex* conflicts and *swapping* conflicts. A vertex conflict occurs in plans where agents occupy the same location at the same time step, and a swapping conflict occurs when agents swap locations at the same time step. The cost of a MAPF solution Π is the sum of steps in the single-agent plans. Prioritized Planning (PP) [9,27] is an extremely popular framework for solving MAPF problems suboptimally. In PP, each agent is assigned a priority such that a total order is formed over the agents based on these priorities. Then a single-agent pathfinding algorithm such as A* [10] is used to find a path for each agent, one at a time in order of the agents' priorities. Importantly, when finding a path for an agent PP avoids conflicts with the paths found for all higher-priority agents. While PP is neither complete nor optimal, it is very efficient computationally, and often returns surprisingly high-quality solutions. PP is popular in MAPF applications such as autonomous warehouses, and has many sophisticated extensions [5,12,14].

POMDP. A POMDP is a tuple $\langle S, A, Tr, R, G, \Omega, O \rangle$ where S is a set of states; A is a set of actions; $Tr : S \times A \times S \to [0,1]$ is the transition function, returning the probability that executing the action $a \in A$ from state $s \in S$ will lead to state $s' \in S$; $R : S \times A \to \mathbb{R}$ is the reward for taking action $a \in A$ from state $s \in S$; $G \in S$ is a set of terminal states; Ω is a set of observations; $O : S \times A \times \Omega \to [0,1]$ is the observation function, returning the probability of observing $o \in \Omega$ when performing $a \in A$ in state $s \in S$. We focus here on finite state, action, and observation spaces. POMDPs solvers often maintain a *belief state* b, where $b(s)$ is the probability that the current state is s. Offline POMDP solvers such as Forward Search Value Iteration for POMDPs (FSVI) [24] and others [21,29,31] compute a policy that maps belief states to actions, and use it during execution. Online POMDP solvers [28,30,38] such as Partially Observable MonteCarlo Planning (POMCP) [28] perform little or no computation before execution and compute during the execution which action to execute next. In our experiments, we used FSVI and POMCP, which are popular examples of offline and online POMDP solvers. FSVI is highly appropriate for environments where sensing actions can be executed en route to the goal, and is thus highly appropriate for our application. However, replacing FSVI in our approach with any other point-based algorithm is trivial.

3 Problem Definition

SMAPF-PO is a MAPF variant: there are k agents moving along the edges of an undirected graph $G = (V, E)$, starting in a set of vertices $s_1, \ldots, s_k$ and aiming to reach a set of goal positions $g_1, \ldots, g_k$. A subset of the vertices $BE \subset V$ contains *beacons*, which can be sensed remotely by the agents. We assume a distance function $d : V \times BE :\to \mathbb{R}$ that quantifies the distance between vertices and beacons, such that nearby beacons can be sensed more reliably. Time is discretized, and at every time step each agent performs either a *wait action*, a *move action*, a *ping action*, or a *declare action*. We define these actions below. At every time step all agents act concurrently. The vector of all single-agent actions is called a *joint action*.

Wait and Move Actions: As in a regular MAPF problem, agents can move to nearby vertices, or stay in the same vertex. A wait action results in the agent staying in its place. While movement actions in classic MAPF applications are from vertex to vertex, under partial observability, we are often unsure where the agent is. Hence, we assume a set of abstract move actions $a_1, ..., a_M$, that apply to all vertices. For example, in grids such abstract move actions can be moving up, down, left, and right. Move actions may have stochastic effects. For each action a_m and vertices v_i, v_j, $Tr(v_i, a_m, v_j)$ denotes the probability that the agent reaches v_j after applying a_m when at v_i.

Conflicts are strictly forbidden, that is, an agent cannot perform a move action if there is a non-zero probability that it will conflict with another agent. More formally, let b be a belief over the current locations of agents, where $b_{i,j}$ is the probability that agent i is at vertex v_j. Given two agents, i_1, i_2, actions a_1, a_2 are forbidden for i_1, i_2 respectively, if there exist nodes v_k, v_n, v_l s.t. $b_{i_1,k} > 0, b_{i_2,n} > 0, Tr(v_k, a_1, v_l) > 0, Tr(v_n, a_2, v_l) > 0$. That is, if both agents may currently be at vertices v_k, v_n, and executing a_1, a_2 may bring them to collide at node v_l.

We do not focus here on avoiding collisions with walls, although that could also be resolved in a similar manner, forbidding the execution of actions that have some probability to cause the agent to collide with a wall.

Ping and Declare Actions: After performing move actions, there is often uncertainty about the current location of agents. The ping action provides some information over that uncertainty by sending a signal to a beacon, receiving back a noisy estimation of its distance from the beacon. More formally, a *ping action* is defined by a pair (v, be) and corresponds to sending a signal to beacon $be \in BE$ when the agent is at position $v \in V$. During ping actions the agent always stays in place. In addition, it receives an observation $o \in \mathbb{R}$ that is related to the *distance* between v and be. The observation function $O_i(v, be, o)$ is the probability that agent i receives observation o when performing a ping action (v, be).

Even with exact ping actions, let alone with noisy observations, there is still uncertainty over the agents' current location, and thus uncertainty over when all agents have reached their goals. A *declare action* is a special action the agent must perform to declare that it is sufficiently confident that it has reached its goal. We assume that the agent cannot perform any action after performing a declare action and it is removed from the graph, similar to Švancara et al. [33]. Other assumptions are also possible.

Objective: navigate all agents to their goal vertices without conflicts, performing the least actions possible, followed by each agent performing a declare action. This complex objective is captured by a reward function $R_i(v, a)$ where i is an agent, v is its position, and a is the action it performed. For a declare action, if $v = g_i$ then $R(v, a)$ is a large positive number, corresponding to a success, and large negative number if $v \neq g_i$. For all other actions $R_i(v, a)$ is a small negative number, corresponding to a cost for each step.

Definition 1 (SMAPF-PO). *A SMAPF-PO problem is a tuple $\langle \Pi, BE,\rangle$ $\langle \{Tr_i\}_i, \{O_i\}_i, \{R_i\}_i\rangle$ where Π is a classical MAPF problem; BE is a set of beacons; and Tr_i, O_i, and R_i are the transition, observation, and reward function of agent i. A SMAPF-PO solver objective is to output a joint action in every time step such that the expected sum of discounted reward collected by all agents is maximized, for a given discount factor.*

3.1 Grid-Based SMAPF-PO

Next, we describe the specific type of SMAPF-PO problem we used in our experiments, where the graph G represents a 4-neighborhood grid where agents' move actions are only up, down, left, and right. We emphasize that the theoretical contributions of this work are not limited to this specific SMAPF-PO problem. Let v_a be the vertex in the direction of a from v. For every agent i, we define $Tr_i(v, a, v') = 0.8$ if $v' = v_a$ and 0.1 for $v' \in \{v_{cl}, v_{cc}\}$, the grid cells that are clockwise (v_{cl}) and counter-clockwise (v_{cc}) from v_a w.r.t. v.

For example, if the agent is currently at grid cell x, y and it executes the down action, then it arrives at cell $x, y+1$ with probability 0.8, and moves to cells $x-1, y$ and $x+1, y$ with probability 0.1. Some grid cells may be blocked, in which case moving towards them results in staying in place. After an agent reaches its goal position, it must execute a declare action. The agent disappears from the grid after the declare action was used, receiving a positive reward if it is indeed at the goal, and a smaller penalty cost if it is not at the goal.

Observations are noisy, providing inexact biased estimates of the Manhattan distance, denoted $d(v, be)$, between the agent's current location v and the chosen beacon be. In particular, the observation never underestimates the Manhattan distance to the beacon. Beacons have a finite (very limited) range. When the agent is too far from the beacon, it observes an infinite distance. If an agent pings a beacon be and receives an observation value of zero, it can deduce that it is exactly at be. This is natural if signal strength weakens as the receiver gets far from the beacon.

More formally, each beacon $be \in BE$ has a maximal range $be.r > 0$. If an agent performs a ping action (v, be), and $d(v, be) > be.r$, it will observe ∞, i.e., $O_i(v, be, \infty) = 1$. Otherwise, the observation is between $d(v, be)$ and $be.r$, with the following observation function:

$$O(v, be, o) = \begin{cases} \frac{2^{be.r - o + d(v, be)}}{2^{be.r+1} - 2^{d(v, be)}} & o \in [d(v, be), be.r] \\ 0 & \text{otherwise} \end{cases} \quad (1)$$

Following preliminary experiments, we defined the reward $R_i(v, a)$ to be 50 when an agent declares at its goal, -20 if it declared not at its goal, and -0.04 if it did not declare.

3.2 Reduction to Single Agent POMDP

As the agents in SMAPF-PO are controlled in a centralized manner, any SMAPF-PO problem $\langle \Pi, BE, \{Tr_i\}_i, \{O_i\}_i, \{R_i\}_i\rangle$ can be reduced to a POMDP problem $\langle S, A, Tr, R, G, \Omega, O \rangle$, as follows. The set of states S in this POMDP is the cross product of all single-agent positions $\times_{i=1}^{k} V$ and a special terminal state s_f. The set of actions A is the set of all joint actions. The transition function Tr is the product of the respective single-agent transition functions Tr_i except that all outcomes in which a conflict has occurred reach the special terminal state s_f. The reward function R is the sum of the corresponding reward functions R_i, and a large negative value for reaching s_f due to a conflict. The set of terminal states G includes s_f and any state reached after all agents have used a declare action. The observations Ω is $\mathbb{R}^k$, corresponding to the joint observation of all agents, and the observation function O is the product of the respective single-agent observation functions O_i.

This reduction allows solving SMAPF-PO problem using off-the-shelf POMDP solvers such as FSVI [24]. Unfortunately, current POMDP solvers cannot solve this POMDP in reasonable time beyond very small problems, as the size of the state space, action space, and observation space are all exponential in the number of agents. In general, solving POMDPs undecidable [16].

4 Online Prioritized Planning

To enable scaling up to larger problems, we propose the *Online Prioritized Planning* (OPP) approach for solving SMAPF-PO problems. As its name suggests, OPP is an online approach that is inspired by the Prioritized Planning (PP) popular MAPF framework [27]. It is *online* in the sense that it does not generate a policy for every possible contingency, but interleaves execution and planning. It is based on PP as it constructs a multi-agent solution by computing only single-agent plans and ensuring they do not conflict. When resolving potential conflicts, we take a prioritized approach, where lower priority agents yield to higher priority agents. We now detail OPP along with several extensions.

OPP starts by generating for each agent i an *individually-optimal policy* π_i, which is an optimal policy for moving i to its goal while ignoring all the other agents. The agents then execute these policies until a *potential conflict* is detected. A potential conflict is a future event that may occur according to the current belief and agents' policies in which a conflict—either vertex or swapping—occurs. At this stage, OPP employs a *potential conflict resolution* mechanism which updates the policy of at least one agent to resolve the conflicts. The agents continue to execute their (revised) policies until either a new potential conflict has been detected, all agents have declared a goal, or sufficient steps have been performed without any agent detecting potential conflicts. The latter condition attempts to capture the case where the agents are no longer in danger of collision, and can return to moving optimally towards their goals. When this occurs, OPP recomputes the individually-optimal policy for the agents that have diverted from their individually-optimal policies to avoid a potential conflict, starting from the current belief.

Algorithm 1. $OPP(\Pi, b_0)$

1: $b \leftarrow b_0$
2: **for** agent r **do**
3:    $\pi_r \leftarrow$ Compute individually optimal policy for r
4: **end for**
5: $\pi \leftarrow \{\pi_1, \ldots, \pi_k\}$
6: **while** Not IsDone(b) **do**
7:    $InConflict \leftarrow$ **DetectPotentialConflicts**(π,b)
8:    **if** $InConflict \neq \emptyset$ **then**
9:       **if ResolvePotentialConflicts**($InConflict$)==False **then**
10:          Fail
11:       **end if**
12:    **end if**
13:    $\{\omega_1, \ldots, \omega_k\} \leftarrow$ Step(π, b)
14:    $b \leftarrow$ UpdateBelief($b, \{\omega_1, \ldots, \omega_k\}$)
15:    **ForgetConflicts**(π, b)
16: **end while**

Algorithm 1 provides the pseudo-code for OPP. The statements "Step(π, b)" and "UpdateBelief($b, \{\omega_1, \ldots, \omega_k\}$)" correspond to performing the joint action specified for the belief state b in policy π, and updating the belief b based on the observations collected after performing the previous joint action. Observe that as the transition and observation functions are factored and the agents share observations, the belief state b is naturally factored to a set of belief states $\{b_i\}_i$ where b_i is a distribution over the possible position agent i may currently occupy. Thus, creating the joint action from b (line 13) involves collecting the actions of the different agents by using their single-agent policies over their respective single-agent beliefs. Note that OPP is incomplete: it may detect a conflict that it cannot resolve, in which case it fails (line 10).

4.1 OPP Components

OPP includes several key steps, described below: (1) generating individually-optimal policies, (2) detecting potential conflicts, (3) resolving potential conflicts, and (4) deciding when to recompute the individually-optimal policies.

Generating an Individually Optimal Policy: To generate the individually optimal policy for agent i, we solve the POMDP Π_i whose state space is V (the set of positions an agent may occupy), the actions are all agent i's actions, and the transition function, observations, observation function, and reward function are Tr_i, $\mathbb{R}$, O_i, and R_i, respectively. This POMDP is exponentially smaller than the POMDP described above, and thus solving it is more practical. In our implementation, we used FSVI [24], a popular POMDP solver. We run FSVI until it either converged or a memory and runtime limit has been reached. As FSVI does not provide optimality guarantees, we are not guaranteed find an individually-optimal policy.

Algorithm 2. Resolve(Π, *InConflict*)

1: $R_{try} \leftarrow \emptyset$
2: **while** *InConflict* is not empty and *InConflict* $\setminus R_{try} \neq \emptyset$ **do**
3:     $r \leftarrow$ **ChooseAgent**(*InConflict*, R_{try})
4:     Add r to R_{try}
5:     $\pi_r \leftarrow$ **FindSafePolicy**(r, Π^{-r})
6:     **if** π_r is safe wrt all other agents **then**
7:        Update Π with π_r
8:        Remove r from *InConflict*
9:     **end if**
10: **end while**
11: **return** *InConflict* $= \emptyset$

Detecting Potential Conflicts: Detecting potential conflicts that may occur in the future requires tracking for all future positions that every agent may occupy, which is prohibitively expensive to compute [3]. Moreover, in an online setting, the agent can limit its attention to conflicts that are possible in the particular execution it is running. Thus, we detect only potential conflicts that may occur in the next d steps, where d is a parameter. This is performed by expanding each agent's belief using the actions dictated by its current policy, considering only sequences of d actions. If there is some vertex v that appears in the expanded beliefs of two agents, then a potential conflict has been detected. If we identify a possible conflict between agents i and j, and another potential conflict between agents j and k, then we assume a potential conflict between i, j, k.

Resolving Potential Conflicts: To resolve one or more potential conflicts between a pair of agents i and j, one agent yields to the other agent. That is, OPP updates the policy of one agent to avoid all possible positions the other agent may occupy when following its current policy. Let F_i and F_j be these sets of possible future positions for agent i and j, respectively (computed in the previous step). We say that a policy for agent i is *safe* with respect to agent j if it avoids all positions in F_j. To find a safe policy for agent i wrt agent j, we solve a POMDP similar to the one described above for computing the individually-optimal policy for i, except that it forbids every action that may result in a non-zero belief in which i is occupying a state in F_j. Note that a safe policy for i may not be able to reach the goal. After the conflict is no longer possible, agent i may continue moving towards the goal. If OPP fails to find a safe policy for i wrt to j, it attempts to find a safe policy for j wrt to i. If OPP fails to find any safe policy, both agents change their policies to stay in their current positions. If there are potential conflicts that involve more than two agents, we repeat the above process but search for a policy that is safe with respect to all other agents. We continue this until all conflicts are resolved or we have failed to find a safe policy for an agent in conflict.

Algorithm 2 lists the pseudo code for the potential conflict resolution method described above. The input is the set of agents that were detected in a potential conflict, denoted *InConflict*. As long as *InConflict* is not empty and we have not attempted to update the policies of all the agents, then one of the conflicting agents is chosen. We search for a safe policy for that agent with respect to the current policies of all other agents (denoted by Π^{-r} in Algorithm 2). If a safe policy has been found, we update the current set of individual policies and remove r from *InConflict*. Otherwise, we iterate and choose a different agent to attempt to find a safe policy. If all conflicts have been resolved, or we have tried to update the policy of all agents, the algorithm stops, reporting whether all conflicts have been resolved.

The above approach to resolve conflicts is but one design choice. An alternative way to resolve potential conflicts includes prioritizing the agents, and limiting the set of forbidden states when planning for each agent to the states potentially occupied by higher-priority agents. In addition, we can repeat the process of searching for a safe policy multiple times for each agent, as the set of potential conflicts may have been changed when trying to resolve some of the conflicts. We have found our implementation to be effective, but future research can explore other options.

Concluding Resolved Conflicts and Replanning: The safe policies created when resolving a conflict may be significantly worse than the corresponding individually optimal policies. Moreover, they are overly pessimistic, in the sense that they forbid reaching any position the other agents may occupy in the next d steps. But, after performing some steps, the set of possible positions the other agents occupy may change, based on the current location of all agents. Thus, it can be beneficial to replan for the agents following a safe policy after every step. On the other hand, replanning requires solving a POMDP and is thus computationally expensive.

As a middle ground, we implemented in OPP the following mechanism. After agent i updates its individually optimal policy to a safe policy in order to resolve a conflict, it executes that policy for T steps. If during those T steps another conflict is detected, then a new safe policy is computed and the step counter is restarted. If no conflicts were detected in T time steps, agent i recomputes an individual policy.

Extensions: We implemented two extensions to the baseline OPP described above. The first extension encourages the agents to perform ping actions instead of declaring failure when a conflict could not be resolved (line 10 in Algorithm 1. We denote this by *Forced Localization* (FL). The second extension is to modify the way the individually optimal policies are computed to explicitly include ping actions, addressing the following known deficit of FSVI. FSVI guides its sampling of the belief space—forward traversals—by solving the underlying MDP. Thus, it is less likely to perform sensing actions, which are ping actions in SMAPF-PO, during its forward traversal, since sensing actions do not provide value in the underlying MDP. Thus, it can be useful to explicitly consider sensing actions during forward traversals. We implemented this concept as follows. A belief is called *movable* if there is a moving action that may not end in a forbidden state. If in the belief collection phase of FSVI the current belief is not movable, the agent will execute every ping action possible and collect the resulted beliefs, thus explicitly considering the sensing actions when needed. We call this OPP extension the *Modified FSVI* (MF).

Table 1. SMAPF-PO benchmark properties, the joint and the decoupled POMDP model parameters.

Grid	Size	Cells	k	Joint |S|	|A|	|O|	Decoupled |S|	|A|	|O|
S_1	7×5	33	2	1056	49	16	33	7	4
S_2	5×5	23	2	506	49	25	23	7	5
S_3	5×5	25	2	600	49	25	25	7	5
S_4	5×5	25	2	600	49	25	25	7	5
M_1	10×10	94	2	8.7×10^3	49	25	94	7	5 d
M_2	10×10	94	2	8.7×10^3	64	49	94	8	7
M_3	10×10	100	2	9.9×10^3	81	81	100	9	9
M_4	10×19	190	2	35×10^3	121	81	190	11	9
M_5	14×11	118	2	13×10^3	81	36	118	9	6
L_1	15×10	138	3	2×10^6	1,331	343	138	11	7
L_2	10×10	100	4	94×10^6	6,561	2,401	100	9	7
L_3	9×19	152	4	512×10^6	14,641	2,401	152	11	7

5 Experimental Results

We implemented OPP and conducted an experimental evaluation of its behavior on grid SMAPF-PO problems.

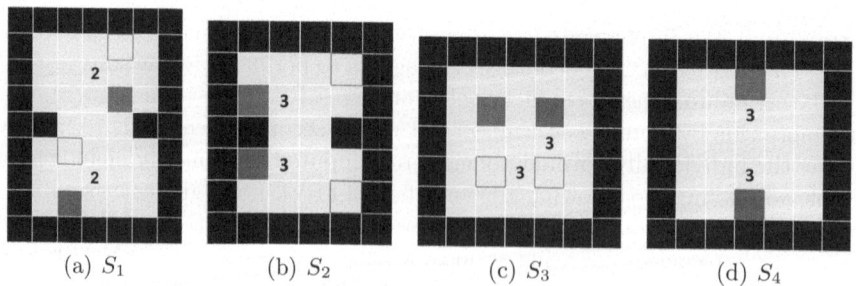

(a) S_1 (b) S_2 (c) S_3 (d) S_4

Fig. 1. The small Grid SMAPF-PO problems in our benchmarks. Each color represents an agent. Initial cells filled, goal cells bordered.

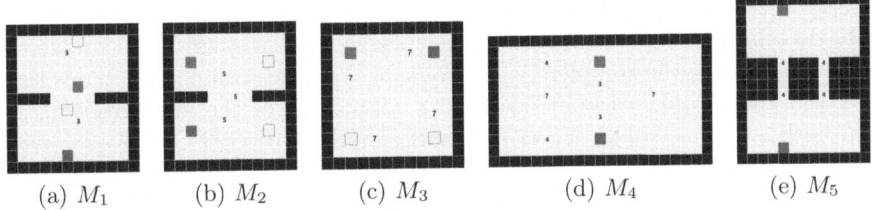

Fig. 2. Medium-sized grid SMAPF-PO problems. Each color represents an agent. Initial cells filled, goal cells bordered.

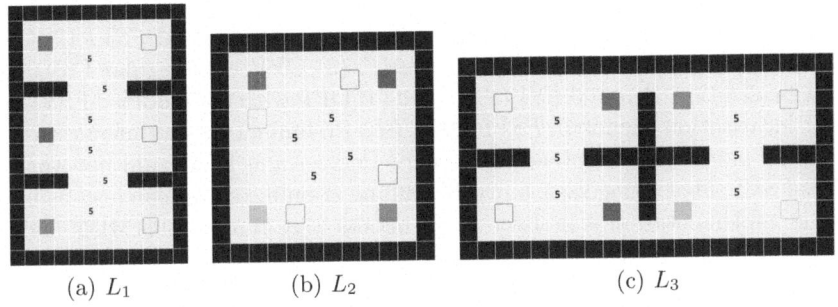

Fig. 3. Larger grid SMAPF-PO problems. Each color represents an agent. Initial cells filled, goal cells bordered.

Benchmarks: Solving SMAPF-PO is much more difficult compared to classical MAPF, and none of our algorithms were able to scale to solve SMAPF-PO problems on standard MAPF benchmarks [32]. Instead, we create a suite of 12 SMAPF-PO problems of different sizes, configurations, and number of agents. Figures 1, 2, and 3 illustrates these problems visually and Table 1 provides additional information.

Agents' start and goal positions are filled and bordered cells, respectively, where each agent has a different color. Cells with beacons are marked with a number that specifies the beacon's maximal range. Our benchmark selection is designed to examine different interactions between the agents and different difficulty levels. Most of these benchmarks are very difficult given noisy partial observability—there are no beacons at the goal positions allowing the agent to know it has arrived at the goal. Goal positions are also not located in places that are easy to reach blindly, such as corners. As such, achieving near perfect success is highly unlikely.

As can be seen in Table 1, the joint problem rapidly becomes unmanageable, due to the huge joint state space, but also due to the joint action and observation spaces. Each additional beacon adds another action, and the number of observations depends on the range of the beacons.

Baselines: An experimental comparison between OPP and classical MAPF algorithms is not possible, as the latter assume only one (deterministic) outcome for each action and perfect localization. The main contribution of our approach is the decoupling method, that allows use to solve smaller single agent problems, rather than tackle the complete joint problem. We hence compare methods that solve the joint problem to our decoupling approach. For the joint problem, we used both an offline solver, FSVI [25], and an online solver, POMCP [28], with a domain specific heuristic that moves towards the goal. We refer to the joint baselines as *Joint-FSVI, and* Joint-POMDP.

For our decoupled approach, we also use both FSVI and POMCP to solve the decoupled single-agent problems. We denote the OPP POMCP version, which we ran with our forced localization method, as *POMCP+FL*. We also experiment with several variations of OPP with FSVI: (1) a vanilla method without forcing localizations and without our modified version of FSVI, denoted *FSVI* (2) OPP with the modified FSVI, denoted *FSVI+MF*, (3) OPP with regular FSVI and forced localization, denoted *FSVI+FL*, and (4) OPP with the modified FSVI and forced locatization, denoted *FSVI+MF+FL*. Preliminary experiments showed that other point-based approaches, namely, Persues and PBVI, did not work as well as FSVI. That being said, any other offline or online solver can also be used.

The implementation is in Java. Experiments were run on an AMD® EPYC 7702P 64-Core with 32 GB of RAM.

Experiment Design and Metrics: For every problem in our benchmark we run each of the evaluated algorithms 50 times. Every such run was terminated when either all agents have declared that their goal has been reached or when the overall number of steps exceeded 200. In the latter case, we forced all remaining agents to perform a declare action.

The main performance metric we considered is the average sum of discounted rewards (ADR), which is a common solution quality measure in the POMDP literature. We also report the standard error of these averages, the average runtime in seconds, and the *success rate*, which is the percentage of runs where all agents reach their respective goal states and performed the declare action appropriately. ADR is not directly correlated with the success rate: when one agent reaches the goal and the other does not, declaring done will produce a positive ADR will not be considered a success. This can be seen in our results, where some cases with 0% success rate still have positive ADR.

Results The results for small problems are shown in Table 2. Columns "P", "RT", and "%S" specify the problem name, runtime in seconds, and the success rate, respectively. We also report the number of resolved potential collisions and the number of times an agent replanned, denoted as "#RC" and "#R", respectively. #RC and #R are always zero for *Offline*, as its initial policy is conflict-free. As expected, Joint-FSVI could only solve in reasonable time the smaller 5×5 problems, S_1, S_2, S_3, and S_4. On the other hand, Joint-FSVI managed in some problems to provide the best policy in terms of success rate and ADR. This is expected, as an optimal POMDP solver on the joint problem, given enough runtime, can return an optimal policy. Joint-POMCP could not scale beyond the smallest problem, due to the large number of joint actions and observations.

Table 2. Results for small problems (S_1, S_2, S_3, and S_4).

P	Algorithm	ADR	RT	% S	#RC	#R
S_1	Joint-FSVI	80 ± 4	671	85%	-	-
	Joint-POMCP	56±6	78	48%	-	-
	POMCP+FL	55 ± 6	3	68%	0.04±0.03	0.04±0.03
	FSVI	80 ± 4	3	88%	0.5±0.1	0.5±0.2
	FSVI+MF	76 ± 4	2	80%	0.3±0.1	0.4±0.1
	FSVI+FL	**79 ± 4**	3	88%	0.5±0.1	0.5±0.2
	FSVI+MF+FL	74 ± 5	5	76%	2±2	4±4
S_2	Joint-FSVI	62 ± 6	692	72%	-	-
	Joint-POMCP					
	POMCP+FL	63 ± 4	106	68%	130±28	131±28
	FSVI	61 ± 5	11	64%	5±0.8	7±1
	FSVI+MF	49 ± 5	23	40%	6±3	10±4
	FSVI+FL	64 ± 6	41	80%	27±5	10±11
	FSVI+MF+FL	48 ± 7	50	62%	41±6	80±13
S_3	Joint-FSVI	3 ± 4	3516	10%	-	-
	Joint-POMCP					
	POMCP+FL	0 ± 4	331	12%	90±6	170±10
	FSVI	21 ± 1	17	0%	2.7±0.1	4.3±0.2
	FSVI+MF	17 ± 3	21	0%	2.4±0.1	3.9±0.2
	FSVI+FL	11 ± 5	68	18%	66±7	128±13
	FSVI+MF+FL	3 ± 4	93	10%	70±6	138±13
S_4	Joint-FSVI	57 ± 6	4735	63%	-	-
	Joint-POMCP					
	FSVI	22 ± 1	9	0%	2±0	3±0
	POMCP+FL	-12.2 ± 0	422	0%	99.7±0.06	199±0.1
	FSVI+MF	22 ± 0.6	5	0%	2±0	3±0
	FSVI+FL	21 ± 5	57	36%	58±6	112±13
	FSVI+MF+FL	-12 ± 0	203	0%	100±0	200±0

The online algorithms perform well on S_1 and S_2, where the agents' shortest path to their goals do not conflict. However, they perform poorly in S_3 and S_4, which represent very difficult problems, where agents must move close together in a tight space. As such, the number of conflicts between the shortest paths is very high, many potential conflicts will be detected and the agents will replan very often. This is clearly observable in the "#RC" and "#R" results, which are high and are inversely correlated with the ADR.

When many conflicts are expected (S_3 and S_4), the modified FSVI technique is not beneficial, but the forced localization works better than the vanilla FSVI.

This is because in such small grids localizing is very helpful, allowing agents to move at least one step without colliding, and then localizing again. Computing the joint policy is much more computationally demanding, as expected, requiring many orders of magnitude additional run time compared to the online algorithms. Indeed, the offline algorithm could not scale to any of the larger problems.

POMCP+FL is slower than all other online methods. This is because even the single agent problems have a relatively large number of actions (movements + pinging beacons), and many observations. Thus, the branching factor is difficult to handle. On the other hand, POMCP+FL creates in some cases good policies, and in S_2, even the best policies.

Table 3. Results for medium problems.

P	Algorithm	ADR	RT	% S	#RC	#R
M_1	FSVI	69 ± 4	21	74%	0.3±0.1	0.4±0.2
	POMCP+FL	52 ± 5	33	62%	15±12	16±13
	FSVI+MF	70 ± 4	19	78%	0.4±0.2	0.6±0.2
	FSVI+FL	61 ± 5	22	66%	0.2±0.1	0.3±0.2
	FSVI+MF+FL	70 ± 4	18	78%	0.4±0.2	0.6±0.2
M_2	FSVI	41 ± 5	146	46%	4±0.4	7±0.6
	POMCP+FL	28 ± 5	946	46%	300±20	300±20
	FSVI+MF	28 ± 4	230	30%	5±0.3	7±0.4
	FSVI+FL	48 ± 5	191	64%	6±0.5	9±0.6
	FSVI+MF+FL	55 ± 4	200	76%	5±0.4	8±0.5
M_3	FSVI	17.8 ± 0.4	253	0%	1±0	2±0
	POMCP+FL	57 ± 3	202	84%	79±15	83±15
	FSVI+MF	17.6 ± 0.3	418	0%	1±0	2±0
	FSVI+FL	56 ± 3	402	92%	10±1	16±3
	FSVI+MF+FL	48 ± 4	535	72%	10±2	18±3
M_4	FSVI	30 ± 3	133	10%	1±0	2±0
	POMCP+FL	73 ± 2	208	94%	63±16	63±16
	FSVI+MF	36 ± 4	91	20%	1±0	2±0
	FSVI+FL	77 ± 7	245	96 %	2±0.3	4±0.4
	FSVI+MF+FL	75 ± 3	125	94%	3±0.7	5±1
M_5	FSVI	-6 ± 3	381	0%	2.1±0.2	3.4±0.2
	POMCP+FL	-11.6 ± 0.6	275	2%	55±5	101±3
	FSVI+MF	5 ± 2	217	0%	2.0±0.1	3.3±0.2
	FSVI+FL	-6 ± 2	896	8%	29±3	55±6
	FSVI+MF+FL	0 ± 2	671	2%	20±3	37±5

Results on Larger Problems. Table 3 and Table 4 lists the results for the larger problems (M_1, M_2, M_3, M_4, M_5, L_1, L_2, and L_3), where the joint problem is too difficult for FSVI and POMCP. In these problems, the benefit of the forced localization (FL) method are obvious. For example, without FL and MF the success rate of the vanilla FSVI was 0 for M_3, M_4, M_5, and L_2, while FSVI+FL and FSVI+MF+FL often succeed. This advantage is also shown in the ADR. For example, in L_1 using FL approximately doubled the ADR achieved.

The benefit of modifying FSVI (MF) to include more pings, however, is less pronounced. Only in M_1 FSVI+MF provides better results than FSVI+FLm while in most cases, using only FSVI+MF in not as good as FSVI+FL. On the other hand, the combined FSVI+FL+MF provides additional leverage, at least in the largest problem, L_3.

POMCP-FL provided competitive results in some cases, but in most problems did not work as well as FSVI-FL. On the largest problems, POMCP-FL failed to provide strong policies, probably because the longer needed planning horizon requires deeper trees, which take a long time to construct.

Table 4. Results for large problems.

P	Algorithm	ADR	RT	% S	#RC	#R
L_1	FSVI	37 ± 6	254	8%	7.2±0.5	10.9±0.8
	POMCP+FL	64 ± 5	1954	64%	372±21	376±21
	FSVI+MF	29 ± 6	433	6%	6.8±0.5	10.5±0.6
	FSVI+FL	97 ± 3	222	78%	8±0.5	12±0.7
	FSVI+MF+FL	97 ± 4	386	74%	10±3	15±4
L_2	FSVI	-11 ± 2	80	0%	2.96±0.02	8.8±0.1
	POMCP+FL	69 ± 12	1950	26%	-	-
	FSVI+MF	-15.1 ± 0.3	57	0%	3±0	8.9±0.1
	FSVI+FL	67 ± 12	182	36%	25±3	50±6
	FSVI+MF+FL	73 ± 11	212	30%	20±3	40±6
L_3	FSVI	67 ± 6	202	8%	8±0.6	12±0.8
	POMCP+FL	35 ± 7	1663	12%	328±23	326±22
	FSVI+MF	59 ± 7	353	8%	9±1	13±1
	FSVI+FL	112 ± 5	183	62%	10±1	14±1
	FSVI+MF+FL	117 ± 6	423	68%	12±1	18±2

In some sense, M_5 is the hardest of the large problems, as the single-agent path of each agent to its goal is conflicting in M_5, requiring much coordination for navigating the narrow corridors without collisions. Additional research is needed to develop methods that can better handle such problems that require strong synchronization. It may be that in such corridors, solving a small, short range joint problem is better.

Summary. For very small problems, finding a solution to the joint problem provides the best policy, but takes a very long time. As such, only OPP was able to scale beyond very small problems, especially when using the FL method. This demonstrates that solving the naive joint MAPF POMDP problem is not practical, and hence, one would need to use some type of decoupling technique, creating single agent problems that allow for much better scaling up.

We also see here that domain specific techniques can help POMDP solvers in creating better policies, with respect to the synchronization of policies. Our localization additions were successful because, when considering a single agent, localization is less important, unless we are near the goal. However, when other agents are nearby, localization can reduce significantly the possibility for collisions, and hence, the need to replan, and the constraints during replanning.

6 Related Work

MAPF with unexpected delays has been studied in different forms [3,4,13,23]. Yet limiting stochastic effects to delays simplifies the problem compared to SMAPF-PO, and these works all assumed perfect observability. UM^* [36] does support uncertainty over agents' locations but it allows agents to risk conflicts as long as their probability of occurring is beneath a given threshold. Similarly, prior work on multi-robot navigation assigned cost to collision and aim to minimize it. The SMAPF-PO is fundamentally different since we require avoiding any chance for having a conflict. Recent work [7] on MAPF with partial observability differs from SMAPF-PO in that they assumed control is not centralized and agents' visibility is based on line of sight. The latter assumption is different from our beacons-based observation model, precluding empirical comparison.

MAPF under movement uncertainty is a special case of Multi-Agent MDP (MMDP) [6]. General-purpose MMDP solvers [8] do not exploit the specific structure of the SMAPF-PO problem, such as the limited interactions between agents. Similarly, online approaches for solving large MDPs, such as FF-Replan [42], are not expected to be effective in our domain and do not deal with partial observability.

Dec-POMDP [19] is often used to model multi-agent problems under partial observability, where agents plan jointly, but execute their policies independently. This is different from our setting, where agents are controlled in a centralized manner and share their observations. Also, Dec-POMDP algorithms tend to scale poorly unless the interactions between the agents are limited to small predefined areas in the state space [17]. Multiagent POMDP [20], where both planning and control are centralized, is an appropriate model for SMAPF-PO. [2] suggest an algorithm based on POMCP which exploits the locality of agent interactions. Their algorithm given singleton sets is similar to our POMCP, which does not scale as well as FSVI. Our approach can be viewed as a particular implementation of FT-POMCP leveraging the structure of the SMAPF-PO problem for factorization, and using prioritized planning to ensure independence.

Factorizing the decision-making process in POMDPs has long roots [26,34, e.g.], and is particularly useful given several independent tasks. Factorization is less effective, however, when the coupling between the tasks increases, as happens in our problem where agents may collide. In tasks with high uncertainty concerning the current state, such coupling is common, and useful factoring is difficult. We used FSVI and POMCP but other alternatives for offline and online POMDP solvers exist [11,37,41, e.g.]. Our contribution is not in an adaptation of a particular POMDP solver to SMAPF-PO, but in our factoring and prioritization schemes. Replacing POMCP with, e.g., ABT, is likely to scale up only slightly, while improvements to the factorization can make a huge difference.

7 Conclusion

We studied the Stochastic MAPF with Partial Observability (SMAPF-PO) problem, which is a generalization of MAPF in which actions have stochastic outcomes and agents do not have perfect observability of the current state. We focused on a centralized control setup. While SMAPF-PO can be modeled as a single-agent POMDP problem, solving this POMDP is intractable even for small problems. We introduced the OPP approach, an online adaptation of Prioritized Planning. OPP has several non-trivial components which we describe, and we also propose two extensions that encourage the agents to actively localize. The results showed that OPP solves larger problems than an offline baseline. Yet, solving larger problems is still an open challenge for future work.

Acknowledgments. This work is partially funded by the Israeli Science Foundation (ISF) grant #1238/23 to Roni Stern.

Disclosure of Interests. The authors have no competing interests to declare that are relevant to the content of this article.

References

1. Amato, C., Konidaris, G., Kaelbling, L.P., How, J.P.: Modeling and planning with macro-actions in decentralized pomdps. J. Artif. Intell. Res. **64**, 817–859 (2019)
2. Amato, C., Oliehoek, F.: Scalable planning and learning for multiagent pomdps. In: AAAI Conference on Artificial Intelligence (2015)
3. Atzmon, D., Stern, R., Felner, A., Sturtevant, N.R., Koenig, S.: Probabilistic robust multi-agent path finding. In: International Conference on Automated Planning and Scheduling, vol. 30, pp. 29–37 (2020)
4. Atzmon, D., Stern, R., Felner, A., Wagner, G., Barták, R., Zhou, N.F.: Robust multi-agent path finding and executing. J. Artif. Intell. Res. **67**, 549–579 (2020)
5. van den Berg, J.P., Overmars, M.H.: Prioritized motion planning for multiple robots. In: Proceedings of the IEEE/RSJ International Conference on Intelligent Robots and Systems (IROS). pp. 430–435 (2005)
6. Boutilier, C.: Planning, learning and coordination in multiagent decision processes. In: TARK, vol. 96, pp. 195–210 (1996)

7. Davydov, V., Skrynnik, A., Yakovlev, K., Panov, A.: Q-mixing network for multi-agent pathfinding in partially observable grid environments. In: Kovalev, S.M., Kuznetsov, S.O., Panov, A.I. (eds.) RCAI 2021. LNCS (LNAI), vol. 12948, pp. 169–179. Springer, Cham (2021). https://doi.org/10.1007/978-3-030-86855-0_12
8. De Nijs, F., Walraven, E., De Weerdt, M., Spaan, M.: Constrained multiagent Markov decision processes: a taxonomy of problems and algorithms. J. Artif. Intell. Res. **70**, 955–1001 (2021)
9. Erdmann, M., Lozano-Perez, T.: On multiple moving objects. Algorithmica **2**(1), 477–521 (1987)
10. Hart, P.E., Nilsson, N.J., Raphael, B.: A formal basis for the heuristic determination of minimum cost paths. IEEE Trans. Syst. Sci. Cybern. **4**(2), 100–107 (1968)
11. Kurniawati, H., Yadav, V.: An online POMDP solver for uncertainty planning in dynamic environment. In: Inaba, M., Corke, P. (eds.) Robotics Research. STAR, vol. 114, pp. 611–629. Springer, Cham (2016). https://doi.org/10.1007/978-3-319-28872-7_35
12. Li, J., Chen, Z., Harabor, D., Stuckey, P.J., Koenig, S.: MAPF-LNS2: fast repairing for multi-agent path finding via large neighborhood search. In: AAAI Conference on Artificial Intelligence, pp. 10256–10265 (2022)
13. Ma, H., Kumar, S., Koenig, S.: Multi-agent path finding with delay probabilities. In: AAAI Conference on Artificial Intelligence, pp. 3605–3612 (2017)
14. Ma, H., Harabor, D., Stuckey, P.J., Li, J., Koenig, S.: Searching with consistent prioritization for multi-agent path finding. In: Proceedings of the AAAI Conference on Artificial Intelligence (AAAI), pp. 7643–7650 (2019)
15. Ma, H., Yang, J., Cohen, L., Kumar, T.K.S., Koenig, S.: Feasibility study: moving non-homogeneous teams in congested video game environments. In: Conference on Artificial Intelligence and Interactive Digital Entertainment (AIIDE), pp. 270–272 (2017)
16. Madani, O., Hanks, S., Condon, A.: On the undecidability of probabilistic planning and related stochastic optimization problems. Artif. Intell. **147**(1–2), 5–34 (2003)
17. Melo, F.S., Veloso, M.: Learning of coordination: exploiting sparse interactions in multiagent systems. In: Proceedings of the 8th International Conference on Autonomous Agents and Multiagent Systems-Volume 2, pp. 773–780. Citeseer (2009)
18. Morris, R., et al.: Planning, scheduling and monitoring for airport surface operations. In: AAAI Workshop: Planning for Hybrid Systems (2016)
19. Oliehoek, F.A.: Decentralized pomdps. In: Reinforcement Learning: State-of-the-Art, pp. 471–503. Springer (2012). https://doi.org/10.1007/978-3-642-27645-3_15
20. Oliehoek, F.A., Spaan, M.T., Terwijn, B., Robbel, P., Messias, J.V.: The madp toolbox: an open source library for planning and learning in (multi-) agent systems. J. Mach. Learn. Res. **18**, 1–5 (2017)
21. Pineau, J., Gordon, G., Thrun, S., et al.: Point-based value iteration: an anytime algorithm for pomdps. In: Ijcai, vol. 3, pp. 1025–1032. Citeseer (2003)
22. Salzman, O., Stern, R.Z.: Research challenges and opportunities in multi-agent path finding and multi-agent pickup and delivery problems blue sky ideas track. In: International Conference on Autonomous Agents and Multiagent Systems (AAMAS), pp. 1711–1715 (2020)
23. Shahar, T., Shekhar, S., Atzmon, D., Saffidine, A., Juba, B., Stern, R.: Safe multi-agent pathfinding with time uncertainty. J. Artif. Intell. Res. **70**, 923–954 (2021)
24. Shani, G., Brafman, R.I., Shimony, S.E.: Forward search value iteration for pomdps. In: IJCAI, pp. 2619–2624 (2007)

25. Shani, G., Pineau, J., Kaplow, R.: A survey of point-based pomdp solvers. Auton. Agent. Multi-Agent Syst. **27**(1), 1–51 (2013)
26. Shani, G., Poupart, P., Brafman, R.I., Shimony, S.E.: Efficient add operations for point-based algorithms. In: ICAPS, pp. 330–337 (2008)
27. Silver, D.: Cooperative pathfinding. In: The AAAI Conference on Artificial Intelligence and Interactive Digital Entertainment (AIIDE), pp. 117–122 (2005)
28. Silver, D., Veness, J.: Monte-carlo planning in large pomdps. Advances in neural information processing systems **23** (2010)
29. Smith, T., Simmons, R.: Point-based pomdp algorithms: improved analysis and implementation. arXiv preprint arXiv:1207.1412 (2012)
30. Somani, A., Ye, N., Hsu, D., Lee, W.S.: Despot: Online pomdp planning with regularization. Advances in neural information processing systems **26** (2013)
31. Spaan, M.T., Vlassis, N.: Perseus: Randomized point-based value iteration for pomdps. J. Artif. Intell. Res. **24**, 195–220 (2005)
32. Stern, R., et al.: Multi-agent pathfinding: definitions, variants, and benchmarks. In: Symposium on Combinatorial Search (SoCS), pp. 151–158 (2019)
33. Švancara, J., Vlk, M., Stern, R., Atzmon, D., Barták, R.: Online multi-agent pathfinding. In: AAAI Conference on Artificial Intelligence, pp. 7732–7739 (2019)
34. Veiga, T., Spaan, M., Lima, P.: Point-based pomdp solving with factored value function approximation. In: AAAI Conference on Artificial Intelligence (2014)
35. Veloso, M.M., Biswas, J., Coltin, B., Rosenthal, S.: Cobots: robust symbiotic autonomous mobile service robots. In: International Joint Conference on Artificial Intelligence (IJCAI) (2015)
36. Wagner, G., Choset, H.: Path planning for multiple agents under uncertainty. In: Twenty-Seventh International Conference on Automated Planning and Scheduling (2017)
37. Walraven, E., Spaan, M.T.: Point-based value iteration for finite-horizon pomdps. J. Artif. Intell. Res. **65**, 307–341 (2019)
38. Washington, R.: BI-POMDP: bounded, incremental partially-observable Markov-model planning. In: Steel, S., Alami, R. (eds.) ECP 1997. LNCS, vol. 1348, pp. 440–451. Springer, Heidelberg (1997). https://doi.org/10.1007/3-540-63912-8_105
39. Wurman, P.R., D'Andrea, R., Mountz, M.: Coordinating hundreds of cooperative, autonomous vehicles in warehouses. AI Mag. **29**(1), 9–9 (2008)
40. Yan, Z., Zheng, H., Wu, C.: Multi-agent path finding for cooperative autonomous driving. In: IEEE International Conference on Robotics and Automation (ICRA) (2024)
41. Ye, N., Somani, A., Hsu, D., Lee, W.S.: Despot: online pomdp planning with regularization. J. Artif. Intell. Res. **58**, 231–266 (2017)
42. Yoon, S.W., Fern, A., Givan, R.: Ff-replan: a baseline for probabilistic planning. In: ICAPS, vol. 7, pp. 352–359 (2007)

Author Index

B
Banaee, Hadi 54
Blondin, Josh 83

C
Chella, Antonio 21

E
Edelkamp, Stefan 1
Esfandiari, Babak 83

G
Garg, Armaan 128
Gatti, Andrea 115
Gaudl, Swen 73
Grand, Christophe 99
Guillet, Victor 99

H
Hagen, Oksana 73
Herynek, Jáchym 1

J
Jha, Shashi Shekhar 128

K
Katz, Inon 145
Kumar, Abhay 128

L
Lesire, Charles 99
Lestingi, Livia 38
Loutfi, Amy 54

M
Mironenko, Olga 54

P
Picard, Gauthier 99

R
Raveh, Itay 145
Rossi, Matteo 38

S
Seidita, Valeria 21
Shani, Guy 145
Stern, Roni 145

T
Tagliaferro, Alberto 38

V
Verma, Kunal 128

SPRINGER NATURE

GPSR Compliance

The European Union's (EU) General Product Safety Regulation (GPSR) is a set of rules that requires consumer products to be safe and our obligations to ensure this.

If you have any concerns about our products, you can contact us on ProductSafety@springernature.com

In case Publisher is established outside the EU, the EU authorized representative is:

Springer Nature Customer Service Center GmbH
Europaplatz 3
69115 Heidelberg, Germany

The manufacturer's authorised representative in the EU is Springer Nature Customer Service Centre GmbH, Europaplatz 3, 69115 Heidelberg, Germany. If you have any concerns regarding our products, please contact ProductSafety@springernature.com

Printed and bound by CPI Group (UK) Ltd, Croydon, CR0 4YY
26/03/2026
02078973-0007